Praise for *Holy See, Unholy Me*

'It is an accurate book and a great read,' – Papal Nuncio Archbishop S.M. Tomasi, Geneva

'[A] delightful new book … [with a] catchy title,'
– Robert Mickens, *The Tablet* (UK)

'Fischer's account of his time as the Australian ambassador there is thoughtful and entertaining. More than a diary, less than a memoir, the book is an amalgam of observation and anecdote of a likeable Australian of the old school,'
– Angela Shanahan, *The Spectator* (UK)

Praise for *Trains Unlimited*

'[A] characteristically breathless but engaging book,'
– Robert Murray, *The Australian*

'[Tim Fischer] uses his heart and considerable mind … to describe rail as a superb vehicle for freight, commuting and pleasure,' – Simon Pinder, *Weekly Times*

'[A] sweeping study of trains around the world,'
– Andrew West, *Sydney Morning Herald*

Former National Party MP and Deputy Prime minister Tim Fischer is one of the country's most prominent ex-parliamentarians. His interests are broad and eclectic and in his new book he combines almost all his favourite things: politics, trains, food, faith, history and Rome!

Also by Tim Fischer

Trains Unlimited in the 21st Century (2011)
Bold Bhutan Beckons (with Tshering Tashi) (2009)
Transcontinental Train Odyssey (2004)
Seven Days in East Timor: Ballot and Bullets (2000)

Holy See, UNHOLY ME
1,000 DAYS IN ROME
Tales from my time as Australian Ambassador to the Vatican

TIM FISCHER

ABC Books

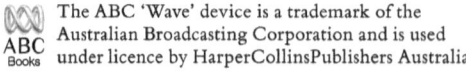
The ABC 'Wave' device is a trademark of the Australian Broadcasting Corporation and is used under licence by HarperCollinsPublishers Australia.

First published in Australia in 2013
by ABC Books for the Australian Broadcasting Corporation
by HarperCollins*Publishers* Australia Pty Limited
ABN 36 009 913 517
www.harpercollins.com.au

Copyright © Tim Fischer 2013

The right of Tim Fischer to be identified as the author of this work has been asserted by him in accordance with the *Copyright Amendment (Moral Rights) Act 2000*.

This work is copyright. Apart from any use as permitted under the *Copyright Act 1968*, no part may be reproduced, copied, scanned, stored in a retrieval system, recorded, or transmitted, in any form or by any means, without the prior written permission of the publisher.

HarperCollins*Publishers*
Level 13, 201 Elizabeth Street, Sydney NSW 2000, Australia
Unit D, 63 Apollo Drive, Rosedale, Auckland 0632, New Zealand
A 53, Sector 57, NOIDA, UP, India
77–85 Fulham Palace Road, London W6 8JB, United Kingdom
2 Bloor Street East, 20th floor, Toronto, Ontario M4W 1A8, Canada
10 East 53rd Street, New York NY 10022, USA

National Library of Australia Cataloguing-in-Publication data:

Fischer, Tim, 1946-
  Holy See, unholy me / Tim Fischer.
  ISBN: 978 0 7333 2835 0 (paperback)
  ISBN: 978 1 7430 9738 0 (ebook)
  Fischer, Tim, 1946-
  Ambassadors – Australia – Biography
  Vatican Palace (Vatican City) – Foreign relations – Australia.
  Australia – Foreign relations – Vatican Palace (Vatican City).
  Vatican Palace (Vatican City) – Description and travel.
  Vatican Palace (Vatican City) – Social life and customs.
327.20924

Cover design by Christa Moffitt, Christabella Designs
Front cover images: Tim Fischer in Rome; Tim Fischer on Caritas Express; St Mary MacKillop canonisation ceremony (courtesy Tim Fischer). Audience with Pope Benedict XVI (courtesy L'Osservatore Romano); coin by Christa Moffitt
Back cover images: Tim Fischer in regalia by the Vatican railway; Father Keith Pecklers SJ, Cardinal Donald Wuerl, Archbishop of Washington DC, and Tim Fischer, deep inside the Vatican on the night after the creation of new cardinals in 2010; Tim Fischer with the Governor-General Quentin Bryce (courtesy Tim Fischer)
Internal images: unless otherwise noted all images are from Tim Fischer's private collection
Typeset in Bembo Std by Kirby Jones

*This book is dedicated to the memory of Joe Grech,
inspirational Bishop of Sandhurst, Victoria,
2001 to 2010*

(born 10 December 1948, Balzan, Malta;
died 28 December 2010, Melbourne, Australia)

In appreciation of my government-provided base in Rome for three years and also the often unsung efforts of staff of the Department of Foreign Affairs and Trade, especially those who helped me in my work, part of the author's royalty proceeds will be donated to:

Anglican Centre, Rome
Aspire Foundation, Bendigo
Bethlehem University, West Bank
Caritas Internationalis, Australia
Country Education Foundation, Australia
East Timor Jesuit project at Kasait
General Sir John Monash Foundation: Monash scholarships
Gross National Happiness Centre, Bhutan
Kalumburu Mission, Western Australia
Lutheran World Service, Australia
Mary MacKillop Foundation
St Benedict's College, Kandy, Sri Lanka
Solidarity with South Sudan

CONTENTS

INTRODUCTION	A Phone Call from the PM	1
CHAPTER ONE	Why Me for Ambassador?	11
CHAPTER TWO	Arrival, Credentials and White Knuckles	21
CHAPTER THREE	Daily Batting for Team Australia	32
CHAPTER FOUR	Who's Who in the Vatican	49
CHAPTER FIVE	Who's Who in the Diplomatic Corps	64
CHAPTER SIX	Frenetic Networking for Your Country	82
CHAPTER SEVEN	Conferences of Solid Gold … and Slippery Silver	98
CHAPTER EIGHT	World Famine, Food Security and the Holy See	119
CHAPTER NINE	The UNSC Campaign	129
CHAPTER TEN	The Vatican and Politics – Oil and Water?	139
CHAPTER ELEVEN	The Canonisation of a Great Aussie Battler	164
CHAPTER TWELVE	Anti-Semitism in the Vatican?	181
CHAPTER THIRTEEN	Towards Religious Freedom	195
CHAPTER FOURTEEN	The Pope's Railway	208
CHAPTER FIFTEEN	Filth in the Church … Light in the Tunnel?	222
CHAPTER SIXTEEN	Papal Resignation?	231
CHAPTER SEVENTEEN	Jesuit Pope Francis Arrives	241

CHAPTER EIGHTEEN	Grand Finale Year	251
CHAPTER NINETEEN	In Salute of DFAT but Not Every Diplomat	261
CHAPTER TWENTY	Which Way the Vatican?	272
POSTSCRIPT	Return to Rome	287
APPENDIX A	Map of Vatican City	292
APPENDIX B	Map of Castel Gandolfo	295
APPENDIX C	Australian Ambassadors to the Holy See	297
APPENDIX D	Popes since 1878	298
APPENDIX E	Departments of the Roman Curia	299
APPENDIX F	Senior Personnel in the Secretariat of State as at 2009	302
APPRECIATION		303
INDEX		305

INTRODUCTION

A Phone Call from the PM

What do you do when the prime minister of the day suddenly rings you, seven years after you have retired from Federal Parliament?

My first reaction was to feel a sense of panic and my second reaction was to be wary.

The phone call in question occurred on a Sunday afternoon in July 2008, and was answered by my wife, Judy. Of all places, we were standing on the promenade deck of the *Queen Mary* floating hotel at Long Beach, about thirty minutes from Los Angeles airport, filling in time with a seven-hour layover on the way home from a family trip in the USA.

As Judy handed the phone to me she whispered, 'It's the PM – it must be something to do with the Pope's visit.' Pope Benedict XVI was about to land in Australia for the week-long World

Youth Day celebrations. We'd had only a few minutes' warning of the possible call when Gary Quinlan, a past acquaintance of mine who was the Senior Advisor International to the Prime Minister in the PM's office, had phoned to check our number.

I said 'Greetings' to Kevin Rudd and established it was him and not a hoax. The PM then asked one question: would I be interested in going to Rome to serve as resident ambassador for Australia to the Holy See? He explained that the government was upgrading the mission to the Holy See to a resident ambassadorship in Rome, and I could contact Doug Chester, the then Department of Foreign Affairs and Trade (DFAT) Deputy Secretary responsible for postings, for more details of conditions and the like.

I told the PM this was all a bit unexpected, but thanked him for the privilege of being considered and added that I would ring back in twenty-four to forty-eight hours to give him my answer.

Then something made me ask him: 'What about an ALP candidate for the Holy See post, not an ex-Nationals leader; would this not be wiser?' PM Rudd replied, not unreasonably: 'Don't *you* worry about that.' It was a clear mobile connection and his emphasis on the word 'you' was very audible. He added that I was the one he wanted for the posting.

Stunned by all of this, I looked out over the shimmering waters of the Pacific and thought about jumping overboard. Instead, I said goodbye to the PM, turned to Judy and said, 'Damnation.'

We had mused in the taxi down to the *Queen Mary* wharf that we had finally got the formula right on this holiday and enjoyed a wonderful family time reconnecting together. I had been stepping down from several boards in recent months and slowing down. I had also just completed a big four-year joint book-writing project, so the busy phase of life was coming to an end – or so I had thought.

Out of earshot of our two boys, Judy and I discussed the pros and cons, reaching no conclusion but developing a dry throat in the process. We went to the *Queen Mary* bar and I had a large Diet Coke laced heavily with rum.

Briefly on the flight home, then for the next two days back in Australia, Judy and I continued to weigh things up, getting more information in the process from the senior echelons of DFAT.

The biggest pro was that clearly the posting would be a great experience. I would be learning on the go, but equally I had some capabilities already: I knew exactly how the Department of Foreign Affairs and Trade worked, being a former Minister for Trade. The main con was the impact on the family, and on the education of our sons, Harrison and Dominic, then aged fourteen and twelve respectively.

Finally, on the afternoon of Wednesday 16 July, in the middle of the Pope's week-long visit to Sydney, I phoned the PM. (I had to cut through the 'praetorian guard' by means of a process he had instructed me to follow, namely ring a certain mobile number, leave a text message and hey presto, within 90 minutes, the PM would ring back.)

I told the PM yes, I would accept the posting, for three years maximum (even though I was offered a fourth year). There was one caveat, namely could I remain in my position as National Chair of the Royal Flying Doctor Service for another three months, due to vital preparations for the organisation's eightieth anniversary. In other words, I said I would go to Rome, but it could not be until January 2009. I thought he might say no to this, but he immediately agreed.

Judy and I had decided that it would be best for her to remain in Australia with our two sons. Harrison is autistic, and we could not find any schooling options that would click, in or around Rome. Meanwhile Dominic was heading in the direction of boarding school for Years 9, 10, 11 and 12. And as it turned out, having Judy back in Australia meant we were still able to maintain a raft of business and farming interests, amongst other things, thanks to the many long hours she spent on the computer at night.

The PM informed me that the nomination would now go immediately to Rome for approval or *agrément* and clearance of an announcement, hopefully to be made at Sydney airport during the farewell ceremony for the Pope who would fly out on Monday 21 July. Governments and even the Vatican can move quickly on occasions, it seems, as this is what happened.

Just as Judy had surmised, the new appointment had been timed perfectly to take advantage of the momentum of World Youth Day in Sydney, which had exceeded expectations in many ways. This proved to be a wise call, as the announcement gained a lot of broadly positive press coverage the next day.

★ ★ ★

Many people pointed out to me that in so many ways my life to date had been a preparation for this role. The rhythm of life is a great song, and over sixty-plus years, my life had had six major turning points.

First was the Korean wool boom of the 1950s which allowed a small Riverina family farm to fund the sending of four children to Catholic boarding schools in Melbourne. My sisters, Carol and Vicki, went to Sacré Coeur, Glen Iris. My brother, Tony, and I went to Xavier College, Kew, and the Jesuit education I received there gave me a deep faith in God, an intense curiosity and a work template based on commitment and motivation. Throughout my life my application of all three has varied but never vanished.

My next turning point was a call-up notice for National Service. This I received at the Darwin General Post Office while on a trip around Australia with mates, not long after finishing school. I graduated from officer training as a second lieutenant with one pip, and served with 1 RAR Infantry Battalion for two and a quarter years in Australia and Vietnam. I marched out of 1 RAR because I declined to go to Malaysia with the Battalion.

Being in the army meant I had to suddenly mature, and be in command of men in a real operational setting. Above all else I had to be organised – so in a sense the clean-desk policy of DFAT – literally, at the end of the day your desk was meant to be clear – was my *modus operandi* from my army years. Being able to schedule carefully and cunningly to maximise, and group together, activities in one part of Rome (or one part of the

Riverina when I was an MP) became second nature because the army teaches you about organisation, about scheduling, about personnel management, and about the need for prior planning.

The third turning point was winning preselection for the then Country Party for the seat of Sturt at the age of twenty-four and then winning election to the NSW Parliament for that Riverina-based seat in early 1971. For thirteen years I belted up and down to Macquarie Street from my country electorate of a mere 20,000 electors, but bigger in size than some European countries. I eventually made it to the front bench and served as Party Whip and also as a shadow minister for various portfolios.

The fourth turning point was switching to Federal Parliament for the seat of Farrer in 1984 and against the odds becoming Nationals Leader in 1990 and then in 1996 Deputy Prime Minister to John Howard for his first one and a half terms. I concurrently served as a busy Minister for Trade from March 1996 to July 1999. In this role I visited Rome and also nearby Castel Gandolfo, where my wife and I were granted a private audience with Pope John Paul II at his Summer Palace in 1998. I stepped down from Federal Parliament at a time of my own choosing in October 2001.

The fifth turning point was marrying Judy Brewer in November 1992 at Dederang, in the beautiful Kiewa Valley of northeast Victoria, and later becoming a parent to our sons, Harrison and Dominic. I believe marriage has made me a softer and more connected person, and Judy gave me a lot of support on those tough days that happen in any job. Judy also just happens to come from an Italian Catholic background:

one more reason why I accepted the posting to Rome. Her great-grandfather Battista di Piazza, from tiny Grosotto in northern Italy, walked hundreds of miles to Genoa, caught a ship to Melbourne, and went to the goldfields and thence to Myrtleford then Mudgegonga, where we now live. (Our family farm is in fact named after this tiny village.)

Finally, the sixth turning point was that phone call from the Prime Minister in July 2008 and the posting to Rome, as first Rome resident Australian ambassador to the Holy See, and hence this book.

Along the way I also had regrets, and one of these was that I did not keep a detailed diary of my ministerial years, in the best traditions of some UK Cabinet Ministers – Alan Clark and Richard Crossman come to mind. Sadly this was not and still is not a strong tradition in Australian politics. So I thought this time, as I headed for Rome, I would make a real effort to keep a good diary to allow others an insight into the life and tasks of an ambassador. I started on the day of the announcement and, with a few breaks, kept it up to date from there, writing three or four paragraphs each day, but not when on leave from the post in Rome. I needed a break from the burden, and it was often a burden.

I had decided never to write an autobiography, as it is too difficult to do well without revealing very personal secrets or offending friends and foes. On top of that I figured there was enough bile in the world without self-justifying recollections from a former NSW and Federal MP. However, a fair and accurate diary as fourteenth Ambassador to the Holy See seemed an achievable and worthwhile task. Unlike some political diaries, it was far from being warts and all; more an *aide memoire* to what occurred on each particular day.

This book is based on the diaries I kept, with every word typed by me in my own time. But it does not use a chronological approach; instead, in each chapter I have looked at a different aspect of my work in the Vatican, and the work done by the Vatican itself.

It is said that all roads lead to Rome; here, then, is what I found at the end of the road down which I ventured unexpectedly at the start of 2009. In revealing much if not most of my work, I have waited a year as a courtesy to current and following ambassadors in Rome. There is much colour, action and movement here, but I confess no secret cable traffic is revealed, for to do so would be, simply stated, not the right thing to do. Further – trust me – the best anecdotes and portraits from in and around the Holy See Embassy are all out there to see publicly, if you know where to look for them. I will now show you where; better still, I will give you chapter and verse, insight and some spice.

An ambassador who is in the activist camp can achieve much for his country and its government, pushing the limits by degrees but never directly contradicting government policies or priorities. You can even bring about a matching of your own hobbies and interests with help for worthy causes, along with an underlying boost to your country's profile.

There is a certain joy in assisting good causes and sharing special and rare experiences with those who might be interested, and to do so by way of a book. In keeping with this dictum, some of the proceeds from this book will go to help education projects. This is all for the better, as it was education and family that gave me my big leg up in an earlier phase of my life.

In proceeding I make one overarching observation. Mainstream religion is in pole position to help rebalance the world, economically and socially. To do this, the templates embedded in Christianity and certain other religious faiths need no fundamental change but do need to be revamped in presentation, in a way that will make them compelling and point to the best road ahead for a deeply troubled world. The hub of Rome is a great starting point to this end.

So all aboard for the read and the ride.

CHAPTER ONE

Why Me for Ambassador?

In the days immediately after saying yes to the PM, I kept thinking about two questions: why upgrade the Holy See post to a resident ambassador, and why me?

Diplomatic relations had been established formally between Australia and the Holy See back in 1973. To save costs, the ambassador had been based elsewhere in Europe. He or she would fly in from Dublin or The Hague about two or three times a year and try to maintain a network of contacts and activities.

At a big Australia Day reception in the ballroom of Government House, Melbourne, in January 2009, Kevin Rudd arranged for me to come half an hour early for a one-on-one meeting. He told me of his thinking and priorities regarding the Vatican upgrade. They were in line with the formal letter of instruction, but he emphasised that a key factor driving the decision was the simple fact that Australia was one of the only members of the G20 that did not have a full-time resident ambassador to the Holy See.

Australia had managed to become a key member of the G20, and the PM was very actively supporting an expanded role for this grouping post the 2008 global financial crisis. He would be strongly involved in the Economic Crisis Summit held in London in April that year. Australia needed a level of gravitas to match its membership of this group, which was seen by some as a Holy Grail.

Whilst I never met with the G20 Holy See ambassadors as a discrete group during my posting, I was always conscious of which ambassadors were from G20 countries, and in the scheme of things, they tended to be better plugged in, more active and with more resources. One or two of the Latin American ambassadors told me shortly after I arrived in Rome that Australia could now be taken seriously, as at last it had a Rome-resident Ambassador to the Holy See!

Perhaps even more significant than the G20 dimension was the decision announced by Kevin Rudd in April 2008 that Australia was to contest the October 2012 ballot for a rotational seat on the United Nations Security Council. It would be a huge period of campaigning, over four years, and Rome was seen as one of the big hubs for this activity. At our meeting in Melbourne, the PM emphasised his absolute determination to see Australia win this ballot, and it was clear that boosting our efforts in Rome was very much part of his strategy.

WHY ME FOR AMBASSADOR?

In addition to the above, the Australian Government had a great interest in the issue of food security. Rome is a hub for discussion of this issue, with the UN Food and Agriculture Organization and several other agriculture-related bodies headquartered in the city. 'Food security' is terminology today for the whole set of issues relating to the sustainable production, distribution and consumption of food worldwide, with the objective that acute shortages and famines are to be strived against and avoided at all costs.

These were probably the three main pillars of the upgrade, but as the three years unfolded, a fourth and fifth dimension emerged. DFAT and the government obviously developed confidence in my work, so they appointed me Envoy to Bhutan (which I remain to this day) as well as to Eritrea and South Sudan. A fifth role was to be a special envoy representing the Foreign Minister or Prime Minister at key conferences and forums.

Also coming with the upgrade was the remit for the Ambassador not only to pursue key issues such as religious freedom and interfaith dialogue, but also to boost Australia's profile and connections at various levels. My letter of instruction from the Foreign and Trade Ministers made that very clear: 'The Government looks to you to leverage the goodwill in the relationship to further Australia's national interests, across the range of issues where the Vatican is active and has influence, including human rights, development assistance, food security, arms control, population issues, refugees and anti-people trafficking, climate change and the environment.'

Kevin Rudd had expressed to me his deep concerns over the drift in religious freedom in parts of Asia, especially at the provincial levels in China and Vietnam. Closer to home, Fiji (covered for the Vatican by its Papal Nuncio in New Zealand) is a work in progress on the religious freedom front, on the constitutional front and on a range of other fronts. The Vatican also continues to keep a close eye on East Timor – a country I know well, having had the privilege of leading an Australian delegation to supervise the 1999 ballot on independence from Indonesia. Today the Catholic Church in East Timor is lively, but it remains a great sadness that there were Christians killing Christians in the immediate aftermath of the ballot. (Local bishop C. F. Belo came all the way to Rome, escaping with the help of the RAAF as his life was at risk, and got a very chilly reception from Pope John Paul II, who took the view that there was only one place Bishop Belo should be, and that was back in East Timor.)

As well as affecting stability in our region, abuse of religious freedom has an even more immediate impact in the form of refugee intakes and people trafficking. Related to this are issues of global poverty and human rights abuse. But just as important are the set of priorities centring on the environment – both for Australia's own future and for the future of the world at large.

By interacting with people in Rome who knew what was happening in each of these areas, my job would be to pick up information which, when it had enough credibility and significance, I would email or cable back to Canberra. So it was a form of continuous reporting on these issues as information was gained by networking, dialogue, attending conferences, or a range of other diplomatic activities, but also by a good deal of reading of various publications that gave pointers to where the Vatican was coming from on critical issues.

Also important would be forming the right relationships with contacts and organisations. Pursuing the issue of development assistance, for instance, meant having really good connections with Caritas Internationalis and other Vatican organisations that do an enormous amount of charity work in Africa and elsewhere. And learning more about climate change involved getting to know the Pope's scientist, Bishop Marcelo Sánchez Sorondo, and attending conferences he organised where that set of issues was very much up front.

At the same time as acquiring information, my role would be to pass on positive information about Australia. I later found part of my practical work was to remind senior Vatican personnel of the size of Asia (including Australasia), the dynamic of Asia, and the need for them to go beyond the comfort zone of Rome and see for themselves what was happening there. Some Curia personnel also turned out to be very curious about the debate going on over how best to boost the education and health levels of Indigenous Australians. And I supplied information to anyone who inquired on this issue.

★ ★ ★

As to the question 'Why me?' the political cynic would argue (as one or two people said to me) that the Prime Minister from the left wanted no static about the cost of the upgrade, and if he hand-picked a retired MP from the right who was also a former deputy PM, then the decision would be accepted without too much fuss. It turned out he was right. Shadow Foreign Minister Julie Bishop was very supportive of my appointment, indeed almost all in the Coalition were supportive, except for a couple of senators.

Now, Kevin Rudd and I are from opposite sides of politics, but we had met often enough over the years, most notably back in 2001, when he was a member of another delegation I led to East Timor. We got on very well under the difficult circumstances of monitoring elections in East Timor as an embryonic independent nation. More recently he had asked me to co-chair the Rural and Regional section of the 2020 Summit, held in 2007 in Canberra.

We also had a mutual acquaintance and friend in Lachlan Harris, the overstretched Prime Ministerial Press Secretary. To this day I figure both Lachlan Harris and my friend in the PM's office from DFAT, Gary Quinlan, had sway on this unusual appointment, the subject of that interesting phone call from Canberra to LA.

I imagine the PM thought, 'Well, here's a guy who's fair dinkum about Team Australia, and not still bogged down in partisan politics.' Both of us acknowledged our political differences, but he had obviously reached some estimate of my capability that led him to make the appointment. What I do know – as I've found out from inside sources – is that it was very much Kevin Rudd's initiative to upgrade the embassy, and Kevin Rudd's initiative (on advice from his department) to put Tim Fischer into the upgraded embassy, and to present these decisions to Stephen Smith, the then Foreign Minister, to execute.

I should emphasise that you can be a Protestant Christian, you can be (as the Israeli Ambassador is) Jewish, you can be Muslim, you can be Buddhist, and still be an ambassador to the Holy See. But I happen to be a practising Catholic and I think the PM was very comfortable with that; he certainly did not want to send an aggressive agnostic or atheist.

I have a broad-based faith from way back: I was brought up a Catholic, I was baptised, I was confirmed, my family and I are regular churchgoers. As I have said publicly before, I am a less-than-perfect practising Catholic, but I do my best.

During my days as a member of John Howard's first Cabinet, every now and then an article would surface observing that a surprisingly large number of Cabinet members were Catholics – yes, there was Richard Alston, Tim Fischer, Peter McGauran, and later on Tony Abbott, amongst others. So what? As a politician and diplomat, you are there to do a job regardless of what religion you happen to practise. I always made a point of not wearing my faith on my sleeve.

In terms of my particular set of beliefs, I am probably middle of the road. I do believe in religion having spine and not being a soufflé. Café-conversational Christianity I am not. But in saying that I believe in religion with spine, with a set of beliefs that you try to adhere to, I would argue that I'm very much in line and comfortable with Vatican Council II

(1962–65), which, amongst other things, introduced the local language into the Catholic Mass, and turned the priest towards rather than away from the congregation. But it also did much more than that: it launched an ecumenical pathway that saw the Catholic Church get off its 'high horse' and communicate more effectively with other Christian denominations and other religions more broadly.

I am very strongly of liberal mind with regard to the ecumenical efforts of the Church. It must reach out, it is reaching out, and I have no problem with the Pope's very purposeful meetings with, for example, the Archbishop of Canterbury, the Primate of the Church of England. Former Archbishop Rowan Williams and Pope Benedict got on very well together and met frequently.

For all that, there will always be areas where different denominations disagree, and one of them of course is the question of papal infallibility: the doctrine that says when the Pope is making an absolute ruling, he is acting in a way deemed to be infallible. I have some reservations about that, but I accept that it is part of the Roman Catholic Church equation – though it must be remembered that it was only adopted in 1870, by Vatican Council I.

Likewise, for the first thousand years of the Roman Catholic Church priests were permitted to marry, and there is no doctrinal reason why this could not be permitted again. I absolutely agree that there could be married priests; equally, I do not agree that there could be female bishops. That, in a funny sort of way, broadly identifies where I stand: committed to finding the best way forward, and not being too hung up on the past; liberal, but not too liberal.

★ ★ ★

Short-lived PM Artie Fadden once said, 'All the good bowlers aren't in the one team.' In politics, the best players are on both sides of the chamber. When you move from being a partisan MP, arguing the cause of your government, to being a diplomat, you find yourself in the slightly broader dimension of arguing the cause of Australia generally. As an ambassador you are representing the Australian Government, the Australian Parliament and the Australian people to (in my case) the Government of the Holy See.

Although there was a broad understanding that I would back the policies of the current Labor Government, it was certainly not demanded that I sever my links with the Nationals. At any rate, my key remits – food security, interfaith dialogue etc – had general bipartisan support.

I was aware that my progression from politician to diplomat would involve considerable change. One interesting twist was that as ambassador I at last had a job where most of my weekends were free and not dominated by electorate and ministerial work. But it also meant I would no longer be able to make any critical statements about current domestic politics and current hot-button debates. In any event, I had stepped out of Parliament in 2001 and moved on, and was not seeking to be an ongoing commentator on Australian political issues. On broader international matters I did occasionally speak up after retiring from politics, and in respect of military history and rail transport I had carved out a bit of a niche for myself over the years. Indeed at all times I advocated efficient rail freight expansion but also positive examination of a High Speed Rail project from Brisbane to Melbourne via Newcastle, Sydney, Canberra and Tullamarine Airport. But even that had to be sublimated during the period when I was ambassador, for obvious reasons.

Much of my thirty years in NSW and Federal politics were about seeking compromises through diplomatic skills, and I led many delegations overseas. I seem to have an ability to cut through directly to the nub of a problem, some would say of me, so perhaps you could say I am a natural pragmatic diplomat.

Naturally, I did have some trepidations about entering an environment where I would have to hold back my opinions on political and other matters. But you've been given a job, you don't want to stuff up, you don't want to be recalled in six months – so I knew I would have to adjust. I was determined, having signed on for the role, to do my very best, which is my approach in all aspects of life.

CHAPTER TWO

Arrival, Credentials and White Knuckles

It was in the pre-dawn half light that I was jolted out of idle thoughts, as I was driven into Rome from the main international airport, Fiumicino.

I saw looming up ahead a building of Melbourne Cricket Ground proportions: the two thousand year old Colosseum in all its floodlit glory. Here was the defining welcoming beacon and superb icon of Rome, built out of a majestic limestone material known as travertine and built to last. Yes, I had definitely arrived in Rome, and in the middle of winter, January 2009. I thought to myself that there was no turning back now from the commitment I had made to devote the next three years of my life to this unexpected posting.

Many ambassadors say the first day of the first posting can be the day from hell, and to some extent it was. Conversely, the location was a bonus: the Eternal City was sparkling in the cool but sunny weather. This was especially so after recent heavy rain had helped wash down the many ancient buildings and cleaned the streets. Even the less than mighty River Tiber was putting on a performance with a vigorous flow, filling the arches of the many superb Romanesque bridges.

My flight from Melbourne had been early by half an hour: a good omen, I felt, but also with thoughts of an old film, *The Ugly American*, in which a new US ambassador turns up at his posting with no officials to welcome him at the airport, just locals rioting at his presence. In my case, an airport courtesy car had whisked me to an empty terminal, where Deputy Head of Mission Anne Giles greeted me with a confidence-building smile.

My first red diplomatic passport in nine years (since stepping down as Deputy PM) had assured my speedy passage through Customs. All of my three bags turned up in about ten minutes – including the big one with the formal court dress of white tie and tails, a black waistcoat, military medals and all the other bits and pieces essential to presenting credentials to His Holiness Pope Benedict XVI. This centuries-old procedure consists of the formal presentation of 'Letters of Credence' from one Head of State to another, naming the letter-holder as ambassador.

Soon we were accelerating along the freeway and the near-empty streets of Rome, then through a raft of very confusing roads to 49 Via Bertoloni, northwest of the city centre.

ARRIVAL, CREDENTIALS AND WHITE KNUCKLES

Apartment 8 used to be occupied by Australian RAAF Group Captain Ric Casagrande and his family, but Defence was shifting the position to Spain. It was a convenient stopgap for accommodation, saving the taxpayer hotel bills and coming with three bedrooms equipped very adequately, and a kitchen big by any apartment standards, be it in Melbourne or in Rome.

Anne said she would be back at 8.50am to take me to the embassy office, then to meetings at the Vatican. I started to unpack, had a long shower, then ate two pieces of toast, and was ready to step out in a new suit, feeling a little concerned and weary but ready to roll with the new posting.

We dived into an embassy car and headed downtown through busy morning traffic to the tiny chancery (office). Anne had

Checking credential documents in a receiving room high up in the Vatican at the Secretariat of State with Protocol Director Monsignor Fortunatus Nwachukwu on day one of the posting.

kept saying how small it was, but in a very good location, with the Vatican just a ten-minute walk away. As it turned out, yes, there was a tiny toilet and a lift from George Orwell days, but my actual office was bigger than any State Parliament or old Federal Parliament House office I had ever occupied, and about half the size of my Deputy PM's office in the new Parliament House in Canberra.

Heaps of mail and papers materialised and to work I went, fired up by the need to address my mission staff in the first hour, in accord with DFAT instructions. But I could see that both Anne and Office Manager Antonia Da-Rin were flat out, so we decided to have a working lunch later around the corner to impart the wisdom of the new HOM. I was quietly laughing to myself at my expectation of delivering a big defining address: in addition to Anne and Antonia there was just one other staff member, my PA, Madonna Noonan. There was also an official driver, Stefano Bernardini.

Just one hour after sitting down at my desk, it was a case of gathering up papers and heading out for my first meeting in the Vatican. Anne and I pounded across the still-swollen River Tiber and through the gates of the Vatican – gates I had peeped through in hectic visits to Rome over the years with never a thought of entering them in an official capacity.

Our meeting was with the Director of Protocol, Monsignor Fortunatus Nwachukwu, a Nigerian. He briefed me on what would take place at the ceremony in a fortnight's time when I would present my credentials to Pope Benedict XVI. Our meeting was friendly but lengthy, leaving little doubt that there were complicated procedures and dress codes from which there would be no departure.

Then it was a quick walk back to the chancery, with a much-needed coffee on the way, and back to desk work and settling in. I was reminded by Anne Giles of the clean-desk policy of DFAT, having already spread papers around in a typical way, but we quickly tidied up and the three of us headed to lunch. Finally I talked through some general issues, including the best method of handling visitors, of which I expected many, starting tomorrow, Saturday, with Monsignor Frank Marriott from Bendigo, who was leading a conference delegation.

★ ★ ★

Soon after lunch I took my leave and was told the embassy driver was waiting downstairs. I failed to spot the car and was about to ring back upstairs when I caught a rather curious look on the face of a man who I suddenly realised was the driver from the airport run, Massimo Aguzzi. My excuse was that it was now broad daylight and he was in a different car!

After this slight embarrassment we returned to my apartment and I headed out to look for a supermarket. I found one about 600 metres away, but promptly got totally lost trying to retrace my steps. There I was with no map, a personal BlackBerry (meaning any help calls to staff would go back to Australia then to Rome) and a growing sense of panic.

As darkness descended, I carefully backtracked to a cinema I had previously noted about halfway along the route. It was showing the film *Australia*, after all! I then adopted a step-by-careful-step approach, and eventually found Via Bertoloni and No. 49. This was just in time to get cleaned up and head out for an informal dinner at the residence of the Australian Ambassador to Italy, Amanda Vanstone.

Our first gathering in Rome was dominated by a combination of recollections and reviews of former ministerial colleagues, along with many practical hints as how best to proceed and work together, sharing aspects of administration that made sense and so eased costs on the taxpayer. Amanda's husband, Tony, gave me a lift home even though it was only a twenty-minute walk. There was no way I was going to get lost twice on day one.

After a long first day, I was exhausted. It was a case of collapse and quickly to bed, reasonably content with the prospects of what the job would hold, and my prospects of being able to handle living in a big city a long way from home.

★ ★ ★

The first fortnight of my posting passed very quickly, especially after the arrival of Judy, Harrison and Dominic for the presentation ceremony, and soon enough it was the big day, 12 February, when I would present my credentials to His Holiness the Pope.

Yes, I had white knuckles, but also a degree of excitement at the idea of stepping forward with my family on this special occasion. I thought of several stories of famous credential presentations – those of Australian diplomats lucky enough to

ARRIVAL, CREDENTIALS AND WHITE KNUCKLES

present to a Kennedy or a Reagan, but also of one Australian career diplomat who presented to then French President Charles de Gaulle. It appears de Gaulle was in a foul mood and launched into a bitter attack on Australia, all in rapid-fire French. Our ambassador of the day, David Anderson AO OBE, stood his ground and went toe to toe with Mon Général, speaking in near-perfect, robust French, and came out of the ceremony shaken but a proud defender of things Australian.

Credential ceremonies vary greatly around the world. At the White House, ambassadors are wheeled in and out quickly – and in the case of Kim Beazley, due to knee surgery from a bad fall on Washington's treacherous ice, literally wheeled in and out on a wheelchair.

Before getting into white tie, tails and medals, I ducked over to the Australian Embassy to Italy for breakfast with all the staff. It was superb bacon and eggs in the car park, a nice and tasty distraction before changing into the formal attire.

At exactly 10.15 we stepped out, but there was no convoy from the Vatican to drive us to the Holy See as promised. It was a five-minute wait before Household Escort Francisco arrived, also dressed in white tie and tails. So Judy (unfazed as usual except for getting the mantilla placed correctly on her hair), Harrison and Dominic (wearing suits and ties for the first time) and I joined the mini-convoy of three cars and sped away to the Vatican.

After a salute by a unit of the Pope's Swiss Guards, we were paraded through a series of corridors and papal apartments of great baroque splendour, many decorated by Raphael, to a corner waiting room that was just below 'The Window'. Every Sunday, the pontiff appears at noon at the second-last window from the corner, and the crowds roar from St Peter's Square. To be in this setting felt intimidating, though on subsequent visits uplifting.

I was then taken in to meet Pope Benedict XVI and to present credential letters in a friendly exchange, which was followed by a one-on-one meeting with the pontiff in his study. I had been told it would last ten to fifteen minutes, and that and a 'cue card' was permissible to guard against a tongue-tied period of silence.

The Pope could speak fluent English and understand the language if not spoken too quickly, and we worked through a list of issues that were in my charter letter, from interfaith dialogue to Vietnam and China. From him came the question: 'How was it that so many could be burnt to death in the State of Victoria in 2009?' (This was just five days after the Black Saturday bushfires.) He expressed deep sympathy to those affected, and asked that I convey that back to Australia. He was also very sincere in his wonder about what had occurred over the week he was in Sydney for World Youth Day. And I found him perhaps a little bit shy, although he's met many ambassadors over the years, but polite and absolutely engaged. An entirely sincere man, but a man for whom the worries of the huge worldwide Church were an obvious burden that he carried with him every day.

At the twenty-minute mark, I thought I should pause and signal that I was happy to bring the meeting to a close. He

ARRIVAL, CREDENTIALS AND WHITE KNUCKLES

hesitated and talked a little more about Vatican Council II before leaning forward and pushing a red button. The doors opened and in came the photographers.

I was able to introduce and present my family one by one, then Anne Giles, after which there were several photos and some light-hearted discussion. Then we were escorted out and down to the Secretary of State (the prime minister equivalent), Cardinal Bertone, for a meeting and second round of proceedings.

Cardinal Bertone, a northern Italian, was also very polite, but more formal than the pontiff. We were able to speak through a terrific interpreter, Monsignor Nicolas Thevenin, who was to become a very close friend of mine. The technical problem was that the Cardinal understood a good deal of English, so would often jump ahead of Monsignor Thevenin, and we would not then know whether to turn to the Monsignor or carry on with the conversation, so we got into a bit of an impasse. But to some extent I felt the pressure was off; I'd got through the meeting with the Pope, and I began to unwind a little. We talked about food security and Australia, but also a recent media saga relating to the Vatican and the Holocaust (which I'll touch on later). Again, after a good twenty minutes or more, we returned to an anteroom for a series of group photos.

I was proud of my family for getting through all of this, especially my autistic son Harrison, who is liable to say or do anything. In fact, three years previously Harrison had been in a fury down in the crowd outside St Peter's. I never thought that one day we would be all upstairs with the Pope. (Three years on again, during the farewell call, Harrison asked the Pope directly how he was and had he had a good day. The Pope said he was all right and then Harrison blurted out that he hoped he would keep the Church together. With a smile the Pope replied, 'I will try!' This raised some eyebrows but also some amusement among the Curia present.)

Then came the third phase of the ceremony, a small procession into St Peter's proper, with tourists cleared back but cameras flashing. My family and I were taken to three altars and invited to kneel and pray at them for one or two minutes each. Then it was through the Prayer Door and out to the cars on the south side. Soon we were hurtling under police escort through the streets of Rome back to the apartment – job completed on behalf of Australia, but in reality job just commencing.

I felt guilty in one sense, as there are many far more devoted to the Church than I could ever be who never get to meet the Pope. I guess that is how the diplomatic system works.

After a snack at home and dictation of a long cable back to Canberra, I dashed to the chancery to handle some media engagements and come back to earth. Then it was a return to the apartment to pick up Judy and attend the Eightieth Lateran Treaty Concert, a performance of Handel's *Messiah*. Several thousand had gathered in the Paul VI Auditorium for the occasion.

I smiled at one unusual twist to the seniority seating policy in the huge auditorium. The Pope sits about halfway back from the stage, and senior ambassadors sit near him and the most junior further away but closer to the front. As the most junior, having presented credentials only a few hours previously, I found Judy and I were in the first row!

The Concert was exceptional, with the famous 'Hallelujah Chorus' performed twice as an encore. It was a superb way to end a great but exhausting day. As it turned out, this was one of the best concerts I attended during my 1000 days of posting in Rome. Judy and I quickly returned home, paid the boys' carer fifty euros and collapsed, happy now that the first fortnight of the job was done and dusted.

CHAPTER THREE

Daily Batting for Team Australia

No matter where an ambassador is in ninety-five different locations around the world, they are part of Team Australia and their job is to promote Australia, and the policies and priorities of the Australian Government, Parliament and the Australian people. All of this helps open up opportunities for companies, sometimes leading nowhere but sometimes delivering millions if not billions to Australia's bottom line. Managing our relations with the likes of China, India and Indonesia all helps underpin trade and investment.

So it's all about generic promotion firstly, then it's about the specific issues that you are allocated – human rights, development assistance, food security, arms control, population issues, refugees, anti-people trafficking, climate change and the environment –

and then there are the campaigns. There was one campaign for me especially, the bid for the UN Security Council seat, but another campaign of great import was Australia's bid to 'host' the Square Kilometre Array (SKA) radio telescope, being developed in the UK with the cooperation of twenty-one nations worldwide (more on which later).

Then, of course, there is the need to oversee a raft of administration issues – handling duty rosters; conducting annual staff reviews; planning ahead for key events, in my case in the knowledge that you have a very limited budget and that it is a very small embassy. The instructions in my ministerial letter were unambiguous: I needed to show 'clear leadership of staff, ensuring the mission in the Holy See is effectively, fairly and ethically managed'. And on the whole I was able to do this, with some creative, lateral thinking.

In some ways, being Ambassador to the Holy See is slightly different from being an ambassador in most locations. Other ambassadors will occasionally visit their host country's parliament, call on various opposition leaders of minor parties and so forth. But in the Vatican there are no parliamentary sessions to attend, because there's no parliament. And there's no leader of the opposition in the Vatican – to which some would say, 'No, there's just the American liberal Church'! But in the course of the average day, there is a wide variety of activities, and the key to managing these is constant networking: everything from attendance at formal functions to casual conversations in the street.

Of course, all of this can't be mastered overnight. Some months earlier DFAT had provided a useful one-day course in

Canberra for heads of mission, covering subjects such as budget administration and security of communications, and the golden rule: no surprises for the Foreign Minister and no contradiction of government policy, ever. DFAT offers nine months' language training for diplomats, but I just didn't have the time to allocate to that before I left. So when I arrived I took three quick weeks to learn basics, at a beautiful place called Montepulciano, on the edge of Tuscany.

But no course can fully prepare you for what awaits once you arrive on location. Suddenly you're doing a different job from anything you'd previously done, while living in a strange city – I'd visited Rome several times before, but living and working there is vastly different. So how do you learn the ropes? You ask lots of questions and you listen to your staff.

My deputy, Anne Giles, was a capable career diplomat who had the courage to tell me when my ideas were not good diplomacy or simply not justified given DFAT's scarce resources. Her Italian language skills were excellent and very helpful at many meetings. She was terrific in so many ways, including handling the administrative side of things. About halfway through my posting she was replaced by the equally able Michael Sullivan, who had a useful previous posting to Israel and who provided stability.

In such a tiny embassy, Madonna Noonan was often a great deal more than just my PA. Working lunches and dinners were her forte, as she could so often anticipate who would not get on so well and adjust the seating accordingly.

Office Manager Antonia Da-Rin also helped as a research

Vibrant Australian Ambassador to Italy Amanda Vanstone, as we got ready to head out from her residence to an informal weekend function, joining other expats in Rome.

officer, and worked on vital projects that will feature later in this book.

The final staff member was Stefano Bernardini, a modern Roman chariot driver whom I had selected from a shortlist. Alas, the vehicle he had to drive had been purchased before I arrived and was a Peugeot. The problem with having a Peugeot as your chariot of choice in Rome is that the width of same is about six inches too wide for the city's narrow streets. (For the record, the Peugeot received only two war wounds: one placed there by Stefano and one by me trying to park in a spot that only an Italian would have attempted to negotiate. We declared a one-all tie!)

Our embassy also shared a Senior Administration Officer (SAO) and Deputy SAO with the Australian Embassy to Italy, known as the bilateral embassy. Throughout most of my posting the SAO was the laid-back but capable Paul Given, followed late in the posting by Kay Rowland, not so laid-back but just as capable as her predecessor. As deputy there was the dedicated and capable Jenny Hobbs. They dealt with matters of building leases, car pool supervision, computer equipment, electricity bills and similar essentials. The consular work, assisting Australians living in or visiting Rome – providing emergency passports, managing body bags involving Australians killed in car accidents – all had to be handled by Jenny or other consular staff. (The consular work was not the responsibility of the Holy See Embassy unless somebody broke their leg within St Peter's Square, but several families under stress were helped by our embassy, such as those seeking access to a general audience with the Pope, for example for their child with cancer.)

As previously stated, the Australian Embassy to Italy was led by Amanda Vanstone when I first arrived in Rome. Amanda was a heavy hitter, both as a politician and as an ambassador. After years in the Australian Senate and before that in the factionally robust South Australian Liberal Party, Amanda was a very different kind of ambassador who could, when needed, give as good as she received.

Throughout her time as ambassador she scored important goals that added depth to the Australian–Italian bilateral relationship. In 2009 Amanda stepped up for an Australian company owed about $18 million. She had the right knowledge and contacts, and arranged the right meetings that led to a two-year outstanding payment being made twenty-eight days after her approach. When the Holy See Embassy moved into a new chancery, Amanda provided great assistance in securing a vital boost to the power connection. This involved getting approval for sixty metres of Via Paola, a historic Roman pavement, to be ripped up for a trench one metre deep, saving over half a million dollars for the Australian taxpayer in the process.

Amanda had brought her huge dog, Gus, with her to Rome, and in his own way, he too was not without influence. 'Great Gus', a rather expressionful Weimaraner, was allowed many liberties, and depending on your point of view he lent great life and colour to some diplomatic occasions – especially when becoming 'friendly' with the Pakistani Ambassador to Italy.

Now, it has long been argued by Amanda that Gus did *not* try to eat the Pakistani Ambassador and definitely did not bite her; it was merely a nick. However, it is accepted that Gus *did* clash with the distinguished ambassador, who required tetanus and rabies shots immediately. Further, Gus has certain form. As revealed (to Amanda's chagrin) on the ABC TV show *Kitchen Cabinet*, Gus had previously had an altercation with a child of Federal MP Christopher Pyne. To be fair to Gus, he is placid unless he is stirred up or you run in his presence.

At one stage I invited Gus and owners to my apartment for dinner. Judy and the boys were staying and I thought it might be fun for them and would also help Gus practise his etiquette, amongst friends, so to speak. Gus was brilliantly behaved and an enjoyable night ensued.

In due course the Gus incidents were raised in Senate Estimates, as the said Gus had been very brave and also tried to bite an Italian security detail policeman. One senator railed against Gus, asking how much he was costing the Australian taxpayer. The correct answer was given, namely zero, and at the end of Amanda's posting Gus departed Europe in style – due to Australian quarantine requirements, via Vienna.

Shortly after the Senate Estimate hearings involving Gus, I was talking on the phone to Richard Maude, my then supervisor at DFAT HQ. When the rest of our business was done, I quietly told Richard that I was greatly missing my sheepdog back home,

At a working conference between the two Australian embassies in Rome; from left to right, Madonna Noonan, Antonia Da-Rin, Toshi Kawaguchi, the two ambassadors – myself and David J. Ritchie – Paul Given, Peter Rayner and Michael Sullivan. These conferences saved taxpayers' money by helping to boost coordination, especially of transport movements, for the heavy load of official visits. David Ritchie delivered considerably at his post, amongst other things securing a visit to Australia of a young Italian MP, Enrico Letta, in 2012. Letta became PM of Italy in 2013.

DAILY BATTING FOR TEAM AUSTRALIA

and asked could I pay for it to come and stay in Rome? There was a chilly silence before I chuckled and said to Richard, 'Relax – I don't even own a sheepdog anymore!'

★ ★ ★

When Amanda departed with Tony and Great Gus in July 2010, she was succeeded by David J. Ritchie, a career diplomat who had been Deputy Secretary of DFAT when I'd been Trade Minister. His wife, Jenelle, had been my Chief of Staff, and I knew her very well. David was a very solid, safe pair of hands who could always advise you on who best to go to in DFAT about the particular thing you were trying to finesse. He and Amanda were two totally different ambassadors, but both went seriously about their work to get things done.

In January 2012, just before my departure, David proved his mettle when he headed up the embassy's response to one of the great disasters to strike Italy in recent years: the sinking of the cruise ship *Costa Concordia* off an island northwest of Rome. The embassy team's effort was superlative in every way. Consul Jenny Hobbs and her team moved through the night to the wharf where those rescued had landed, setting up a help centre in a coffee shop with a big Australian flag erected out the front, and by sunset all 23 Australians had been accounted for and assisted. With a million Australians overseas at any one time, it demonstrates why we need a network on the ground in key locations, with fast-moving, professional staff, ready to issue passports and help out many people, often very distressed.

The Deputy Head of Mission to Amanda Vanstone and David Ritchie was Peter Rayner, whom I'd known from many years ago, having met him when he was posted to Indonesia.

I judged it one of my most important duties to maintain close informal and formal contact with the Australian Embassy to Italy and its key staff, since so many of them were my staff as well. There are a few parts of the world where more than one ambassador is stationed – Geneva, Paris, Vienna, New York, Washington – and over the years, human nature being what it is, there've been situations where those ambassadors at the one location were not even on talking terms with each other. I was well aware of that as former Deputy Prime Minister, and I was determined to see that that did not happen to me.

And so I'd go over to Amanda's or David's place or on one occasion to Peter Rayner's place and have a quiet dinner and vice versa, and mix around and learn. David Ritchie was out of town a bit, because he was up in Milan or down in Sicily doing his job, but we connected regularly for coffee in his office or mine. As two heads of missions, we also had a quick bite to eat round town about once a fortnight, just to keep across everything that could go wrong between the two embassies.

In fact, the two embassies shared a lot more than just staff. We were all batting for Team Australia, so everything was geared towards maximising efficiency and effectiveness on a limited budget and with limited resources.

On one notorious occasion, I invited Bishop Marcelo Sánchez Sorondo, the Pope's Chief Scientist, to a lunch in his honour – which I called the Primavera Lunch (Springtime Lunch). We would focus on food famine issues and agriculture with others of the same bent in that regard. And at the time I didn't have a big enough venue to do a proper lunch for twenty-four people, so I borrowed, surreptitiously, the kitchen and dining room of Amanda Vanstone's residence. (Amanda fortunately was out of Rome at the time, and just for once, Gus was not in attendance!)

It probably stretched half a dozen protocol rules within the Vatican, because the two embassies are meant to be absolutely separate addresses, but I got around that by making the declaration at seven that morning that the dining room and kitchen of the Australian Embassy to Italy were for the next ten hours to be leased by the Australian Embassy to the Holy See. The lunch went extremely well, but right at the end one senior ambassador was starting to twig to what was happening, so I discreetly bundled her out of the room before she could ask too many more questions! Some ambassadors are very correct and chip those who bend the rules.

(I hasten to add that this was very much a one-off exercise – partly because the Australian Ambassador to Italy's residence in Parioli has since been vacated, as major reconstruction takes place to stop it from falling down the hill into the Tiber.)

This sort of close cooperation between embassies ultimately received its reward. From time to time the DFAT HQ conducts in-country reviews of the performance of ambassadors and embassies, which is always a good idea. They're done at arm's length and a performance report drawn up. In the second half of my posting, I proudly recall that one of those reports indicated that the Australian Embassy to Italy and the Australian Embassy to the Holy See had achieved a great deal of positive liaison, saving taxpayers' money in the process. In fact, it was judged that we worked together better than any other two embassies at locations where Australia had more than one DFAT unit.

I thought, 'Well, we should celebrate this: David Ritchie and I will hire a canoe and paddle gently down the Tiber, with photographers stationed on a bridge!' One side of the Tiber was in a sense the responsibility of the Australian Ambassador to Italy, and the other side of the Tiber, where Vatican City is, was my responsibility, so it would have been a very symbolic gesture. I suggested this to David and got a sort of wry smile from him – and almost everyone else I raised it with – implying that this was just one of those ten ideas a day I have that should be rejected by all and sundry! It was.

★ ★ ★

During my early days in Rome, it was joint staff member Paul Given who helped me find a permanent apartment. We looked at a couple of three- and four-storey villas a bit out of town, but a slightly less luxurious apartment on Via Nomentana was the one that appealed to me. It was two floors underneath the Eritrean Ambassador's apartment, alongside the Libyan Embassy and not far from the Iranian and Turkish embassies, but a fair way from downtown Rome.

For several months there were regular demonstrations outside the Iranian and then the Libyan embassies, bringing out huge police contingents, though no shots were ever fired. It was certainly interesting living next to these two missions and near the always-polite Eritrean Ambassador. This later tied in well with my side job as Envoy to Eritrea. The apartment was one of the best calls I made over the three years: it was in a compound, with gardens, and allowed me to do a lot of reading and writing from that location.

A typical day started at the apartment at 6.30am, with a quick flick through my emails from home and my diary for the day. There would also be a Skype session with my family. As Minister for Trade I'd been away a fair bit, but I'd never been separated from my family for this long before, and without Skype it would have been tough. Our morning catch-ups gave me a chance to debrief about the good moments, the critical moments and the moments where additional advice was helpful.

Thanks to the time difference, first thing in the morning in Rome, the front pages of the likes of the *New York Times* or *Washington Post* could be read online. I would also look at the ABC news website and read the Australian morning newspapers, if I hadn't managed to see them the night before. They would tell me what was happening in Australia, and what was happening elsewhere as seen through an Australian lens.

I remember, as a young boy, going with my father to buy the Sunday papers on a Monday night when the mail train finally reached Boree Creek from Sydney, thirty-six hours later. In Rome, if I had more than a thirty-six second delay in downloading the *Australian* and other papers, I would hit the roof; that's how crazy it's become. Unfortunately the outbreak of paywalls some time during my posting meant I needed to use legal loopholes to still download for free, until they gradually became impossible to bypass. As this began to happen I switched to key UK newspapers, particularly the UK *Financial Times*.

After all this reading it was out the back gate for a quick cup of coffee before meeting up with my Deputy Head of Mission at 8.30, and together we would drive or be driven into the chancery. After another quick coffee at nearby Café Nero (yes, two bursts most mornings, but usually none after noon), it was to my desk to read the stream of emails from Canberra and the DFAT clips, which list every story printed about DFAT anywhere in the world.

All this information gathering meant that if there was something governmental that was breaking in Australia, you could anticipate and prepare a response. I was on deck in Rome when Australia changed its prime minister very suddenly in 2010. The day before that happened, I could see the ground moving, and I remember saying, 'By sunset tomorrow, Australia will have a new prime minister.' 'How can you be so sure?' asked some of my interlocutors. I answered, 'Well, they've called a special Caucus meeting and they don't call that kind of Caucus meeting unless they've got the numbers.' (As Deputy Prime Minister I had had leadership spills against me on occasions, so I knew the drill only too well.)

And sure enough, by Rome sunset time the next day, there was a new Prime Minister – Julia Gillard. There was a lot of interest in that, because Kevin Rudd was well known around Rome, had made a couple of visits by that stage as Prime Minister, and people were generally wanting to understand how this had happened, and you're obliged to answer those questions. I did so in a careful, informational way, without any emotion.

★ ★ ★

Around 10.15 each morning there would be a staff meeting, then at 11 there might be a call and meeting with a senior Vatican figure such as Bishop Marcelo Sánchez Sorondo on food security issues or Father Mapelli from the Vatican Museum on exhibiting some great artifacts from the Tiwi Islands. Then there might be a light working lunch or a more formal working lunch, often enough with ambassadors but always with other key Vatican or university personnel, such as from the Jesuit Gregorian University, present. In one week I fitted in functions with former Trade Minister Bob McMullan, now Queensland Transport Minister Scott Emerson, Geraldine Doogue from the ABC, US-based Jesuit Professor Dan Madigan, Lesley-Anne Knight from Caritas Internationalis, Dr Cary Fowler from the Global Crop Diversity Trust, and several others, including the delightful Dutch Ambassador Henriette van Lynden-Leijten, who very sadly died mid-posting after a big contribution for her country around the Mediterranean and beyond.

After lunch I often took the opportunity to go to the secure section of the embassy to read the classified cables. There are three different areas in the chancery: there's a public reception area, and then you are admitted through a double-door airlock, through airport-type screening, into an open area and a set of offices. Then through another set of door locks there is the secure area of the embassy, to which only my PA, my deputy and I had access. This housed the DFAT Satin High computer, where highly classified material from Canberra could be read.

Around 3.30pm there might be desk work to tidy up, to satisfy the DFAT clean-desk policy. Or there could be visitors from Australia seeking to call on me. I soon decided to open up the chancery to as many Australian taxpayers as possible, as an opportunity to explain what the embassy does. So a steady stream from the ordinary to the high-powered, the deeply religious to the atheist, political friends to former political foes all made it through and signed the visitors' book.

School groups, including school choirs, visited from many parts of Australia. Many families came through, sometimes with very sick children, and the embassy team always pulled out all stops. One family came from Queensland with a young daughter who was terminally ill and wanted to see the Pope. Against all odds, her wish was granted and she obtained a front-row seat at a general audience with His Holiness, receiving a greeting and blessing. (The trick was not to ask too often for tickets to the vital front row, whose occupants generally got to meet the Pope briefly one-on-one and have their photos taken.)

Outreach of this kind was not exactly the highest DFAT priority; it needed to be managed so that the time required did not get out of hand. But I would argue that it was a win-win outcome. The chance to restate the fact that I was representing the Australian Government and Australian Parliament to the oldest organisation in the world, and was not a conduit from the Australian bishops to their boss, was useful. Indeed, it was a very beneficial reminder of the fundamentals of my job.

★ ★ ★

As the office working day came to a close, it was a case of getting ready for the diplomatic peak hours. From 5.30 to 7.30pm there was usually a lecture followed by a reception at one of the big universities, or a national day function, or a conference plenary session, or the opening of an exhibition.

Then, on many but not all nights, a diplomatic dinner would take place, usually at 8pm (though on one night the invitation actually said '9 for 9.30'). Eventually, after a long dinner, I would walk home if it was still before midnight – or get public transport or a taxi if it was any later. Then, if I had the energy, I would boot up my computer to see the Australian newspaper headlines and sometimes listen to the 7.45am ABC Radio news.

Occasionally, when my family was not in town, I had house guests to stay at the apartment – everyone from official guests to friends. I commend to new ambassadors two great rules I developed from experience and listening to the woes of others: firstly, no friends of friends to stay, and secondly, a maximum of three nights to minimise the impact on a busy ambassadorial schedule and protect your own 'time out'.

I tried to organise fewer long official functions at night during the precious weeks when my family was staying in Rome. It worked out that they visited me twice a year, and the boys very much enjoyed their trips to see me. The *quid pro quo* of not having their dad around most of the time was that they got to attend Christmas in Rome, they got to attend the canonisation of Mary MacKillop, and they got to go to parts of Italy and Prague, Seville and Granada as side trips. On one occasion we even travelled to the village of Grosotto in the Valtellina area, where Judy's great-grandfather came from.

Harrison got into the habit of long walks in the area round the apartment, and on free nights we resumed a custom of family Scrabble battles, with Dominic and (on occasion) Judy's sister Rosie dominating. As a family we went to as many official Masses as could be fitted in, and Judy accompanied me to a couple of diplomatic dinners in the Vatican Gardens, which was a great delight to me. As the wife of a former Deputy Prime Minister, and in her own right in various university roles, she knew how to mix well so she was very comfortable with this sort of activity, and got to know many of the ambassadors' wives.

Though the gaps between the family visits were not too long, the visits were always memorable and it was a letdown when they came to an end and I had to say goodbye.

★ ★ ★

Amid all this activity, there was certainly never a dull moment throughout my 1000 days in Rome. Some parts of my job were better than others, but there was always a certain buzz, interesting issues and people, and sheer purpose, to ensure that the three years were over almost before I knew it.

CHAPTER FOUR

Who's Who in the Vatican

So who does a Holy See ambassador engage with in the Vatican, and what can they learn in return as they go about representing their country to the nation state of the Holy See? This was another area I had to get my head around during my first months in Rome – though in fact, I don't think you ever fully do.

The Swiss Guards are a powerful body, controlling access to many parts of Vatican City. I had been told that if you established relations early and they got to know you, a lot of time was saved. So my first formal official working lunch on arriving in the Holy See, hosted at my apartment, was designed as an ice breaker to help me get to know some senior members of what is the oldest regiment in the world.

I had been given a magnificent black cattleman's Akubra to take to Rome, and I must admit I wore it or waved it repeatedly on seeking ambassadorial entry into Vatican City, thus expediting the process of dealing with the Swiss Guards, who could on odd occasions proceed with a slow, detailed inspection of your Vatican ambassadorial pass.

Anton Kurmann was one of a handful of Swiss Guards whom I got to know on first-name terms. He has an aunt who lives in Victoria and who met me when she came through Rome; Anton himself had been to Australia a couple of years before. One morning I was taking a delegation led by Queensland Senate President John Hogg into the Vatican City for meetings. The Swiss Guard on duty saw my hat, said 'Hello, Tim,' shook my hand and waved us through. I responded 'Hello, Anton,' and away we went, with John Hogg spluttering that he could barely believe what he had just witnessed.

I was certainly assisted in negotiating the Vatican by the head-of-mission course I did before I left Australia, and the briefings of my Deputy Head of Mission, Anne Giles, upon arrival in Rome, who (as related) had me in to see the Director of Protocol on the very morning I got off the plane. Finally, I was also greatly helped by a course that was offered to diplomats from Greater Asia (including Australia) in May 2009. It was entitled 'The Catholic Church and the International Policy of the Holy See', and was run jointly by the Gregorian Foundation and the International Jacques Maritain Institute. For me it could not have been better timed, coming in the first few months of my posting, and it proved very useful indeed, giving me a lot more background than I'd received from any other source.

The second week of the conference was held in Turin, where

I was asked to chair a session on 'International Policy of the Holy See'. One speaker, Geneva-based Archbishop Silvano Maria Tomasi, covered a great deal of ground relating to the Holy See's relationship with international organisations such as the World Trade Organization (WTO), the Rome-based UN Food and Agriculture Organization (FAO) and other UN agencies. I found this session very helpful in broadening my understanding. For example, I learnt that the Vatican has 'Official Observer' status at the FAO, with generally a senior archbishop in attendance. The extent of the Holy See's involvement with so many world organisations, and its use of soft power to promote its position on issues such as population growth and food shortage, were real eye-openers.

The two star speakers at the conference were Vatican Assessore (Chief of Staff) Monsignor Gabriele Caccia, and Undersecretary (Deputy Foreign Minister) Monsignor Pietro Parolin (both later promoted to archbishop). These two monsignors gave freely of their time, had a sense of humour and were helpful and informative. In a wide-ranging address, Caccia detailed the history of the Holy See, the distinctions between the Holy See and its capital, Vatican City, and the key units within the structure of the Holy See.

Important to my role was the Prefecture of the Papal Household, which organises all audiences with the Pope, including credentials ceremonies, as well as the Pope's travels within Italy. Because in the modern world he who controls the diary is the one who says yes or no to access to the Pope, that becomes a very powerful unit within the Vatican.

Then you had the actual governing body of the Holy See, known as the Roman Curia. The Secretariat of State was the political and diplomatic unit, led by the prime minister equivalent, Cardinal Bertone, and divided into two sections: the Section for General Affairs and the Section for Relations with States. Then there was a series of units that administered the affairs of the worldwide Church at the most senior level, including nine congregations, three tribunals, eleven (later twelve) pontifical councils and three offices, as well as pontifical commissions, academies, committees and a range of other institutions – overseeing everything from Catholic doctrine to the Church's vast museum collections. It is, as you might expect, an extremely complex structure, to govern what is one of the world's most complex organisations.

But one telling difference from most organisations – and most governments – is that there is only one ultimate decision-maker, and that is the Pope (and to some extent the Secretary of State, Cardinal Bertone). While there is a kind of democratic approach to the ballot process of the conclave (papal election), once elected the Pope rules as Supreme Pontiff, a kind of absolute monarch. Yes, he consults; he can chose any number of people to advise him individually; but at the end of the day the decisions are his. This applies to every area from key questions of theology to the appointment of each bishop and archbishop throughout the world. (Of course, the big danger in this is that, unless the right people are advising him, these decisions may not accurately reflect the state of affairs in individual churches around the world – which is why the Pope is so often exposed to accusations of being 'out of touch'.)

WHO'S WHO IN THE VATICAN

While I was ambassador, there was no cabinet or parliament to help the pope of the day with coordination; however, new Pope Francis in April 2013 appointed a group of eight cardinals to advise him. To date, the various departments of the Curia rarely, if ever, meet as a group. Each meets individually with Cardinal Bertone, and of course on occasions with the absolute ruler. In the case of the heads of the two departments handling nominations for archbishops and bishops, generally these meetings were weekly, and the Pope selected each candidate from a shortlist of three names: around twenty new appointments a week. (On my farewell call on the Pope in January 2012 we had to wait forty-five minutes for one of these meetings to conclude.) But for other department heads, opportunities to meet with the Pope could be much rarer.

As a result, there were often breakdowns in coordination. Quite often the various units simply did not know what their next-door neighbours were doing, even though it might relate to the same part of Africa, or whatever the issue might be. Sometimes the left hand didn't quite tell the right hand that it had just scheduled a major conference in Asia that clashed with, for example, the elevation of archbishops to cardinals, requiring the Archbishop of Manila to be in Rome to be promoted to cardinal, because that's an absolute necessity, so consequently the conference had to be rescheduled.

Now, as the Vatican is a hierarchical organisation, and the Pope has absolute power, I don't argue that there should be a cabinet as we would understand a cabinet in any other Western State, making decisions. No, the Pope makes the big decisions and promulgates all changes to Canon Law, the laws of the Catholic Church. (The absence of a cabinet or a parliament does not mean the absence of any form of judiciary; there are the various papal tribunals and even a kind of magistrates' court.) The new overarching advisory body, however, is sensible; eight senior cardinals, with all but one from outside Italy, to shape reforms.

Occasionally there is swapping around of internal information – 'A popular archbishop is being sacked in Country X; the news will come out next week – how are we going to handle it?' – but this phenomenon was rare. More coordination between departments would mean the Vatican wasn't caught flat-footed, and might even have a stratagem in place so that those that who are going to be upset by the sacking of the archbishop might still have some olive branch offered, rather than having this decision presented as a *fait accompli* by Rome, with no room for explanation or discussion. Removal of key personnel who are under-performing is one area the Vatican does not handle well – more on that later.

I noticed countless disconnections of timing, of coordination, of exchange of information, over my 1000 days in Rome. I once asked whether even the secretaries of the various Holy See departments met on, say, the first Monday of each month for coffee, simply to exchange useful information, and especially to coordinate the timing of big events. The universal response was laughter and usually a rejoinder: 'If only, but not likely any time soon!' The Vatican is driven by tradition. It hates modernity – or elements of it hate modernity – and when a new monsignor discusses imposing key performance indicators on his staff, or a thing called a budget, they go purple with apoplexy.

Ambassadors like me weren't going to alter this 'silo mentality' so we simply had to adjust to it. In fact, ambassadors sometimes became conduits of information between the various silos, almost accidentally. For me, it also allowed some scope to elevate certain priorities in accordance with DFAT instructions, such as the food security issue. There are so many issues bubbling around Rome that half the battle is to bring focus to any particular one.

One further point: I also think the Catholic Church will be more rounded out when there is a majority of non-Italians running aspects of its central administration (with the one exception, perhaps, of Governorato of the Vatican City, equivalent to the lord mayor). The tension between the non-Italians, who see Roman Catholicism as the universal Church, and the Italian majority, who regard it as the universal *Italian* Church, continues to this day. Of the senior appointments to the Curia that Pope Benedict made, the majority of them favoured Italian personnel. And so the hold of the Italians on the Vatican Curia was in no way diminished by having a German Pope. (It might have helped if there were also a non-Italian Secretary of State, instead of Cardinal Bertone.) Yes, there are many non-Italians in senior positions in the Curia, but somehow the resident Italians still hold it with an iron grip – even though, as one wily American monsignor has pointed out, 'More money for the funding of the Vatican comes from the USA than from Italy; we should have more share of the action.'

So, to repeat the question I asked at the start: who were the major players that I particularly related to as Ambassador to the Holy See?

Within the Secretariat of State, clearly the key senior personnel were Archbishop Mamberti, the head of the Section for Relations with States (the foreign minister equivalent), and his deputy. Then there was the network of over 140 papal nuncios, the Holy See's ambassadors stationed around the world. They are constantly reporting back to their HQ in Rome, and are repositories of much information and knowledge about complex situations in places such as the Horn of Africa. Unfortunately ambassadors to the Holy See cannot automatically tap into these valuable flows of information, although the occasional briefing is held, such as was the case after the Pope's successful visit to the United Kingdom in 2010. Here often frosty relations between the Catholic and Anglican Churches were enhanced and Pope Benedict gave a terrific and thoughtful address in Westminster Hall on the things that unite all mankind.

Maltese Monsignor Antoine Camilleri was effectively the personal assistant to Archbishop Mamberti and his deputy. He did all that he could do to facilitate key meetings in the diplomatic area of the Curia. After a few weeks I developed the habit of only asking for a meeting at a senior level in the Vatican if I had a specific issue to raise, and then I always kept the meeting tight. Once the main business of the meeting was complete, generally within twenty minutes or so, I would ask if there was anything the Curia person wanted to raise with me, and if not I would stand and politely bring the meeting to a close.

There was real purpose to my method, because you maximised your chances of getting further meetings if you were judged not to be a time waster and if you were prompt and punctual. The senior Curia members frowned on any ambassador who stayed over an hour and took half an hour to get to the subject at hand.

For the duration of my posting, Archbishop James Harvey from Minnesota, USA, was Head of the Papal Prefecture, and he decided, amongst other things, who got to sit in the coveted front row at general audiences with the Pope. So he was on everybody's visiting list, especially when you had a head of State or another VIP coming to Rome. A pleasant Mid-Westerner, he has now been promoted to cardinal and head of St Paul's outside the Vatican Walls.

Another key person to know when making arrangements regarding the Pope was his Principal Private Secretary, Monsignor Georg Gänswein ('the power behind the throne' who has since taken over Archbishop Harvey's role). The monsignor once called himself 'the Pope's window on the world', adding, 'the cleaner it is, the more he can see.'

As with all huge organisations that have been around for decades and even centuries, it is halfway down the Vatican hierarchy that you can often gain the most useful contact. On the one hand, the very senior are rarely accessible; on the other, the very junior are often available but too far down the information chain. Falling plumb in the middle are those in the rank of monsignor, many of them very dedicated, younger in age than the cardinals, archbishops and bishops, and more open to new ideas and information. They were also more interested in arrivals in Rome, such as new ambassadors to the Holy See. And almost all spoke English, which was a practical help. So in the first few weeks, and indeed the first year of posting, it was a good idea for a junior ambassador to mix well with this rank of personnel in the Vatican. They knew a lot about what was going on and were prepared to pass on a lot of (non-classified) information.

Monsignor Fortunatus Nwachukwu, the Director of Protocol, was someone to whom all ambassadors had to relate in a formal sense: he decided exactly when a credentials ceremony would start, and when a farewell ceremony would take place at the end of an ambassadorial posting. He was distinctly non-Italian, and he was great value; his mother had visited Melbourne at some stage, so that gave us an extra point of connection.

Each country with diplomatic relations with the Holy See had an allocated desk officer, and for Australia it was the Irish Monsignor Joseph Murphy, who performed his role covering a wide clutch of diverse countries including Pakistan very professionally. There were many other good monsignors around this Secretariat of State part of the Vatican, for example Monsignor Leo Cushley from Scotland via South Africa, to name one of many who did so much to make an ancient system work as well as possible.

In most of the key departments of the Holy See, I found monsignors and others to connect with, such as the Secretary of the Pontifical Council for Social Communications, an Irishman, Monsignor Paul Tighe. He had a cheerful disposition and a surprisingly deep and finely tuned knowledge of not only the Internet but all aspects of social media.

Perhaps the two most powerful monsignors of all were the Chef du Cabinet, or Assessore – Monsignor Gabriele Caccia and later Monsignor Peter Wells – and the Deputy Minister for Foreign Affairs, or Undersecretary for Relations with States – Monsignor Pietro Parolin, later Monsignor Ettore Balestrero, and most recently Antoine Camilleri. These two key positions were a fulcrum to some extent and involved facilitating the reaching out across the various silos of the Holy See and even across the world, to alert key international cardinals and archbishops of storm clouds breaking in the media. When the Pope travelled overseas, these two remained at post in the Vatican and were the most senior Curia members from the centrum still in town.

Some key monsignors were based out of Rome. They included the extraordinary Monsignor Robert Vitillo, who handles a huge swag of policy issues for Caritas Internationalis from the office of Papal Nunciate in Geneva, including Health and HIV-AIDS policies. This makes sense, as the World Health Organization is headquartered in Geneva, but because his work saw him often having to come to Rome, he happily doubled up as the Caritas representative on the Caritas Express steam train project covered later.

Monsignor Nicolas Thevenin was another worthy fulcrum within the inner circle, on most days sitting just outside the door of the Pope's official study or formal receival room, closest to the Pope at most times but rarely dining with him upstairs in the private quarters. We had many shared interests, especially in the progress of the railways of the world but also in India and Bhutan. Monsignor Thevenin had held many postings way beyond Rome, including in India, Congo, Belgium, Lebanon, Cuba and Bulgaria. He is fluent, as so many are around the Vatican, in many languages: English, French, Italian, German, Spanish and even Portuguese. This meant he had rare insights into many regional issues, which will be beneficial in his latest deserved promotion and posting as Papal Nuncio to Guatemala.

My interactions with key monsignors besides being useful and interesting and mostly enjoyable, also assisted my necessary interface with those more senior officials such as the Curia bishops, archbishops and even cardinals. Some became good friends and one, namely the same said multi-lingual Nicolas Thevenin, returned hospitality by cooking a simple but sumptuous farewell meal in his tiny apartment on the rooftop of a Vatican building just south of the Bernini Colonnade, for Judy, Dominic and myself. Maybe he was anticipating new Pope Francis and his ability to ride subways and cook for himself!

Even the many Australian monsignors are good networkers who know their way around, such as Monsignor Frank Marriott, ex-Wodonga and now at the superb Sacred Heart Cathedral in Bendigo. Frank turned up in Rome a couple of times, in fact on the day after my arrival in Rome back in 2009, with a group of delegates to a Wellbeing of the Family conference, and so on my second day I hosted an informal lunch in a strange city in a new job with this group. Only a monsignor with a great mixture of bravado and dedication would ensure this all came about; it was good fast networking.

★ ★ ★

But the Vatican was really just the tip of the iceberg in terms of those doing church-related work around Rome. And several religious orders with HQs in Rome had Australians in charge, due to appointments made on merit. It was said that the Australians were often favoured because they had a practical bent, did not stand on ceremony, and above all else did not bring any imperial baggage with them. Many put in long hours dealing with complex tasks, some in very senior leadership positions.

To name just some ... Abbot General of the Silvester grouping within the Benedictines Father Michael Kelly; also his classmate Father Robert McCulloch, who has recently completed years of service in Pakistan to become Procurator General of the Columbans in Rome. Sister Mary Wright, for most of my posting, a former worldwide head of the Loreto Order, was technically the most senior Australian in the Vatican. Meanwhile, Sister Sue Phillips from Tasmania heads an order of several hundred nuns known as the Franciscan Missionaries of Mary (FMM). FMM nuns are often located in very hostile territory, such as remote parts of India, where Australian missionaries have been attacked and even burnt to death. Sister Sue as the head of the congregation has enormous responsibilities, including the ever-present problem for many clerical orders and congregations:

maintenance of huge properties now often half-empty. These and other women I met in the Vatican were unsung heroes in so many ways, beavering away largely below the radar screen, but they emerged on *my* radar screen more and more as my posting continued.

Australian seminarians and young priests doing further studies were scattered all over Rome. The biggest group was resident at the Pontifical North American College up on the hill just south of the Vatican and nicknamed Fort Nac. I played tennis with some of these hard-working dedicated men, including Michael Gallagher and Daniel McCaughan. Father Stuart Moran lived in a tiny cell on the noisy Corso. He was from Melbourne and did well at his studies, gaining his doctorate and returning to work at the East Kew parish but also to shoulder a heavy load of lecturing at the Catholic University in Melbourne. Ken Brimaud was another Australian studying in Rome, ex-head of the Board of Trustees of NSW Powerhouse Museum but now completing a huge thesis on the Johannine writings and helping out at the Caravita Community parish. The universities of Rome are a great magnet for so many, some students spending years if not decades in a form of purposeful captivity.

I met many of these hard-working Australian nuns, priests and religious students at an informal gathering convened by Sister Helen Simpson and held on a Saturday about once a month, on rotation in one of the religious houses, normally one of the many headquarters where Australians were posted. The chance to swap information and talk through practical issues such as visas and the cheapest flights in and out of Rome was very useful. Sister Helen had been in Rome several years and maintained a tight list of contacts and information flow.

I found these Australian men and women of faith to be very dedicated, in the main very practical, types, with feet firmly on the ground, just getting on with their jobs. Some were not all that extroverted, befitting a life of vows and prayers, but they were all very polite. Likewise I also got to know many from the other 'Anglo' or English-speaking countries, especially the British, Canadian and Irish brigades.

★ ★ ★

There were so many other extraordinary lay and ordained Catholics whom I encountered on my three-year posting to Rome, with many more deserving of attention in this book – from key cardinals to hard-working nuns and exceptional lay personnel in the Curia. It would not be possible to write in detail about them all when there are so many – but I hope I have provided a taste of the structure of the Vatican, and the kinds of dedicated men and women who devote their time to the work of the Church around Rome, and throughout the world.

CHAPTER FIVE

Who's Who in the Diplomatic Corps

Representing the Government of Australia to the Government of the Holy See was never dull and never other than reasonably busy – in part because I was an activist and determined to deliver as much as I could for Australia. Along the way, I learnt much from the more experienced ambassadors of the Holy See diplomatic corps.

There are around eighty of them resident in Rome, with about another 100 of them based elsewhere. Over fifty of the resident ambassadors are also ambassadors to the Sovereign Order of Malta (a sovereign entity without territory), which for decades has been headquartered in Rome. And a couple of ambassadors are accredited to the tiny but beautiful San Marino near Bologna, the oldest continuous republic in the world: a testament to the powers of good diplomacy!

For the first six to twelve months I was one of the most junior ambassadors, and I had to be conscious there was a pecking order from which I could not budge – for instance, where there was free seating at an event and suddenly a more senior ambassador loomed large, you made space. In the Vatican, formal seating arrangements were always done strictly by seniority.

I was representing Australia, so I didn't want to be a shrinking violet, but I always had to know my place in that pecking order, which is measured from the day you present your credentials to the Pope. Generally I found it no trouble – being ex-army, and an ex-backbencher in two parliaments, I knew how to work out my place at a conference, a function or wherever. And almost every month there were rotations of ambassadors, so I soon moved up from being the most junior.

During my very first few days in Rome, I called on the Dean of the Corps at his chancery, as is the correct procedure. Often but not always, the Dean of the Corps is the most senior ambassador accredited to the Holy See in terms of years of service, and throughout my posting this was the amiable Honduran Ambassador, Alejandro Valladares Lanza. He came to Rome on this posting way back in March 1991, and has nigh on two decades of seniority.

The Dean, as the most senior, gave the three big speeches each year on behalf of the Corps: to the official gathering with the Pope in January; to the Secretary of State, Cardinal Bertone, at the Corps Dinner that same day; and a third speech later in the year at the Summer Dinner in the Vatican Gardens. He also took up collections to buy a plaque for departing ambassadors. But his main job always remained representing his country, Honduras.

Due to language difficulties, even with the valiant help of my deputy, Anne Giles, I could not communicate with the Dean beyond basic pleasantries. This resulted in my having a polite and correct but very narrow and limited relationship with him during my posting. Perhaps in some diplomatic corps this could be an issue, but it really did not matter a great deal in the scheme of things in and around the Vatican. This was partly due to the fact that key administrative matters such as diplomatic vehicle registrations and identity cards were handled by either the Vatican or the Italian Embassy to the Holy See, rather than the Dean, who is meant to help iron out wrinkles in administration matters.

In every diplomatic corps there are both activists and minimalists. The minimalists are the types who attend the compulsory functions but are not too often sighted beyond these appearances. Pleasant and diplomatic in the extreme, I guess they are happy for others to make the running, or – as has often been the case in recent years – they have severe budget limitations. None of the minimalists will be mentioned here; instead, I concentrate on the activists, from whom I tried to learn throughout my posting.

In the activist camp were many of the career diplomats, some of whom had held critical postings in locations such as London, Moscow, Warsaw and Washington. The Canadian Ambassador,

WHO'S WHO IN THE DIPLOMATIC CORPS

Anne Leahy, and the French Ambassador, Stanislas de Laboulaye, are both ex-Moscow ambassadors, and with a string of other key postings before that. The capable Irish Ambassador until July 2011 was Noel Fahey, who had a string of heavyweight postings to his name, including roles in Washington and Germany. The Brazilian Ambassador, Luiz Felipe de Seixas Corrêa (ex Berlin and Geneva) was a powerhouse who helped mastermind many Brazilian victories, including a narrow win for the Brazilian candidate in 2011 for the post of Director-General of the Food and Agriculture Organization (FAO).

Then there were the non-career ambassadors, who tended to be ex-MPs like me, or had served in other roles close to the political action. It meant the diplomatic corps was not so incestuous. When I arrived in Rome there was already a number of these trail-blazers – and we brought, I think, a bit of diversity and colour to the diplomatic corps, and different angles on things, which on occasions opened the eyes of very experienced career diplomats. In fact, I think both groups of ambassadors learnt from each other.

The other subset of non-career diplomats for some particular reason seemed to be ex-academics. The ambassadors from the Former Republic of Macedonia, Slovakia and Slovenia all fell into that category. Israel's ambassador, Mordechay Lewy, was a noted history scholar. Turkey had Kenan Gürsoy, a professor of theology with a deep interest in old maps. The United States Ambassador, Miguel Humberto Díaz, and his wife, Marion Diaz, were *both* theology professors. (The US Embassy is perhaps the largest of the Holy See embassies in terms of staff;

it mounted many initiatives in the course of each year and ran well-planned conferences, generally on topical subjects such as HIV-AIDS.)

Some embassies, such as Canada's, did not have the budget for a deputy head of mission, meaning an even bigger burden on all counts for the ambassador. The deputies of the various larger embassies were generally a younger crowd of career diplomats who saw the role as a stepping-stone, and they seemed to enjoy life more than their superiors. Why wouldn't you want to be posted to the Eternal City of Rome, and able to step out for a big night near the Spanish Steps, the Farnese Palace or the district of Trastevere?

While it isn't possible to detail all members of the Holy See diplomatic corps during the period 2009 to 2012, I can honestly say that every one of them was friendly and broadly helpful in exchanging information. Right from the beginning, if I had a query about my role, I would ask a fellow ambassador, because I knew they would know the answer, and most of them would try to assist.

There were a few who were standouts, from whom I learnt not just through asking questions, but through observing the exceptional way they did their job.

The Italian ambassadors to the Holy See were a vital part of the machinery, including helping with various administrative requirements from the Italian Government, as we all actually lived in Italy. Antonio Zanardi Landi was very helpful and practical; he once drove from Rome to a previous posting in Teheran, Iran, and he was promoted from the Holy See to

Italian Ambassador to Moscow. His successor was a proud and equally helpful Italian, Francesco Greco, from Lecce.

For more than a decade Poland has been very well represented by Hanna Suchocka, who was Prime Minister of Poland in the early 1990s, just after democracy was established – some would say a less shrill version of Margaret Thatcher. Hanna was one of the best diplomats in town, with a no-nonsense but thoughtful approach and a sharp eye for detail. She handled many incredible situations, including the giant funeral of the Polish Pope John Paul II, and the one million people in town, many from Poland, for his beatification on 1 May 2011.

I will never forget driving past her residence and the local Polish church one Sunday where weeping crowds had gathered in response to the plane crash at Smolensk, Russia, on 10 April 2010 that killed all on board, including the then President of Poland, Lech Kaczyński and his wife. They were flying in for a memorial service in recognition of the 1940 Katyn massacre.

★ ★ ★

The larger-than-life Francis Campbell served as a lively and creative British Ambassador from December 2005 until early 2011. He had worked at No. 10 Downing Street during the Blair years and simply applied for the post in response to an advertisement from the Foreign Office (though he is also a former Catholic seminarian).

Full of energy, he lifted the performance of the diplomatic corps as a whole by dint of his activities. On the occasion of the

Pope's visit to the UK in September 2010 (the first ever by a Pope as Head of State), he made sure that the other ambassadors were briefed on the structure and purpose of the Pope's visit, then after the visit put on a further briefing on the outcomes. In a long-overdue breakthrough, he spearheaded a four-part BBC TV documentary on the duties of an ambassador to the Holy See, giving many practical examples of the work and problems encountered.

He was the principal ambassador I called on for advice. He was always forthcoming, and generally his advice was very good. His successor, Nigel Baker, was also very outgoing and soon learnt the ropes around Rome.

★ ★ ★

The ambassador with whom I probably worked most closely was Anne Leahy from Canada, because Canada had a saint being canonised at the same time as the Australian Mary MacKillop, in October 2010. Anne was French Canadian, extremely capable, no-nonsense, and a good practitioner of her craft. And she was a very courteous hostess.

As an upshot of our work on the canonisations, I initiated the Triangle Christmas Drinks, involving the Australian, British and Canadian embassies. It happened that we were often working together on particular things and it was a fact that we all got on well together at the ambassadorial and deputy ambassadorial level, and I thought, 'Well, we've only got five in our little office – we need a few more for a decent party for

Christmas drinks.' And it wasn't going to cost taxpayers any more because we then rotated the responsibility, so Australia hosted the first year, then Canada, then Britain. This was just a minor way of building connections with these two other Commonwealth embassies.

★ ★ ★

The ambassador from one of the world's smallest countries, the Greek Cypriot George Poulides, was a giant of a man and giant-hearted as well. He did not miss a beat. He was able to maximise scarce resources to boost his country's profile, as so many ambassadors from small countries did, and – as I suspect – ambassadors from even large countries are going to have to learn to do in the future. Cyprus was a perfect example of how a tiny embassy can manufacture momentum, right through to scoring a visit by the Pope in 2010, against all the odds.

George's achievements demonstrated something that distinguished the Holy See ambassadors from other corps: dint of personality had a bigger bearing than size of country. In the diplomatic whirl of New York or Paris or Washington or London, existing alliances give every new Australian ambassador an immediate footprint and starting level. In the Holy See, because no one is competing to sell a million tonnes of iron ore or trying to stitch up aviation rights, I think individual initiatives have more play.

Instead of competition, in the Holy See it was all about sharing of information – or working together to extract more information from within the impenetrable walls of the Vatican. The ambassadors, together with the more helpful monsignors, were all on a unity ticket where, inch by millimetre, we sought to draw information out of this deep well, and as the odd gremlin crept out we would tend to share it where it was purposeful to do so.

This was another reason to be plugged in to your fellow ambassadors, because sometimes someone would hear something and pass it on. 'Oh, I should mention to you that yesterday Cardinal X was going on about Australia's role in East Timor, and I thought you should know,' one of my ambassadorial colleagues would say to me. So I would then go and make a call on that cardinal, and open our conversation on the matter of East Timor.

It was at yet another function that the non-resident ambassador for Sweden, Ulla Gudmundson, raised a very delicate issue which I can't write about, except to say that it involved Mediterranean politics in real time, ahead of the Arab Spring.

Ulla was as sharp as all getup regarding affairs in the Vatican, even though she was resident in Stockholm. She'd been a diplomat for many years, and she knew exactly where to go to for information on her precious few days in Rome. She always wore quaint national folk dress in the receiving line at diplomatic papal audiences, so the Pope knew exactly when he was about to be upbraided by this feisty ambassador. She would come down to Rome three or four times a year, and she'd always call on me to catch up on what was happening, and share her own findings.

On one such visit, she gave me a copy of what is called a 'non-paper' that she had recently produced. In the world of diplomacy, these non-papers are used as a way to increase the currency of ideas. A government will sometimes float a strategy or a proposal amongst a group this way and still be able to disavow it if it hits the front page of a newspaper.

On this occasion, the press never got hold of the paper at any stage, and that's why I can't speak of it in detail, other than to say it was an excellent non-paper, and extremely well argued. It put a particular proposal relating to various tensions within the Mediterranean, most notably in respect of Christian minorities of the Maronite Church, to a working unit within the Vatican. It was purposeful enough for me at the time to quote its contents back to Canberra by way of the confidential cable traffic. It obviously didn't head off the death and destruction of the Arab Spring, but it was an example of a high degree of fast-thinking flexibility that existed within the diplomatic corps. I learnt never to underestimate non-resident ambassadors: some of the better ones were indeed a force to be reckoned with.

★ ★ ★

As a group, I worked most closely with the Asian or Greater Asian ambassadors – an important grouping for Australia as we seek to build more and more links with Asia. At the start of this chapter I mentioned the importance of the pecking order within the diplomatic corps. But there was one position that was not the subject of seniority, and that was the role of Convening Chair of the Greater Asian Group of Ambassadors.

I didn't at first chase this job, but I could see it was heading my way so I made sure it did, because I thought, for various reasons, that it would be useful to head this body. I could see ways in which I could make it a far more purposeful group, as a unit of information exchange, and so against the odds I jumped ahead of more senior ambassadors to become its chair early on in my posting.

'Greater Asia' without fail was represented by activist ambassadors, and this group included Turkey and Egypt, right through to Japan, Australia and New Zealand (which had a non-resident ambassador). Other members included Lebanon, Iraq, Iran, India, South Korea, Chinese Taipei (Taiwan), the Philippines, Singapore, Indonesia and East Timor. Russia was not in the Asian Group, notwithstanding that it is physically the largest country in Asia (east of the Urals), and so we did not have the wise counsel of Nikolay Sadchikov, especially his advice on Russian Orthodox Church matters of interest and relevance to Greater Asia.

I felt a particular empathy with both the ambassadors from Iraq during my time, Albert Yelda and his successor Habeeb Al-Sadr; for them home leave meant facing the gauntlet of travelling to Baghdad and belting in and out of the airport, along a corridor subject to many bombings. Also due to mutual contacts and interests, linkages were easily formed and built on with the Japanese ambassador, Kagefumi Ueno, who was a former consul from a posting to Melbourne and who resented the Vatican using predominantly languages that few spoke; it was a view shared by his successor, Hidekazu Yamaguchi.

One interesting thing was to see the happy way in which the Indonesian Embassy, led ably by Suprapto Martosetomo, worked with the tiny East Timor Embassy team whose ambassadors changed during my posting, but the deputy, Chargé d'Affaires Armindo Pedro Simoes, was always on deck; there seemed to be no lingering tensions after all that happened over the 1999 ballot and the subsequent granting of independence.

Another was to see the Philippine ambassador, Mercedes Tuason, a lady of no mean age, actively step up and network as well as helping to build linkages amongst former ambassadors to the Holy See. Lebanese Ambassador Georges El Khoury was

Three ambassadors on the margins of a ceremony in Paris when key Monsignor Nicolas Thevenin was awarded the Legion of Honour: George Poulides, the white bear from Cyprus on my right, and Georges El Khoury of Lebanon on my left, fresh from a visit to Beirut.

the Greater Asia Ambassador representing a nation quite close to Rome, meaning many from his country would descend on him with short notice, from the President downwards.

There was one national day I was not allowed to attend, namely that of Chinese Taipei, or Taiwan, because Australia had not had diplomatic relations with it since switching to recognising mainland China some forty years ago. Still, I was allowed to liaise with its observant ambassador, Larry Yu-yuan, in his role as a member of the Greater Asia group. It was a tricky situation, as I had learnt years ago when China criticised me for visiting Taipei as a shadow minister. The Vatican is contemplating switching diplomatic recognition from Taiwan to China but there are many complexities to be resolved.

Geographically this Asian region embraced much of the heartlands of the Muslim, Hindu and Buddhist faiths. So it wasn't just a case of sharing information about what was going on within the Vatican; I was getting information on the ground about some very tempestuous parts of the world. Much of this information involved the fates of Christian minorities, in Vietnam, in China, in Egypt and in many other nations where there is widespread abuse of constitutional provisions regarding religious freedom. And I was able to feed a lot of this information back to DFAT, directly and indirectly, when it was relevant.

Part of my role as chair was to ensure there were proper welcomes and farewells for Asian ambassadors as their postings rolled over. But I also tried to ensure that the group met usefully on a regular basis, to do different things such as travelling to the Vatican Observatory and receiving a lecture there, then going onto the nearby rooftop of the Pope's Summer Palace to observe sunspot activity through the solar telescope, and ultimately a working luncheon at a nearby restaurant, as part of promoting Australia's cause in the bid to host some of the Square Kilometre Array (SKA) radio telescope.

On another occasion we met the Pontifical Council for Culture, which handles the Holy See's relations with other cultures. We talked through the efforts of that pontifical council to better understand the Hindu, Buddhist and Muslim faiths and their rich cultural heritages. It was in Australia's interests to promote Asia in this key hub of Europe, as many in Canberra reminded me – though I had always held this view myself. So during my time as chair, I used my energies to highlight the importance of Asia and the need for the Vatican to focus way beyond Europe. I reminded all and sundry that one of the fastest growing and largest Catholic-population countries was the Philippines, yet many senior active cardinals had never even been there.

Towards the end of 2011, I then provided, as a good chair should, for transition to a very capable Vaticanite, an ex-lay member of a Pontifical Council, Korean Ambassador Thomas Han, who arrived during my posting, and I know the group continues to do interesting things and thrive.

★ ★ ★

I may have had most to do with the ambassadors from Greater Asia, but, it was those from the Balkans who stood out. This group has emerged from nowhere over the last twenty years following the breakup of Yugoslavia – contributing to the modest expansion in the Holy See diplomatic corps over that period. These ambassadors as 'new arrivals' on the scene tended to be more active, pragmatic and lateral thinking than others – though many of them had years of diplomatic experience to bring to the task.

They and their families had endured a great deal of personal danger and hardship over the previous two decades during the violent disintegration of Yugoslavia. Gjoko Gjorgevski, the Ambassador of the Former Yugoslav Republic of Macedonia, had even served as a corporal in Sarajevo. It was hard not to admire this level of personal experience. The group also had a different take on affairs in Europe, being (apart from Slovenia) outside of the European Union.

The Balkan ambassadors turned out to be very strong supporters of Australia's UN Security Council vote. Though Australia is a long way from the Balkans, many of its populace immigrated to Australia from that part of the world, to help build the Snowy Mountains Scheme among other things. The migration linkages continue; by way of example, the Mayor of Sarajevo elected in 2013, Professor Ivo Komsic, has a daughter living in Melbourne.

The most capable and colourful member of the group was the can-do Jasna Krivošić-Prpić, Ambassador for Bosnia-Herzegovina. It was at a Gregorian conference in my second month of posting that we first met, and she helpfully provided some translations and information as we sat through a session in fast Italian, where unusually no translation was offered.

Jasna did not stand on ceremony, and – I guess a bit like me – when conversation lulled at a diplomatic function or when something needed to be done, Jasna stepped up. Married to a Muslim, Jasna had some sharp views on interfaith dialogue. She gave me some terrific insights into the horrific wars that devastated her region throughout the 1990s.

I found the Balkan ambassadors both illuminating and enjoyable company. They were not always in agreement on the big political issues of Europe, but they covered the ground and liaised far more broadly than I thought would be the case, given the bloodshed of the 1990s, when most of the world showed their region little support.

One no-go area in conversations with this group was the name 'Former Yugoslav Republic of Macedonia'. It's an issue that remains very emotional, especially for people from the northern parts of Greece, because of the linkages to Alexander the Great and various other complexities. Occasionally I would say, 'Why not just simply call it "*New* Macedonia", instead of "the Former Yugoslav Republic of Macedonia"?', thinking, that's hardly an exceptional change of name. But after a while I desisted, because it generally led to strongly argued ripostes from the Ambassador of Greece or the other ambassadors from around that part of Europe.

I also once informally suggested that the intense boundary dispute between Croatia and Slovenia over the Bay of Pirano could be settled by offering a lease of sovereignty to the Holy See for, say, 999 years. At least the headlines could read well: 'Holy See All at Sea Again'! I was gently reminded that in diplomacy words can be bullets, but was forgiven because of the undoubted advantage at times of being a non-career diplomat with a strange sense of humour. Australians tend to call a spade a spade, but after a while I learnt to call a spade a silver shovel. Whilst I had no spades to wield, I did have a tennis racquet, and so with some of the Balkanista, especially Professor Vladeta Janković from Serbia, I occasionally played tennis. With others, such as the dynamic ambassador for Slovenia, Maja Lovrenčič Svetek, it was no sporting contact but pleasant family encounters – after all, her husband was an expert on European rail freight logistics.

Perhaps I pushed the margins, but there were many other ambassadors in the Vatican with a great sense of humour. After all, this was a diplomatic corps in which personality counted more than in most. But you always used the humour for a purpose: it was a way of breaking the ice, and moving conversations on.

Once, in the middle of a serious dialogue with the French Ambassador, Stanislas de Laboulaye, I told him, 'Congratulations.' He said, 'What for?' I replied, 'This week is the centenary of the famous or infamous night theatre club Folies Bergères in Paris!' He roared with laughter. I think he enjoyed a bit of levity as Holy See Ambassador after a grim posting to Moscow. (He was also happy to display the star attraction of his official residence: the guest bedroom on the ground floor, featuring an oversized double bed specially made to accommodate the ample length of French President Charles de Gaulle.)

★ ★ ★

It has to be said: never underestimate the wit or wisdom of the members of the Pope's diplomatic corps, and never put up a loose argument in front of a senior diplomat, or you will be ever so gently taken apart and left high and dry. New Pope Francis moved quickly to address the diplomatic corps during his first week of official duties following enthronement, extolling their role and reminding them that St Francis of Assisi was not only a champion of the poor but also a man of peace. In fact St Francis walked across no man's land to try to bring peace between the crusaders and the Muslims centuries ago.

There is good sense in being plugged into the diplomacy of the Holy See, the oldest organisation in the world and one that has been 'doing' diplomacy for well over 1000 years. This is best done by having a small embassy on the ground in Rome, with a modest budget but an active ambassador using leverage of every relevant kind to advance 'Cause Australia'.

CHAPTER SIX

Frenetic Networking for Your Country

Incessant networking is at the very heart of diplomacy – building contacts and relationships, promoting Australia at every opportunity. This means you convene meetings that are purposeful for the particular issues your government has asked you to pursue; it means that you attend useful meetings that other ambassadors have convened – which could be concerts, conferences, national days, working lunches or dinners within and without the Vatican, or even informal encounters. Simply walking between your embassy and St Peter's Square, you could bump into people, often resulting in a useful exchange of information.

It must be said that much networking is done at events involving large quantities of very good food. Is it not a heavenly experience to be paid to eat for your country, and to do so in

FRENETIC NETWORKING FOR YOUR COUNTRY

the magical city of Rome? This question was put to me by visitors from time to time, and yes, it would be difficult to argue otherwise. Still, there were plenty of pitfalls along the way.

First I should explain that Italians do not 'do' breakfast, and see any function tied to the time of early morning as being beyond the pale. The trial team-building breakfast on the day of my credentials ceremony was never to be repeated. Italians simply don't 'do' bacon and egg rolls, so I generously helped out by eating more than I should have on that occasion! Australian inter-embassy liaison later developed using other types of functions. Fair enough, as when in Rome do as the Romans do.

I also hasten to add: do not think that half the time is spent boozing away for one's country with other ambassadors. Even at the very long functions I encountered no drunkenness, and the Italians in particular have a capacity to drink much wine with next to zero impact. It is a case of prosecco rather than champagne, very pleasant but half the whack.

For the first twelve months you are advised to attend every single function you're invited to, until you get the hang of things. In my case, because of the UNSC campaign and other factors, I continued to go along to everything I was available to attend.

An essential event for every embassy was the annual function to celebrate their country's national day. Now, for many the national day circuit is avoided like the plague. The problem is if you do one, then by degrees you are obliged to do them all. They take time, and they often consist of a series of one-minute conversations that lead nowhere. Be that as it may, I wanted to be courteous, and I wanted the host to come to the next function *I* was planning, so I had to help create that obligation by turning up at their national day.

The food at these events is usually of the greatest quality and abundance; as a kind of expression of the standing of the country. In fact, it was often enough the case that the smaller the country, the bigger the national day function.

Tiny Monaco and its experienced, friendly ambassador, Jean-Claude Michel, chose a superb venue at a grand villa on a distant hill of Rome, with a four-course dinner in the gardens for its national day in 2010. Now, this was a chance to network seriously and get updates on current issues fixating the Vatican, rather than just gossiping about who is about to be posted and who are the top two cardinals most likely to be the next Pope.

The announcement of the engagement of Prince Albert of Monaco occurred about a fortnight before the Monaco national day function and it led to the attendance of the über-VIP couple at the reception – by way of two high-quality cardboard cutouts. In the long receiving line in the early evening twilight I looked ahead to see the couple in the distance and thought: 'Could this really be them?' I laughed when the truth emerged and told the ambassador he had shown great initiative, but that I wanted the real thing on one of his future national days.

Then there was a magnificent but awkward annual function put on by the Egyptian Embassy on Ash Wednesday, the first day of Lent. It was hosted by dynamic Ambassador Lamia Aly Hamada Mekhemar, at her residence on the Aventine Hill, which happens to lie along the path of the Pope's Ash Wednesday procession. Egyptian hospitality is such that there is a huge meal, yet practising Roman Catholics are meant to be eating very lightly that day, if at all. So you could tell which ones were the Catholics – and which ones were the less-than-perfect Catholics, which was my category! Then at the appointed hour we would all step out and line up in front of the Ambassador's residence, and the Holy Father would walk in procession to the nearby Church of Sant'Anselmo, say some prayers and then walk back down to the Basilica of Santa Sabina.

The first year I went to it, Ash Wednesday fell in late February and it got dark quite early. I'd dismissed my driver, Stefano Bernardini, and told him I'd make my own way home. I'd only been in Rome a few weeks and I got completely lost; I couldn't even spot St Peter's Dome. I couldn't find a taxi, and I didn't want to re-encounter any of my fellow guests and reveal my embarrassment (and they'd have gone home by then, anyhow, in their official cars). The only rule you can follow in these circumstances is to walk steadily in one direction until you hit either the River Tiber or one of the major roads, and then you can get your bearings. I did that and finally found an underground station. Fortunately, navigating my way around was easier on subsequent Ash Wednesdays – though resisting temptation was not.

★ ★ ★

I have already mentioned how, for the first half of my posting, the tiny size of the Australian chancery made it difficult to host functions of our own. So we became very friendly with the staff of Zagara, a nearby family-run restaurant, in Via Paola. After we moved into a larger chancery in mid-2010, Zagara still did a lot of the catering, and even handled a couple of our extra-big lunches, such as on the day when the Governor–General, Quentin Bryce, met with Pope Benedict XVI. At other times we used Grant Kinnear, a Kiwi resident in Rome, who made great lamingtons when required.

The new chancery, with its large board room, made a big difference: I was able to hit the ground running and catch up on a lot of owed hospitality. This varied from large and small receptions (typically occurring between 6 and 8pm), to workshops on key topics for thirty or forty people, to formal lunches for up to sixteen. I could open up the doors and hold Australia Day functions for zero venue cost, and these events became very popular. If there was a visiting Australian parliamentary delegation, I would work out the entertaining in conjunction with the Australian Embassy to Italy; they would tend to do a big luncheon and my embassy might do a smaller reception.

I might have the occasional visiting Australian bishop home to my apartment, but I generally did all my entertaining in the chancery. (As related, I did on one occasion 'borrow' Ambassador to Italy Amanda Vanstone's residence.) Had my family been permanently in Rome it might have been different; as it was, I could not justify a chef or other staff in my own house.

FRENETIC NETWORKING FOR YOUR COUNTRY

Checking documents with Keith Copper (right) and lawyers before the move from the temporary chancery to the new chancery around the corner.

If it was just a quick lunch with a senior officer of DFAT handling a particular policy – disarmament, for example, or HIV-AIDS – rather than using the board room I would usually step out to one of the many nearby restaurants. Sometimes it got down to planning important events over a quick cup of coffee. Everything's done over a cup of coffee in Italy!

Sometimes these meetings were completely impromptu. On one occasion I ran into a Spanish diplomat I knew quite well who was always a useful bouncing-off point for matters relating to Europe. I thought, 'I'd better shout him a coffee,' because he was at secretary level and I was at ambassador level and that was the correct protocol. Unfortunately I managed to pick a coffee shop on the main drag up to St Peter's – Via della Conciliazone – where you get charged far more than at a cafe just fifty metres to either side of this 'clip the tourist' street. Lesson learnt – I'll never go there again – but at least the occasion served its purpose. Complaints relating to overcharging of tourists continue to this day: $600 for a meal for two, $60 for four ice-creams. My suggestion is to complain and threaten to take it to the media first, the tourist police second.

About 500 metres from the chancery, off Corso Vittorio Emanuele II, there's a lovely square, Piazza Sforza Cesarini, where in summer you can sit outside, away from the traffic a bit, because the square is quite deep. It is the location of a well-known restaurant, Trattoria Polese, where I liked to take people if they were visiting from Australia. On one occasion I'd just finished a working lunch there, and was walking around the square and back towards the chancery, when I noticed a certain shop front. To the best of my knowledge of such things (which is not extensive), it was a fetish shop, full of whips and straps and all sorts of exotic leather gear for erotic purposes (I gather).

Rome being Rome, this is a fairly unusual sight, and I had just paused for a moment to take it all in when I heard the voice of a long-serving woman ambassador in my ear. 'Hello, Mr Fischer,' she said. 'What are you doing looking in this window?'

I promptly replied: 'I have just discovered this extraordinary shop, and was just trying to work out exactly what it was; having established what it is, I shall now move on, Your Excellency.' So after that I renamed the piazza 'Fetish Square', and was very careful to stay away from that particular shop front!

★ ★ ★

FRENETIC NETWORKING FOR YOUR COUNTRY

With all this entertaining there was a self-evident danger: was I going to end up so overweight as to engender a heart attack from all this eating for my country? Only by cutting back on other meals on a day when I had a big formal lunch or dinner was the battle of the bulge to be won and weight gain minimised.

It also helped to walk long distances through Rome as opportunity permitted, and to play frequent games of tennis. I found this a great networking activity in Rome, playing mainly with other ambassadors but also with other diplomatic staff and occasionally staff from the Vatican. Due to my often busy schedule, it was not always possible to get in a weekly match, but I always felt so much better and mentally fresher after a set or two.

I also took advantage of the pharmacy at street level below the new chancery (and just around the corner from the old one) to get my blood pressure checked. As in Australia, pharmacists in Italy are somewhat protected as a sector, but unlike in Australia they actually have to give something back, namely a free blood pressure check for anyone asking for it. As I was eating for my country and putting on weight, even after eliminating cooked breakfasts, I thought it wise to keep tabs on my blood pressure.

Throughout the three years of the posting, it hovered at 120 over 80, very satisfactory for someone in their mid-sixties. However, one weekend when I was heading up to the monastery at Bose on the edge of the Alps, I decided to check my blood pressure immediately before and after the weekend. After a couple of days of meditation, mountain walking, listening to solemn chanting, and eating and drinking less, I rechecked and found about a five per cent reduction. Clearly over the centuries the monks have perfected the art of meditation and capturing the add-on benefits.

★ ★ ★

Not all networking involved large amounts of eating and drinking. One time-consuming activity – enjoyable at times – was the concerts often put on by European embassies and larger non-European embassies. On occasions these involved intense folk singers from Eastern Europe, or a large choir with a bent for singing complex works written by long-forgotten composers with unpronounceable names. School choirs often like to have in their CV that they have sung in Rome, and quite often ambassadors are asked to organise concerts and invite people to come.

It might have been the fifth night out in a row on a work activity, and it generally meant listening to speeches in languages unknown to me, with no translators available. Was I tempted to skip these concerts? Well, yes; I'm only human. Did I skip them? Absolutely not, as there was always some redeeming feature. So it was that I met various visiting foreign ministers and other VIPs, and so it was that more were reminded of Australia and our interests.

It also meant that when *I* was hosting musical events, I could lean on these ambassadors to reciprocate by attending. One of the greatest venues for school choir performances was the beautiful Caravita Oratory, where Mozart once played. The ancient church in the centre of Rome is laid out for Mass 'in the round' with seating around the altar. It was my parish church of choice. I hosted a number of these school choir performances there, and they were a win-win opportunity. It was good for the choir to step up in the glorious city of Rome, fostering interest in Australia and the Australian style of handling church-orientated music. And it was useful for the embassy's profile to entertain a variety of guests as they ate, drank and mixed in the aftermath of some beautiful singing. A number of ambassadors generally came, unless it was a busy conference week or something. Sometimes these events would be slightly more formal, because I needed to control the numbers, but I tried to keep them as public as possible, and circulate invitations all over Rome.

★ ★ ★

Often less enjoyable – though probably better for the soul – were the many official functions I was obliged to attend in the Vatican. Around a dozen of these a year required the diplomatic corps to wear formal dress, which was of great colour and diversity. Many African ambassadors wore national costume, while others such as the British and Peruvian ambassadors wore outfits that looked as if they came straight from a production of Gilbert and Sullivan's *HMS Pinafore*.

It was a bit irksome getting into the white tie, tails and medals that I was obliged to wear, but I eventually got it down to a very fine art so that it wasn't a twenty-minute exercise, but a five-minute exercise. (I must confess that I discovered it was better not to tie your white tie, but to buy a pre-tied one.)

For diplomats, the year formally begins with the Diplomatic Papal Audience in the Royal Gallery, which is between the Sistine Chapel and the Gallery of Blessings, high up in the inner Vatican.

It is always a privilege to attend for many reasons, including soaking up the incredible setting, and walking through corridors of overwhelming size and ornateness. The baroque artwork and design dominate, but for me there was something else that I valued equally. It was the chance to pace out the steps taken by a newly elected pope – about 140 steps from the Sistine Chapel, where the papal conclave is held, directly into the Royal Gallery, then up a half flight of stairs, then into the Gallery of Blessings, just behind the balcony above the main doors of St Peter's Basilica.

This formal day of pomp, dialogue and circumstance, the starting gun for another year of intense diplomatic activity, was a must-attend for all ambassadors, resident and non-resident. The Pope enters and delivers a formal address on world affairs, in the diplomatic language of French, which is a language Pope Benedict spoke reasonably well. The Dean of the Corps responds in front of the gathering and then each ambassador is received in order of seniority. During this procedure you get a chance to make just one brief statement to the Pope.

After this the entire diplomatic corps stand in allocated spots and the Pope and key members of his entourage join

FRENETIC NETWORKING FOR YOUR COUNTRY

them for a round of photographs. This is terminated on the command of the Pope's Principal Private Secretary, during my time Monsignor Georg Gänswein, raising his voice and yelling 'Basta' ('Enough') until the clutch of official and media photographers desists. The Pope then departs with a smile – and possibly the thought that he does not have to face every ambassador together for another twelve months.

★ ★ ★

Also required at the Vatican was attendance at some of the big Masses in St Peter's Basilica and elsewhere. At the Maundy Thursday night Mass, in the superb St John Lateran, every ambassador had the right to receive communion from the Pope, which was a tremendous gesture. This was the case up until 2012 when a roster system was introduced to ease the burden. But the most gruelling event was the four-part Easter Saturday liturgy. It got underway at about 9pm and ran one year till very close to 1am (after which they decided to tighten it up a little bit). It was, literally, an endurance test, because there was no toilet break. Quite often I would point out to newer ambassadors where the best set of toilets was located just outside the Basilica in an underground Vatican carpark, to save them the embarrassment of having to go and get a Swiss Guard to escort them in and out during the course of the Mass.

★ ★ ★

Functions in the Vatican could be just as useful for networking purposes as those put on by the diplomatic corps. It was a case of knowing which functions were more freewheeling to allow that, and therefore to spend more time at. It was also a case of arriving on time, or even ahead of time, when you knew there would be opportunity to spend more time with key people. At other functions it actually paid to be late – tactically late – because things didn't free up until the end of formalities. If you weren't wanting to sit through a two-hour concert, and you knew there was going to be a reception afterwards, you could time it to arrive just in time for that.

It took some time to meet all of the Vatican high-flyers, because they're busy and out of town a lot. In the early days of my posting, before I got to know many of them, I developed a few subjects as bridge builders at Vatican functions. The first of these was to raise the success of World Youth Day celebrations in Sydney. It helped that many senior Vatican personnel had travelled with Pope Benedict XVI to Sydney and returned with him on the special Qantas jumbo flight. All were greatly impressed by the sparkle of Sydney, especially the ferry ride on a glistening Sydney Harbour, under the Harbour Bridge and past the Opera House. All I had to do was mention Sydney and the smiles would appear, accompanied by a certain wistful comment or two, such as 'Sydney was magnificent; I wish I could return one day'. Some even said that the Pope was still commenting favourably about Sydney months after visiting. At least one Italian monsignor who did not get to do the trip was heard to say he was sick of hearing about the city!

FRENETIC NETWORKING FOR YOUR COUNTRY

Certainly it was a positive subject to break the ice or stir a conversation along.

Once I did get to know the Vatican heavies, I could carry conversations further. I would always keep up with the friendly Cardinal Antonio Maria Vegliò, the head of Pastoral Care of Migrants and Itinerant People. That provided opportunities to emphasise the high level of official migrant intake that Australia has maintained over the last twenty years, and equally to emphasise that Japan (for instance) has had next to zero migrant intake over that time. Why was I making that point? Because I wanted not only to highlight the countries that were making an enormous contribution – Canada and Australia – but also to remind the Vatican that countries that should know better (most notably Japan) prefer a declining total population to the intake of any large numbers of migrants.

This type of subject often raised eyebrows, but I was of the view that you needed to avoid a conversation of clichés or talking about the weather. I became quite adept at picking up where I last left off with people, and I enjoy the cut-and-thrust of doing that: employing your brain but working out exactly what you want to get across early in the piece. And then others would join the group and the conversation would drift – that's fine, but in the meantime I would have made a point, or asked for and received observations from the Curia on what's happening, what's fixating the various pontifical councils and other units.

Most of the senior Vatican personnel had had fascinating careers: many of them had been to Baghdad, for instance, and served there for a couple of years – the deputy prime minister equivalent, Archbishop (now Cardinal) Fernando Filoni, to name one; Monsignor Michael Crotty, to name another. They were anxious to unburden themselves in some cases, because they rarely had the chance to step back from their official roles and talk to someone with a genuine thirst for more information about their experiences.

Another very good example was the Vatican's 'foreign minister' equivalent, Archbishop Mamberti. At a particular dinner I ended up sitting next to him and thought, 'This is going to be hard work' – but I'd read his CV and discovered he had served in Ethiopia, Eritrea and South Sudan as papal nuncio. South Sudan was just at this stage building towards independence, which was finally granted in July 2011, and I went there in June 2012 for the UN Security Council campaign (in my capacity as Australian envoy). The Archbishop reminded me that the creation of an independent South Sudan was supported by the Church, and that it would be a strongly Christian country, but he said, 'There are a million displaced South Sudanese in the north of Sudan, and we are deeply concerned as to what is going to happen to them.' This was becoming quite a major focus of the Holy See through its UN representatives, and a formal program was being developed to help shift thousands of people of South Sudanese ethnicity from Khartoum, the capital of Sudan, to Juba, the capital of the new South Sudan. The Archbishop explained some of the dynamics – and this was very useful to me when I was later appointed Envoy to South Sudan.

FRENETIC NETWORKING FOR YOUR COUNTRY

I could cite many instances of the concrete gains I made through this kind of networking. The attendance at one particular function in January 2010 led to a special meeting I had with Archbishop Fernando Filoni over a matter I came to refer to as 'Project Baghdad'. (I'll touch on that later.) On another occasion, I stumbled across the fact that Bethlehem University in Jerusalem was created by the Holy See. This came out of a reception that I was attending with the de la Salle Brothers, in their big monastery near St Peter's, and resulted in a couple of excellent briefings on the tensions in that part of the world, and ultimately a spellbinding visit to the university itself.

★ ★ ★

Ultimately, though, my networking success must be judged by others. In the Vatican there was one particular small, windowless room, less decorated than the rest, and the rumour was that if any ambassador was ushered into that room, it was for a very negative reason, because the Holy See was wanting to remonstrate with them over a position of their government, or some other offence. It was a sort of 'sin bin room'.

As good management (or luck) would have it, the Australian Ambassador was never ushered into the 'sin bin room'. It probably was a narrow call, thinking about it!

Maintaining balance and positive momentum, especially through key relationships that I developed, whilst batting for Australia generally, this was the key to getting the job done in the eternal city.

CHAPTER SEVEN

Conferences of Solid Gold ... and Slippery Silver

Conferences of all kinds were a big part of the action of the Australian Ambassador to the Holy See. Why? Because, like concerts and formal ambassadorial functions, they allowed for extended networking, for boosting the priority of issues that were part of my remit from the Australian Government, and for gaining more information on key subjects related to Australia's interests. And Rome is an incredibly underrated world hub: many, many, many conferences are held in Rome, as many as London and New York.

Because it's Rome they tend to be filtered out a bit by the Australian media; not one Australian media outlet had a bureau in Rome, preferring places like London, Washington and also Jerusalem. I had not realised the impact of the UN Food and

CONFERENCES OF SOLID GOLD ... AND SLIPPERY SILVER

Agriculture Organization (FAO), the Global Crop Diversity Trust, Biodiversity International and several other agriculture and immigration organisations, all headquartered in Rome.

After the first year of my posting, when I'd gained confidence and become better known, I was invited to conferences as a guest speaker. One of these was at the Pontifical Beda College, which trains English-speaking candidates for the priesthood; another was at the Istituto Tevere (Tiber Institute), set up by two young Muslim academics to encourage intercultural relations. I gave a lecture there presenting an Australian view of East–West relations, with a particular focus on Australian–Indonesian interfaith dialogue. At other times I was invited to chair a session of a conference. Such invitations became yet another vehicle for boosting Australian priorities, and I was always quite pleased to receive them, because it meant that I was obviously being accepted and could make a worthwhile contribution on that front.

More often I was simply a delegate or participant invited to listen to the opening session of a conference, then to stay on for the more interesting sessions. And then, on the margins, I would mix strategically, zeroing in on those who were not necessarily readily available otherwise. If the conference was within the Vatican, around the edge of the huge Paolo Sixto Auditorium (which seats several thousand people) there is a number of lecture rooms that each seat several hundred people. So I had plenty of room to manoeuvre.

I would arrive early and work out where best to sit so as to observe my fellow guests as much as the speaker. Secondly, I would be armed with the program of the day and would note the generous coffee breaks Italians have in the mornings, and whether there was a buffet luncheon – which was my preference, because then you could mix while you ate and work the room in a quite focused way.

Sometimes an ambassador hosting a conference would even put on a special dinner for the guest speaker, and ten or twelve of us would be invited to the ambassador's residence to kick on a bit more with our discussions.

Some of the bigger European countries sponsored a large number of conferences because they could bring some of their best professors in with no great cost factor. And so there was a steady stream of visiting European academics – for example, Father Patrick Desbois, Director of the French Episcopal Committee for Relations with Judaism. He came to Rome to speak about the almost unknown 'Eastern Holocaust', which he has uncovered almost single-handedly, inspired by the incarceration of his own grandfather at the Nazi prison camp Rawa Ruska (on the Poland–Ukraine border). The truth of this second holocaust was hidden behind the Iron Curtain after World War II, covered up by Stalin, but it is now known that the Nazis committed dreadful atrocities against the Jews of Ukraine and Belarus. According to Father Desbois, more than 2.5 million Jews and thousands of Roma (Gypsy) people were executed. He has written about many of his findings in his book *The Holocaust by Bullets* and helped form an organisation called 'Yahad – In Unum', to continue the investigation.

CONFERENCES OF SOLID GOLD ... AND SLIPPERY SILVER

Such a conference was on the margins of my priorities, on the one hand; on the other hand, the diaspora – those who have immigrated to Australia from Ukraine and Belarus and other parts of Eastern Europe – feel that this should be as important a part of World War II history as Dachau and Auschwitz. And so I took particular notice of conferences like this that touched on Australia's interests.

There were even cases where I attended a conference simply because I wanted to learn from some of the key speakers. The Pope's Chief Scientist, Bishop Marcelo Sánchez Sorondo, once spoke at a conference at the Angelicum University. It was on a subject of very little interest to me, but the bishop was a priority target for me; I wanted to get to know him and understand his work more, especially with regard to food security and agriculture. And so I made a point of attending for that reason alone.

The information I gained at such conferences might not be enough to warrant an immediate cable to DFAT, nevertheless it was part of a broad interpretation of my remit. It might not be of use until I had something to hook it on to – until something of significance was happening that related to Australia.

There was certainly a huge variety of functions to attend: scientific conferences, conferences on migration or interfaith dialogue. The purely theological ones I tended to duck and weave around, because I did not consider them important to my work as Australian Ambassador. But others particularly stand out, both in terms of the information I acquired, and in terms of what I was able to achieve on the sidelines.

* * *

Heavyweight conferences in the twenty-first century are a dime a dozen, but there is something special about a heavyweight conference framed within the majestic setting of a 500-year-old university. The Gregorian University (which educated many future popes) is one such institution, run by the Jesuits and located near the Trevi Fountain in the centre of Rome.

My first conference at the Gregorian was timed to commemorate both the 200th anniversary of the birth of Charles Darwin and the 150th anniversary of the publication of his theory of evolution. It was in the category of solid gold – worthwhile on all fronts – as distinct from slippery silver – of dubious value.

The opening session started with a bang: a forthright statement from Cardinal Gianfranco Ravasi (head of the Pontifical Council for Culture) that there is nothing incompatible between science and Christian religion, nothing incompatible between Charles Darwin's theory and the Catholic Church with its teachings from the Bible.

In fact, the overall message of the conference was about the *convergence* of science and religion, rather than the traditional take of the last 500 years that the two are not compatible. This was not helped by the fact that the Catholic Church for 1500 years believed that the earth was flat, until science upended that tenet comprehensively. Science having won that victory around the sixteenth century, helped by the great minds of Copernicus and Galileo, then moved back into its separate corner to some extent.

CONFERENCES OF SOLID GOLD ... AND SLIPPERY SILVER

This conference very cheerfully overturned all those centuries of disagreement. It was as if the Church were getting off its high horse at last, engaging with scientists and modern thinkers; that had probably happened previously but without so much fanfare until this Charles Darwin conference loomed large at the Gregorian University. Some of the speakers were also taking the essential theories of Charles Darwin into the twenty-first century and dealing with developments that have enhanced Darwin's work, such as the study of modern stromatolites ('living fossils'), which bear a great similarity to life forms of 3.5 billion years ago.

As the long opening day of the conference wore on, I pinched myself and thought what a privilege it was to have the time to attend and just soak the information up, and to at last have a job that gave me time to think and learn outside a narrow portfolio of issues, while contributing to Australia.

At the very end of the day, we heard Professor Lynn Margulis, a key lecturer from Boston University, state with gusto that the best stromatolites in the world are in Shark Bay, Western Australia. I dined off this statement in the post-session networking, and even rang ABC Perth later to alert them to this endorsement of an aspect of Western Australia. Immediately Eoin Cameron, the capable breakfast announcer, put me live to air, and this in turn led to some follow-up interviews with local experts on stromatolites. (In accordance with the DFAT rules, I informed the Media Liaison Service Duty Officer of this, and neither reproach nor approval of this initiative was given. You might describe this type of response as 'risk-adverse neutrality':

yes, as an ambassador today you are allowed to initiate media activity, and if the Foreign Minister's office does not go berserk then it is okay.)

The plug for West Australian stromatolites, minor in many ways, was still an unexpected bonus – part of being an active ambassador and attending as many functions as possible. Now, I could have knocked this invitation back – and I remember thinking, 'Oh, I'm too busy.' And there's no way I would have picked up on the reference to Australia had I not been not only at the opening session, but still sitting there eight hours later at the close of a long first day. I went back on the second day, although I had to juggle other things as a consequence. But this is the kind of priority call ambassadors are making around the world every day of the week. Sometimes you get lucky, sometimes you are unlucky in missing a particular conference, or attending a conference that is not worth the trouble.

The Charles Darwin conference was well run, featuring stunning speakers saying interesting things, and the conference deliberations were noted worldwide. There was also controversy when an anti-Darwinista tried to ask a question but had the microphone removed before he could finish.

Another conference that fell into the worthwhile category was an unveiling the original petition by King Henry VIII for divorce from Catherine of Aragon, a magnificent document with the various red wax seals still in good shape. The conference marked the 500th anniversary of the document's formulation. What tipped the balance at this conference was a vibrant UK lecturer – could it have been Professor Eamon Duffy of

CONFERENCES OF SOLID GOLD ... AND SLIPPERY SILVER

Cambridge in full flight? In fact it was renowned historian David Starkey. He contended that had Pope Clement VII moved more quickly to consider and process the petition, he probably would have granted the divorce, and history might have been very different. Pope Clement had already given Henry VIII the title Defender of the Faith, because Henry had actually been quite helpful against Martin Luther and the Reformation emerging in Germany. But the Pope declined his divorce petition; with that Henry VIII famously went his own way and set up what would become the Church of England.

The main contention of the lecturer was that, faced with promoting a Church whose spark of creation was the divorce of a king rather than any rift in biblical interpretation, Henry's advisers were forced to construct a raft of propaganda against Rome and Catholic Europe. They built a compelling case for the necessity of the Church of England, and why it was essential to the security and religious freedom of England that they cut links with Rome. This led to a great deal of scepticism and anger between the average Englander and the average continental European – helped a good deal by England's 'island State' mentality. In turn it led, often enough, to war – the Spanish Armada and the Hundred Years' War being notable examples.

When the European Union gradually emerged after World War II, the British Government was obliged to switch from 500 years of gentle bashings of Europe to a more creative approach. But you can't make so massive a switch by pressing a button, and you can't turn around Britons' entrenched scepticism and criticism of Europe overnight. And the lecturer's closing comment has rung loudly with me ever since: 'You are looking at a document that has impact to this day, and explains why the default position of all members of the House of Commons over 500 years is to be firmly Euro-sceptic.' This set off fierce debate about the Brits' scepticism in all matters relating to continental Europe that carried on into the evening.

I came away from that lecture reflecting on another dimension of that famous divorce petition. In a sense the Euro-scepticism it created was enough to cause the PM at the time the euro was being devised, Tony Blair, to hold back from embracing the euro and abolishing the pound. It gave life to the strong campaigns of then Leader of the Opposition William Hague, then Chancellor of the Exchequer Gordon Brown and others. Today this is regarded by most observers of currency matters as having been a very wise call.

So what was in this particular conference for me was not so much any gain for Australia as a better understanding of aspects of the UK's ongoing relationship – and lack of relationship – with continental Europe. It also helped me work at relations with the Anglican Centre in Rome, headed up by an Australian, the Very Rev. Canon David Richardson. I saw this as part of building unity between Christian denominations, and through that building dialogue between Christians and those of other faiths.

During visits to the Anglican Centre I got to meet often enough the Archbishop of Canterbury, Rowan Williams (now retired, as is David). One famous day, Rowan Williams was coming across to Rome to speak at a big Vatican conference and I was invited, with a handful of guests, including heavies

At a Sunday night supper at the Anglican Centre with great networkers, from left to right, the Very Rev. Canon David Richardson, hostess Margaret Richardson, official MacKillop postulator Sister Maria Casey and Father Keith Pecklers SJ, a New Yorker well established in Rome.

from the Vatican, by the Richardsons to lunch with him ahead of the conference. What happened was that there was heavy fog at Heathrow that morning, which would not budge until late morning. The first phone call from the Anglican leader's PA said that the plane had loaded and moved away from the terminal with warnings of 'slight delays'. So the lunch schedule remained in place, and on arrival we were told the 'guest of honour' would be a little late.

In fact, the Archbishop of Canterbury was more than two hours late. But the Richardsons did not bat an eyelid and served the lunch after swapping the seating around to ensure the conversation flowed ahead of the Archbishop's arrival. The

Archbishop eventually turned up, slid into his seat, skipped a couple of courses and entered the conversation as if he had been present since the first drink. To top it off, he made it across the Tiber on time and delivered a stimulating and solid address on interpretations of art in the Old Testament that had some cardinals almost stranded in his wake.

★ ★ ★

Another illustrious late arrival at a conference I helped chair in October 2010 was Cardinal Peter Turkson, fairly new in town from his native Ghana, and driving himself around Rome to prove a point – good luck to him!

The occasion was the Tenth Anniversary Symposium of the English-speaking Caravita congregation, convened by Father Keith Pecklers SJ, under the title 'How Firm A Foundation: The Role of the Laity and the Church's Mission in the Third Millennium'. It was held at beautiful Villa Aurora, which is tucked away in a complex set of one-way streets, and hard to find first up.

The Cardinal – who was the keynote speaker – arrived an hour late. But he spoke well and then he took questions. He had told me he had a luncheon appointment with the Pope, so at one point I whispered to him, 'Hadn't you better get going?'

'Oh,' – he looked at his watch – 'Oh, one more question.' And it was a long question and answer.

After he finished his answer I escorted him out and he threw open the back of his four-wheel drive vehicle and hurriedly put

CONFERENCES OF SOLID GOLD ... AND SLIPPERY SILVER

on his formal cardinal's cassock, so that he would arrive dressed correctly for the lunch with the Pope. I said, 'Do you know how to get from Villa Aurora to Vatican City?'

'Oh, I'll be all right,' he replied.

I asked, 'Do you have a GPS?'

He said, 'No, but I think I know the way.'

With that, away he went. We learnt a few days later from another person who was at the lunch – and you're not often invited to lunch with the Pope on a Saturday – that the good Cardinal Turkson had arrived just in time for the last of the desserts. The Pope was relaxed and thought it amusing; dare I say some of the 'praetorian guard' would have taken a dim view of it!

So the conference on that occasion was noteworthy not chiefly for the speeches and discussion, but for the chance to discover that the senior clergy of the Vatican are human after all. It was also memorable for the opportunity it gave to take a look inside the magnificent Villa, which contains (among many other treasures) the only ceiling ever painted by Caravaggio. The Villa is owned by Prince and Princess Boncompagni Ludovisi, and Princess Rita is a fascinating figure. A Texan, who for a period was married to US congressman John Jenrette, over the years she has done many things, including appearing in *Playboy*, attending Harvard Business School and helping write a key report for the then Presidential Commission on World Food Hunger. Metre by square metre Nicolo and Rita are restoring Villa Aurora to its former magnificence, including the delightful central salon where opera singing was initiated 500 years ago by Vittoria Archilei.

An ancient wooden trunk recently uncovered by Rita in the family cellar will set the world ablaze when the curators and restorers complete their work. Spellbinding writings dating back as far as the thirteenth century await the world: never-before-seen letters from extraordinary people such as Pope Gregory XIII who gave us the Gregorian calendar, emperors of Spain and kings of France and Marie Antoinette, written just before going to the guillotine. In a generous way, steps are being taken to ensure many in the world will get to see the contents of this trunk of 'pure gold in the written form', as part of a major travelling exhibition.

Many Italians regard themselves as citizens at large of the Holy See, especially those who have had associations with the Vatican over the centuries. The Colonna family, for example, with Prospero Colonna carrying out honorary duties at various key gatherings, sets a noble pattern. Likewise in her own way the daughter of the inventor of radio, Marconi, namely Elettra Marconi, was a great friend of Australia and attended many functions. Over seventy years ago she turned on a radio beam on her father's yacht in Genoa that activated the Sydney Town Hall Christmas lights.

★ ★ ★

After my first few months at my post had elapsed with no great upsets, DFAT obviously gained some confidence in my abilities. So I, with many others, was appointed as special envoy to attend key international conferences if ministers could not

CONFERENCES OF SOLID GOLD ... AND SLIPPERY SILVER

get there, for instance because Federal Parliament was sitting. When there was no minister available, it was believed to be useful to send a former Deputy Prime Minister who also happened to be a current ambassador to conferences. DFAT could be confident it was sending someone who was used to the international conference circuit, and knew how to work those conferences and how to target the key people and highlight Australia's activities.

Suddenly I was needed to go to conferences in Buenos Aires, Belgrade, Bali, Madrid or Manila. In Buenos Aires was the forum for East Asia–Latin America cooperation-building; in Belgrade and Bali were meetings of the Non-Aligned Movement; and Madrid and Manila were both interfaith dialogue conferences, which was more my direct remit, and I was the obvious person for the job. There are conferences every week of the year, and many ambassadors get sent to these events.

During most of my posting there were at least two of these conferences a year, but in the final six months I was directed to attend some five overseas conferences. I sensed that I kept meeting the same brigade of delegates at many – dedicated representatives but firmly entrenched on the conference circuit – but who was I to talk?

The worst overseas conference by far was the week-long African Unity Conference, conducted in a huge tent with chandeliers just east of the Libyan capital of Tripoli. It was mid-2009 and during the last hurrah of the Gaddafi regime. Many countries had been encouraged to send envoys to 'celebrate' the fortieth anniversary of the Gaddafi-led revolution. The call was made that someone from Australia should go, and I drew the short straw.

I was given some very specific instructions. I was to be seen to represent Australia, but was *not* to shake the hand of Gaddafi or be photographed with him.

Most conferences are all about handshakes and networking, so this was a prescient move by DFAT. There was plenty of other work to be done on the margins for the Australian Trade Commission (Austrade), which is linked to DFAT but comes under the Minister for Trade. My host for a week of hectic activity was the larger-than-life Austrade Consul-General in Tripoli, Tom Yates.

Tom met me at Tripoli international airport, about thirty kilometres south of the city on the edge of the desert. There was no sign that Libya was within twelve months of imploding – second cab off the rank after Tunisia with the Arab Spring – but the way you can tell what's happening in bad regimes is to keep your eyes open at airports.

The bigger the gap between rich and poor, the larger the special air terminal for the leader, separate from all other buildings. It can generally be spotted, if you know where to look, at key airports throughout the Middle East. There are all the public terminals, but then right away on the other side of the runway there's a glorious palace-like building, and the penny suddenly drops: that's where the royal family or the president's family arrive and depart. Sometimes you'll see the heavily laden VIP planes fly back in from shopping missions

CONFERENCES OF SOLID GOLD ... AND SLIPPERY SILVER

to Paris and Rome and London. The Gaddafi regime was no exception to this. Clearly the senior elements lived in a time warp, speaking of freedom and justice as they enriched themselves beyond belief.

As Tom and I drove from the airport into the city and later around Green Square (now called Martyrs' Square), everywhere there were signs saluting the fortieth anniversary of the revolution and giant airbrushed photos of the 'fearless leader'.

The ceremonial part of the event was just the sort of thing a forty-year-old dictatorship might be expected to present, involving massive expenditure, but with everything clunky and disorganised, running hours behind schedule. On the second day of my visit a big anniversary parade took place, but only after the diplomatic corps had been sitting about five hours in Green Square waiting for it to begin. There was a long procession of tanks and a fly-past, for which they had to hire the Italian Air Force's equivalent of the RAAF's Red Roulettes.

This was followed by a big banquet on a small ornamental island nearby, and I managed to get Tom into the VIP section with me. On the way to our table, Tom and I passed about half a metre from Colonel Gaddafi's shoulder; I glanced over furtively but he was bailed up by the President of Sri Lanka – God bless the President of Sri Lanka, because that allowed us to escape, straight through to the table section.

This is called a 'brush-past' – part of the terminology DFAT uses; another is the 'pull-aside' (where you pull someone behind a pillar at a conference and speak for five minutes on some important subject). I did a 'brush-past' with Silvio Berlusconi at the Lateran Reception in Rome, and I 'brushed past' Romanian head Nicolae Ceaușescu years ago as a backbencher, when he came to Canberra. And so I've also had the 'honour' of 'brushing past' Gaddafi.

It was around midnight by the time the banquet started and some had already bailed out, including the King of Jordan, who had flown out of Tripoli in his personal jet well beforehand. The lavish servings of lobster and good wine reinvigorated me, and so Tom and I wandered around doing some selective networking, before taking in part of the post-banquet open circus show and then wilting.

Of course, then there was the conference itself. One problem with conferences the world over is that they are rarely spontaneous, rarely fluid enough to accommodate the dynamic that emerges on the floor from delegates' interactions. Quite often, when I was Deputy Prime Minister and Minister for Trade, a week before I went to a conference a document would turn up on my desk: 'For Ministers' Information'; this would be a communiqué arising from the conference I hadn't even packed for, already done and dusted. It would have been based on meetings between the various officers of each country attending, and where there *was* an area of disagreement that the officers were going to graciously allow ministers to discuss, they would put it in square brackets, as a section where the words were not yet quite finalised – in case ministers might actually do something spontaneously at the conference for a change!

CONFERENCES OF SOLID GOLD ... AND SLIPPERY SILVER

I don't believe I attended any conference as representative of the Australian Government during my three years as Australian Ambassador to the Holy See where there was a major change in the communiqué driven from the conference floor. And in the case of the African Unity Conference, it was very much a ceremonial communiqué: African leaders expressing absolute unity and peace as they go to war again!

One morning we were all taken by bus to a huge set of tents about twenty minutes from Green Square to attend the opening session. Ambassadors and envoys were seated up the back, but in my case not far from President Robert Mugabe of Zimbabwe. At any stage during the hour we were kept waiting for Gaddafi to arrive I could have easily entered into a conversation with this despot who has wrecked the economy of a once-vibrant country, but for once I bit my lip and chose not to.

On another night, the diplomatic corps and envoys were bundled into coaches and driven to the ancient Roman theatre at nearby Sabratha for a rock concert. While sitting on hard rock, I noticed that fifty metres further around the old stadium, big leather chairs had been installed, in case 'the Gaddafi family' turned up. They were empty the whole night, but I managed to sit on one of them for two minutes before being asked by stern-faced guards to move on.

During that week I got to know the British Ambassador to Libya quite well; there was a lot of cooperation between the ambassadors in that very tough posting. And I learnt from him and from Tom that the situation in Libya was very fluid, and the Gaddafi regime's shaky grip on reality was clearly weakening its power. I also gained the confidence of younger people in the course of that visit, and had quiet conversations with them. I discovered that they didn't want to challenge the politics of the day so much as they just wanted the right to get on with their lives.

All in all it was an incredible week, and full marks to Tom for the great job he has been doing in Libya, especially (much later) in helping hundreds out of the country during the revolution. By day Tom and I took the opportunity to visit a number of Australian companies doing great things in Libya, from training offshore platform workers to designing new inner suburbs. On the last full day of the visit we travelled by charter flight from Tripoli to Tobruk and visited the two Commonwealth War Cemeteries and the famous fig tree growing over a cave that was used as a regimental aid post. This was an unexpected bonus, as it had been on my 'to do' list for some time. If Hamel with John Monash was a turning point in World War I, and it was, Tobruk was the Western Front of World War II. I wanted to see where the diggers gave Rommel and the Nazis their first bloody nose.

World War II besmirched Libya in a way that World War I did not. Recalling a conversation I had with Tom Yates's father, Bill Yates (ex British diplomat and former MP in both the UK House of Commons and the House of Representatives in Canberra), I said to Tom we should give Bill a ring from Tripoli as he had served from Tripoli (Libya) to Tripoli (Lebanon). This we did on the last night and I asked Bill was he still of

Welcoming Consul-General Tom Yates back safely to Rome, after his escape from Libya, where he helped hundreds to rapidly exit the country as the Gaddafi regime collapsed.

the view Lawrence of Arabia came to Australia, well after the motorbike accident that Bill maintained Lawrence survived. Bill replied 'Yes', but added he refused to talk about it as it remains sensitive. Sadly Bill is no longer with us so we will never know more about this interesting twist.

Soon enough I was heading to the airport with Tom. Never had I longed for a flight back to Rome so much. I left Tripoli reflecting that it had been one of the most self-indulgent and mediocre conferences I have ever attended, run by one of the most bizarre leaders I have ever encountered. But my mission had been achieved: I had been noted as being present, but had not gone anywhere near Colonel Gaddafi.

This conference definitely fell into the category of 'slippery silver', and only served to remind me of what a good conference should be about. For an ambassador, a solid gold conference is about gaining information that is of use for your country, and it is a bonus if you can also boost the profile of your country in a meaningful way.

CHAPTER EIGHT

World Famine, Food Security and the Holy See

Are the Himalayan glaciers melting to extinction, and will this have a big impact on South Asia, if not the world? Will millions be displaced and go on the move in search of food?

In the glorious gardens of the Vatican is the Pontifical Academy of Science, led by a great Argentinean thinker and doer, Bishop Marcelo Sánchez Sorondo, whom I have mentioned before. He has travelled widely, studied a great deal and absorbed much about the world and its scientific endeavours.

In April 2011, a handful of ambassadors, including me, were invited to join a four-day conference on the Himalayan glaciers, featuring scientific heavyweights from around the world and held in the very pleasant conference room of the Academy. The sessions continued throughout the entire first weekend of

April and on to the Monday; discussions carried on late into most nights. I was happy to surrender a springtime weekend of glorious sunshine to soak it all up.

After four days of gripping but sober scientific assessments, delivered by several expert key speakers in a down-to-earth way with no hint of hyperbole, the conference adjourned but with the promise of a post-conference summary statement. This ended up taking weeks, not days, but it was worth the wait. Although there are aspects of the statement that I do not agree with, it is a powerful wake-up call.

The statement is entitled 'Fate of Mountain Glaciers in the Anthropocene', and is available on the Internet. It argues that there is a ninety per cent chance that global warming is a result of the observed increase in anthropogenic (man-made) greenhouse gas emissions. Essentially it urges caution in relation to the high levels of carbon dioxide being pumped into the atmosphere, and it emphasises that it is fact that glaciers are vanishing around the world.

Whatever might yet be determined as the real cause of climate change, and whatever might yet be determined as to whether recent prolonged drought periods in parts of the world were merely pendulum swings or signs of long-term irreversible change, there are some hard-edged impacts that cannot be denied.

It is irrefutable that the rate of glacier melt in the northwest Himalayas is close to neutral, but that in the central and eastern Himalayas it has accelerated at an alarming pace, with smaller glaciers vanishing altogether. The modelling for the next few decades in relation to the great southbound rivers flowing from the Himalayas to the Indian Ocean points to huge changes in about twenty-five years' time, as the glaciers feeding these rivers become no more.

More immediately, large natural lakes and dams formed by many glaciers as they melt can eventually lead to flood water that hurtles down a valley, sweeping all before it. The glacial Lake Imja was cited as posing real danger for the Nepalese living in that valley, especially as the lake is expanding rapidly.

South of Nepal, the flood plains of many parts of Myanmar, India and Bangladesh are essential to production in the region's food bowl, and will also be affected. In these areas, the advent of a blanketing brown cloud, arising from areas of intense industrialisation, adds to the burden, as reduced sunlight on crops is having an impact on crop growth and yield.

So a perfect storm looms. And not just figuratively: recent rises in weather volatility mean that violent hurricanes, typhoons and tornadoes increasingly abound across the world. Even the Riverina and New South Wales–Victorian border region has to put up with tornadoes these days. These may bring some much-needed moisture-laden air with the destruction, but they can never be as reliable as the annual flooding of big rivers like the Ganges.

The conference spearheaded by Bishop Sánchez Sorondo and the Vatican was a wake-up call to both sides of the climate debate, and also to those neutral about it but keen to be assured that there will be enough food to feed the world over the next few decades.

The general conclusion around Rome — home to the HQs of the UN Food and Agriculture Organization, the UN World Food Program, Biodiversity International and the Global Crop Diversity Trust — is yes, in theory the world can produce enough to feed its population of seven billion (and growing). Further, steps have been made to take out insurance of a clever kind. The Global Crop Diversity Trust stores safely in Norway, in the Svalbard Vault, thousands of seed samples of rice and wheat and many more crops, as a hedge against the possibility of a form of super rust wreaking havoc.

For all of this, the world's population is predicted to be nine billion by 2050; the food deficit in parts of the world is getting worse, not better; and conversely, there is a huge problem of food *waste* in many of the world's developed nations. This wastage, along with massive distributional problems, will still cause famine, and not just in Africa. The rising middle class of Asia, eating more protein, will be another crunch factor.

This is an issue for every nation on earth, our own included. Since World War II Australia has given much to agricultural research: we have not only been the supplier of many agricultural research scientists and funded a great deal of research within and without Australia, but we have also benefited very directly. The ACIAR (Australian Centre of International Agricultural Research) channels funds to the CGIAR Consortium (Consultative Group on International Agricultural Research), which has various research centres around the world, such as the International Potato Centre in Peru, the International Rice Research Institute (IRRI) in the Philippines, and the International Maize and Wheat Improvement Centre (CIMMYT) in Mexico. Sadly the International Centre for Agricultural Research in the Dry Areas (ICARDA) at Aleppo in Syria has been trashed, destroyed in the Syrian civil war but not before the GCDT helped rescue the seed bank, transferring it out of Syria to safety.

Australia has aided CIMMYT in the development of dwarf wheat varieties, which are less prone to wind damage and moisture stress and produce more grain per head. This has led to a huge increase in wheat yields in the Mallee and Riverina and many other parts of our arid nation. CIMMYT is now looking at a newer 'super-wheat', while a 'super-rice' crop is being cultivated by IRRI in the Philippines.

So Australia has had — and will continue to have — much to contribute in this area, for some financial gain but also for the improvement of food production around the globe. This is why food security was one of the key issues I had been publicly instructed by DFAT to pursue in Rome. But there was a political reason too: it afforded yet another vehicle for giving well-focused, well-targeted aid to parts of Africa, at a time when we were seeking votes for the United Nations Security Council.

As part of this remit, towards the end of my three-year term I decided to host a conference in Rome, in liaison with Australian Ambassador to Italy David Ritchie.

The two key speakers were easy to nail down: Australian science communicator Julian Cribb, who as luck would have it was due to visit Europe, and Bishop Sánchez Sorondo. The theme was Food Security and World Famine, the venue was the conference room at the new Domus Australia (more on that later), and I was the convenor and conference chair.

To save money, I invited Julian Cribb to stay in the spare bedroom at my apartment, which also allowed for some fine tuning and a better understanding of his position on food security, as set out in his recent book *The Coming Famine*. (I in fact presented a copy of this book to the Pope on my last visit to him.)

In his lecture, Julian Cribb laid out succinctly the problems associated with peak water – in essence a critical shortage of fresh water, particularly in politically unstable parts of the world such as the Middle East. To this he added the issues of good agricultural land scarcity, peak phosphorus, finite natural nutrient supplies and many related aspects, notably food wastage adding to the world famine equation.

One statistic above all, included in Julian's book and backed up by independent research, should make us stop and think. On current trends, by 2020 the world is likely to be burning, in the form of biofuels, around 400 million tonnes of grain annually. Now, here is the scary part: this is the equivalent of the world's current annual rice crop. Yes, logically some farmers will create and use their own biofuels, but this is different from doing it on a huge scale to feed the world's indulgent needs, including the excessive use of motor vehicles in some large OECD countries.

Bishop Sánchez Sorondo reminded everyone: 'Our security, even our survival, will depend on the world forging a triple commitment: to end extreme poverty; to ensure human rights

WORLD FAMINE, FOOD SECURITY AND THE HOLY SEE

for all; and to protect the natural environment from human-induced crises' (for instance, the brown cloud over much of South Asia, and the glacier melt in the central and eastern Himalayas).

There was a good, diverse roll-up on the day, and the great presentations were matched by vibrant question-and-answer sessions plus discussion periods. But when all is said and done there still seems to be a critical gap in European thinking, leading to what might be termed the falsehood that a 'nostalgia agriculture' approach will still fix all.

Senior Curia personnel believed that somehow farming in the twenty-first century would be best if it reverted to small lots and a kind of cottage farming, carried out by extended families and using local markets. One cardinal was adamant that this was what people really wanted, and further, that farming was best done on an organic basis, with no fertilisers, no chemical sprays and no big machines. In a perfect and population-stable or shrinking world, this might just work, but I do not think so.

Traditionally Europe has been opposed to genetically modified (GM) crops, and has supported various kinds of farm subsidies under its Common Agricultural Policy. As Australian Minister for Trade in the last few years of the twentieth century, I (and my successors from both sides of Australian politics) spent much energy railing against the distortions created by the Common Agricultural Policy, especially the poverty it creates for developing countries in Africa – such as Uganda, trying to export bananas into Europe.

Conversely, the younger thinkers in the Curia, along with Bishop Sánchez Sorondo, were much in favour of modern agriculture: large-scale, efficient farming with advanced machinery, using GM crops in a cautious way (and preferably in a way that does not allow mega seed companies to dominate). Most of them are absolutely in favour of exploring all aspects of modern science and agriculture. If rainfall is scarce, you must maximise crop yields on the precious hectares where it falls adequately, and if you can modify rice varieties to protect eaters from deteriorating eyesight with no adverse ramifications, then why not do so?

The Australian Government and both sides of the Australian Parliament remain strongly in favour of modern agriculture. This accords with the worldwide school of thought arguing that with increased weather volatility and a growing world population, famine awaits on a huge scale unless large-scale agriculture continues to expand using the best cropping science and best modes of operating. Equally, efforts to eliminate food waste must gain momentum.

Pope Benedict XVI has his own farm up at Castel Gandolfo. In an Angelus Address in November 2010 he made an interesting reference to agriculture that hit the nail on the head: 'There is a need to review all aspects of agriculture, not for any nostalgic reasons but because of its fundamental importance for the future of the world.' I sent messages of commendation to the Vatican following this address, praising the Pope's words as Head of State. (Occasionally I would meet the actual speech writer, buried in the Office of the Secretary of State – they never admitted directly to the role, but did allow that they made contributions to the speeches of the Pope and other senior figures.)

WORLD FAMINE, FOOD SECURITY AND THE HOLY SEE

Tucked away in various parts of the Vatican, not just the Pontifical Council of Justice and Peace or the Pontifical Academy of Science, there are many with a deep interest in the issue of food security and the related possibility of world famine, stretching far beyond Africa. That said, exactly what can the Vatican do to ease the burden of starvation worldwide?

Through organisations like Caritas Internationalis and the Sovereign Order of Malta, there are many practical programs that are working to relieve hunger on the ground in distant parts of Africa and Asia. In following the mandate of Jesus to love the poor, I expect the Church will continue to shoulder a huge role at the coalface, from setting up soup kitchens for the less well off in OECD countries to establishing flood recovery programs in the deltas of Asia, to speed up the return to normal levels of food production.

Food shortages are driven by problems on both the supply side and the demand side, and some say that until the Holy See alters its approach to the question of birth control, it denies the use of weaponry that could make a great difference to demand in predominantly Catholic countries. It is unlikely that there will be changes in the Vatican's attitude to this issue in the near future, but I have no doubt that the Holy See will maintain a deep interest in food security and will continue to explore issues such as GM crops and many other aspects of modern agriculture.

The Holy See will always go in to bat for the oppressed and those under-represented in the halls of power. It is the pathway laid down by so many early saints such as Francis of Assisi, and pursued by all modern-day popes. My beef is that the raw media capability of the Holy See is immense, but this does not mean the views of the Vatican will get huge coverage, as too often the silo mentality undoes media efforts. The need to use social media and similar resources is very well understood in the Pontifical Council of Social Communications – but they are not necessarily in a position to drive the Holy See forward in a coordinated way. Previous popes have been listened to carefully by powerful leaders; it is my hope that current and future popes will continue to pursue both spiritual and scientific endeavours to help build a better and more sustainable world.

Food security should be near the top of the list of priority issues to be sensibly articulated and taken forward by the Holy See and all of its relevant arms. The Vatican has made a difference in the past and it can and should in the future. God alone knows that the clock is ticking fast. This huge problem must be addressed if massive disasters are to be avoided.

CHAPTER NINE

The UNSC Campaign

When, in July 2008, the decision was made to upgrade the Australian Embassy to the Holy See, my posting came with very firm instructions attached. An overarching priority for all Australian ambassadors was to do whatever they could to boost momentum and votes for Australia in its bid for a rotational seat on the United Nations Security Council.

As the UN's primary peacekeeping body, in a sense the UNSC is the apex of the whole of its activities. Membership would bring Australia international gravitas, and recognition as a significant middle-ranking power. Critical votes on the Security Council matter, in respect of the Middle East and elsewhere, and sanctions being imposed on countries like Iran. Australia itself would be within rocket range of North Korea, if everything went absolutely pear-shaped. So, what was our reason for going on the UNSC? To do our very best to see that things *do not* go absolutely pear-shaped in the second decade of the twenty-first century. It's not a dollar-and-cents equation; it is about obtaining the wherewithal for a better world, and Australia does have a stake in that.

The UNSC is composed of five permanent members with veto powers – China, France, Russia, the UK and the US – along with ten rotational members: five from the African and Asian States; one from the Eastern European States; two from the Latin American and Caribbean States; and two from Western European and other States. Each year, five new non-permanent members are elected for a two-year term.

Our pool of nations from which two were to be elected was 'Western European and other States'. Finland and Luxemburg were the other two countries contesting. Finland was in the race early, and quickly tied up a number of key European countries, arguing that it had a strong track record of giving international aid over recent decades. Tiny Luxemburg had one point to pursue above all others: it had never ever had a turn on the UN Security Council. And Australia said, 'It's almost thirty years since Australia served; it's about time we had another turn.'

There's a small degree of sniping that goes on between nations as they manoeuvre for the votes. Finland monitored Australia closely and was not backward in bad-mouthing us from time to time around the international conference circuit as the campaign gathered momentum. In other zones, we had to be careful who we were voting for, because we really wanted

THE UNSC CAMPAIGN

to reciprocate voting support as much as we could. It was never going to be easy to win; every vote by every country with potential to help Australia win the ballot was to be systematically canvassed and sought.

Our generals in the campaign were easily identifiable: the Prime Minister and Foreign Minister of the day, Kevin Rudd and Stephen Smith respectively, then from mid-2010 Julia Gillard and Kevin Rudd. At departmental level it was DFAT Secretary Dennis Richardson and Deputy Secretary Gillian Bird.

At the coalface, bearing the brunt of the burden created by the countless hours of campaign endeavour, burning the midnight oil literally, were Caroline Millar at DFAT HQ and Ambassador Gary Quinlan, our man at the UN in New York (formerly of the PM's office). Officially he is Australia's Permanent Representative to the UN, with the title of ambassador. (Before Gary took up the role in mid-2009, it was occupied by former South Australian senator and minister Robert Hill.)

These two alone, Caroline Millar based in Canberra and Gary Quinlan based in New York, could make or break the campaign, and I had good relationships with both after many contacts in various capacities over the years. I say 'make or break' because Australia suffered a huge defeat in the UNSC ballot of 1996 under the stewardship of the then Ambassador to the UN for Australia, Richard Butler, in which the final ballot saw Portugal on 124 votes and Australia on just 57 votes.

These were our generals, but it was to be a case of all hands on deck, and each embassy was a cog in the giant wheel of the campaign. Each ambassador had to maximise the grip of his cog if Australia were to have a chance of winning.

Before departing on my posting, I had various briefings with DFAT detailing the key focuses of the campaign and the possible pitfalls. The greatest pitfall was a matter of public record: namely Australia's voting record on sensitive Middle Eastern issues, especially relating to the Palestinian question.

It was recognised that small embassies with junior ambassadors were not going to make a huge difference to the campaign, but I was told that every attempt was to be made to help Australia gain vital early momentum.

★ ★ ★

It is a useful early phase of posting when new ambassadors are expected to call on more senior ambassadors, both as a courtesy and to learn from them about the best ways to proceed, but also to engage in useful dialogue and representations on key issues for one's country. So, soon after taking up my posting, I launched down the path of making it well known that Australia was contesting actively for the UNSC seat and making sure all key ambassadors were aware of this.

The largest grouping of ambassadors to the Holy See is not from Europe, as you might expect, but from Latin America, reflecting the aggressive colonisation of the South American continent by the strongly Roman Catholic countries of Spain and Portugal. This was a group I targeted in particular.

Australia's relations and trade with Latin America over

THE UNSC CAMPAIGN

the decades have been minimal, but around 1990 this began to change. My Labor predecessors, myself and my Coalition successors, as ministers for trade, made many visits to South America and more generally Latin America (that is, everything south of the USA–Mexico border). In opening new embassies in such places as Peru and upgrading others in recent years, the Australian Government has broadened its character as a credible middle-sized power that deliberates seriously on the business of the world.

I do not claim that my overtures to the Latin Americans swung any individual country's votes but as former US Speaker Tip O'Neill once said, 'People like to be asked for their vote.' In my book you cannot do that too often at any level in an international contest. Further I had observed the heroic and comprehensive efforts of the Brazilian Ambassador to the Holy See, my friend Luiz Felipe de Seixas Corrêa, swing a result in the FAO against the odds, with Brazil defeating Spain as previously mentioned, for the key director-general position.

It also greatly helped that the Vatican was across the details of our campaign. A formal request for assistance was made by Minister Kevin Rudd to 'Foreign Minister' Archbishop Mamberti and repeatedly backed up by me, so that at functions attended by Vatican officials involving interface with delegates from all over the world, Australia's very active campaign would be to the fore and (hopefully) spoken of in a positive way.

Above all else, Rome is one of the super-hubs of the world, along with Geneva, London, New York, Paris and now several

Asian super-cities such as Singapore. There was much activity – conferences, seminars, canonisations and all – that dovetailed with my work in support of the UNSC campaign. After I was appointed a special envoy to represent the government at key international conferences, I made sure everyone at these conferences knew I was there from Australia, and that Australia was running for the UNSC.

I later took on an even more direct role in supporting the campaign. In the second half of my posting I was also appointed Envoy for the Prime Minister of Australia to Bhutan, Eritrea, South Sudan and (initially) Rwanda. This latter proved to be a bridge too far; I simply could not fit in a visit during this very busy period of the last half of my posting. Bhutan was right up my alley, as I had been there eight times in various capacities, met the two very impressive kings and come to know PM Jigmi Y Thinley and senior cabinet ministers very well. South Sudan has a very strong Christian population, and thus good connections with my work in Rome; Eritrea happens to be an old Italian colony, so there was a link there as well. Envoys who could speak Portuguese fluently, or Spanish, or French, were assigned countries where these language skills would be of benefit.

My main role with regard to the three countries I was allocated would be to present formal letters from the Prime Minister to each head of government, elevating onto the radar screen of each government how serious Australia was about seeking a seat on the UNSC. 'We have a track record, we've served on the Security Council before, we are a major player

THE UNSC CAMPAIGN

in providing overseas aid to Africa and other parts of the world, and we are purposeful members of many multilateral organisations. And you, the President of Eritrea, or you, the President of South Sudan, or you, the Prime Minister of Bhutan, might like to keep that in mind, please.'

Specific promises to vote in these countries' interests on the UNSC were matters for the Foreign Minister, who knew the full width and depth of the UNSC campaign. But in my view, since no government can predict the wording of resolutions, or the nature of proposed sanctions, or world security developments over the course of the two years of incumbency, it would not be wise or easy for a government to pre-commit to supporting country X over country Y on problem Z, or boundary dispute ZZ.

Another less directly handled dimension was to craft AusAID programs and initiatives that would benefit countries that were showing a good deal of interest in our campaign for the UNSC. Now, I wouldn't put too fine a point on that. Were we buying votes, per se? No, because those AusAID programs had to stack up on their own merit. Nevertheless, extra deserved tertiary scholarships for the students of Bhutan, who compete with vigour for Australian university places, was a win-win situation for everybody.

So during my time in Rome I took the time to travel to the 2010 Trento Festival of Economics in northern Italy to witness a rock-star reception for the Bhutanese Prime Minister. He gave a great lecture one very hot summer Saturday, and over a quiet dinner with him and one or two of his entourage, I presented Julia Gillard's letters and was able to advise that the much sought-after tertiary scholarships were being increased in number. The vibes were good that night on many issues, including the UNSC.

Meanwhile, I worked at 'cultivating' the Eritrean Ambassador to Italy, Zemede Woldetatios, who just happened to be my upstairs neighbour. This was a little unusual, but it was too good an opportunity to waste and he was an interesting fellow in his own right. Of course I kept my colleague David Ritchie informed, and any formal approaches to the Ambassador were through David. This led in June 2012 (after my posting ended) to a three-day visit to the Eritrean capital, Asmara, with Australian Ambassador Dr Ralph King from Cairo (who covers Eritrea), where we received great access right up to and including the President.

In the case of South Sudan, I had to wait until it actually gained independence and became a separate country, in mid-2011. As the world's newest nation, for the time being it has elected to have Juba, situated on the White Nile, as its capital. I flew into Juba with Ambassador Geoff Tooth again in June 2012, and again gaining high-level access to the President and senior ministers.

In both Eritrea and South Sudan I found issues of religious freedom were to the fore, with many large Christian churches and Muslim mosques to behold, almost side by side. These two small countries were happy to support Australia, however they are not without major problems and we will need to continue to provide measured assistance and advice when asked.

THE UNSC CAMPAIGN

All this travel was not without the odd humorous moment. One morning a delegate stepped back and fell into an ornamental pool. My assistant, the quick-witted Peter Stone from the Australian UN Mission, observed that the delegate was from a country that was voting for Finland and Luxemburg so we should not race to his rescue! The delegate *did* emerge from the shallow pool with a somewhat sheepish look.

★ ★ ★

The 2010 Federal election in Australia nearly derailed our attempt at the UNSC seat, with the Coalition saying in essence: yes, it was OK to seek a UNSC seat, but not now. When the ALP Government was sworn in post-election after a very tight result and negotiations with the independents, DFAT rebooted its efforts, but I recall overhearing some static at that time from Finnish sources trying to make mischief by saying Australia was split on the UNSC attempt.

All in all, the UNSC campaign provided much activity and some very interesting times for Australian ambassadors around the world, as the clock counted down to the vote in New York in October 2012. What would the result be? No one knew, but there was much speculation, and also prods from on high to redouble our efforts. I recalled all the attacks levelled at DFAT after the defeat of Australia's UNSC bid in 1996 and I did not want to see a repeat of these.

I very much hoped that Australia would succeed, as I for one and so many others had put in considerable effort way beyond so-called regular office hours. Even though I was only a bit player in the campaign, it gave an extra sense of purpose and focus to my work in Rome. The incredible outcome and result is covered in the Postscript to this book, as the vote took place in New York after my posting had ended.

CHAPTER TEN

The Vatican and Politics – Oil and Water?

Stalin once famously asked how many divisions of soldiers the Pope had, and of course the answer is none – just one regiment of Swiss Guards. The Holy See is certainly not a military power, nevertheless it does have influence on the world stage. This flows from the curious fact that it is not just the governing body of the Church, but a political entity as well. It is an associate member of the United Nations, with, in fact, the same status as the Palestinian National Authority. But it has been around for centuries longer, with a network of 140 ambassadors around the world.

Outside the Holy See, the divide between Church and State remains firmly fixed. When a bishop in Australia speaks forthrightly about film censorship and protecting under-fifteen-year-olds, he does so as a bishop of the Church. There has recently been a bishop of Paraguay elected president, but he ceased to be a bishop (more so when it was discovered he had a child!).

Where it gets badly mixed up is where you have a sort of Christian Democrats saga, as they had in Italy for decades after World War II, when the Church was deeply entwined with a particular and ultimately corrupt Italian political party. Senior elements of the Curia still spend hours each week on Italian politics, though without wielding any great power: even Italy tends to vote against the Church's position on matters of divorce law and so forth.

So is it the Church's place to interfere in politics at all? Certainly Jesus was never a political leader. Yet I would argue that the Catholic Church has been involved in politics for a very long time, and (in line with Jesus' mandate to his apostles) the outcomes have generally been for the betterment of the world.

A thousand years ago the Vatican helped create the nation of Portugal. It was formally recognised by Pope Alexander III in 1179 and popes regularly intervened in political disputes. Since the loss in 1870 of the Papal States – once including a chunk of central Italy and even pockets of southern France – the tools of influence and war it had in the form of armies separate from the Swiss Guard, have been more limited.

In more recent times, I think World War II remains seminal to those in the sixty-plus age group. It will always be debated whether the Vatican could have done more to prevent the atrocities that occurred, but it did take action to protect

THE VATICAN AND POLITICS – OIL AND WATER?

thousands of Jews in Rome, a fact that some people want to airbrush out of history (and a subject for another chapter).

Skipping forward to 1973, Paul VI created Bethlehem University on the West Bank, as a beacon of light in a land of turmoil. It remains so today, with 1000 Christians and 2000 Muslims gathering there each academic day to go about their studies in relative harmony, on a superb campus above the Square of the Manger, but with the huge Israeli-built concrete wall nearby, cutting off access to Jerusalem.

Yet it was the twenty-six year papacy of John Paul II that left such a huge legacy that it continues to be felt in Rome to this day. For more than a quarter of a century he was a central force to be reckoned with; he had no guns but he had a hard-edged soft moral power.

My wife, Judy, and I met John Paul II on two occasions. The first was in 1994, on his arrival in Sydney for the beatification of Mary MacKillop. I represented the Opposition, and had a magicial two seconds with Il Papa. Later, when I visited Rome as Deputy Prime Minister in 1998, I had a spare half Saturday, and Judy and I had a private meeting with the Pope at his summer palace, Castel Gandolfo. The Pope was already beginning to tremble slightly with the onset of Parkinson's disease, but he could not have been kinder, and he happily recalled his visits to Australia and the names of key personnel.

The former Cardinal Karol Wojtyła had had a tough upbringing and narrowly missed a roundup of young men by the Nazis on the streets of Krakow. He later saw the Berlin Wall go up – from the 'wrong' side. For years, as cardinal, he closely observed the workings of Communism from behind the Iron Curtain.

In looking at the long public life of this man who became pope, it is reasonable to state that he was no shrinking violet and he played the cards available to him with maximum leverage. After 1978, he accepted that part of his designated role as pontiff was not to step back from the international stage. He wanted to give real help to good causes.

The first big political cause was the startling deterioration of relations between Argentina and Chile in the early 1980s, a dispute that had at its core the international boundary between these two giant countries that dominate a large part of Latin America. In a nutshell, the problem related to the fact that the highest point along the spine of the Andes is not the point that equally divides the flow of water to the lowlands of Argentina and Chile respectively. Also underlying this dispute was the desire to maximise the gains to be obtained from the huge oil and gas deposits in the region.

So the generals running Argentina at the time muscled up on Chile and prepared to bomb its capital, Santiago, as a kind of opening salvo for one-sided negotiations. The prospect of conflict was ringing alarm bells all the way to Washington and Rome.

Enter Pope John Paul II, who had been just a few years on the papal throne and had recently bounced back from a 1981 assassination attempt in St Peter's Square. He offered to mediate, and set up a papal commission to examine the border in detail and recommend alterations. In the end, there

THE VATICAN AND POLITICS – OIL AND WATER?

were more than 900 alterations recommended, which were wrapped into the 1984 Treaty of Peace and Friendship and delineated clear-cut boundaries for almost all the length of the Argentina–Chile border in South America. Both Chile and Argentina accepted the outcome and modern maps reflect the papal intervention, especially near the critical Beagle Channel and Magellan Strait. In 2009, in the Pontifical Academy of Science building in the Vatican Gardens, a plaque was unveiled commemorating the twenty-fifth anniversary of the Treaty of Peace and Friendship, with the Presidents of Argentina and Chile both present.

The ground-breaking treaty was a huge achievement, which by degrees made Latin America a more stable and peaceful place. It was an outcome that Pope John Paul II could be proud of. But he did not have much time to dwell on it, as other crises loomed.

In late 1980 Ronald Reagan had won the US presidency and was keen to forge links with the Pope of the day, particularly since he was a Slav pope from behind the Iron Curtain. Reagan arranged to meet with John Paul II during his first term.

Reagan was of the view that the 'evil empire' of the Soviet Union was ripe for change and the Eastern bloc close to the point of being unsustainable as a united power bloc. At the time, Europe was a basket case. There were huge industrial troubles, bouts of damaging inflation and too much unemployment. Drugs and booze were to the fore, especially among the young.

Over his two-term presidency (1981–89), Reagan had the spine to follow through and keep challenging the Soviet bloc.

To some extent he was supported by British Prime Minister Margaret Thatcher, though she was very concerned about what a united Germany could mean to the world.

Throughout this period Reagan found in Pope John Paul II a fellow traveller, who was deeply opposed to Communism and sensed that the first hints of fundamental change were beginning to emerge from behind the Iron Curtain.

Already the Solidarity movement had sprung up in the northern parts of Poland, led by Lech Wałeşa, later Poland's president. The Pope provided both spiritual comfort and financial support for this rapidly growing movement. It is accepted today that he supplied around US$100 million through various channels, greatly helping Solidarity through its darkest days of formation.

Gradually Solidarity gained sufficient momentum to manoeuvre Poland towards free elections in 1989 and up-end the four and a half decades of Communist rule. The unwavering support of the Pope and the Holy See was critical to ensuring Poland broke out of the Soviet bloc, and this in turn brought massive pressure to bear on East Germany. At the time, the Kremlin had its hands full, as the Soviet Union itself was also starting to show signs of breaking up.

The year 1989 brought a European summer with much tension and many people on the move. The dismantling of Hungary's border with Austria saw thousands of East Germans moving south to (then) Czechoslovakia and Hungary and crossing into the free world. As the northern autumn wore on, the Berlin Wall itself came under direct pressure. The remnant

THE VATICAN AND POLITICS – OIL AND WATER?

East German Government finally gave orders not to shoot at those seeking to jump over the Wall. Within hours it started to come down as the 'stand still and do not shoot' orders were absorbed and obeyed by the East German police.

The Kremlin blinked, but did not – or could not – intervene. Soon the famous scenes of West Germans embracing East Germans were beamed around the world, as people climbed over the Wall during the night, or came through holes that quickly opened up in the Wall's structure. Within weeks all Communist regimes between Poland and Bulgaria had collapsed, with the hated Romanian dictator and his wife being executed on Christmas Day 1989. History was being made.

At the twentieth anniversary of the fall of the Berlin Wall in 2010, the US Secretary of State, Hillary Clinton, gave particular credit to Pope John Paul II's contribution to the fall of Communism in Poland. She highlighted that this vital work became a critical factor in bringing pressure to bear on the East German Communist Government. In turn, this created the conditions for the collapse of the Wall and the overthrow of the Communist regime.

As we see Communism survive in various guises in the twenty-first century, such as in China and Cuba, we are reminded that the fall of Communism in the Eastern bloc was never going to be easy to achieve or facilitate.

Over the centuries, the Holy See has seen nation states and national capitals come and go. It is unlikely to be the decisive and lead player, but it is often instrumental in these monumental events. After the fall of the Berlin Wall and the collapse of

Communism in Eastern Europe and the Soviet Union, it could be said that the Holy See and its leader the Pope continue to matter.

★ ★ ★

There is no doubt that Pope Benedict XVI had a very different personality from his predecessor, John Paul, who was much more outgoing and really liked to mix with people; anyone in Rome could apply to attend a pre-breakfast Mass in his private chapel and break bread with him afterwards. This sort of socialising was never the German Pope's *modus operandi*.

It is often stated that Pope Benedict did not appear as strongly motivated by the international agonies of the world. But allowance has to be made for the fact that there could not be a repeat of the spectacular events that so changed Europe, leading to the long-hoped-for fall of Communism, and reunification of East and West Germany to create a deeply democratic and productive country.

The first few years of the papacy of Pope Benedict XVI were more stable times – until the unfolding of the global financial crisis in 2008 and the Arab Spring in 2010. Since then, he played the difficult cards he was dealt as well as any pope might have played them.

But even before these events, a particularly brutal incident in the Middle East gave the new Pope an opportunity to make his mark. In the summer of 2006 there was an ugly war between Israel and Lebanon (or elements within Lebanon). This saw

THE VATICAN AND POLITICS – OIL AND WATER?

Israeli aircraft bomb parts of Beirut International Airport, occupy many sections of southern Lebanon and engage in fierce tank warfare with the Lebanese militant group Hezbollah.

Casualties mounted on both sides; worse still, Corporal Gilad Shalit, whom Israel had been seeking to free at the start of the war, was nowhere to be found. (He was finally released in a prisoner exchange in October 2011.)

The White House and others stepped in to negotiate a ceasefire and it was agreed this would come into effect on 14 August 2006. Against the odds, the ceasefire held and brought an end to immediate hostilities, with the Israeli forces withdrawing.

However, in the last forty-eight hours before the final implementation of the ceasefire a very nasty operation took place, conducted by elements of the US and Israeli military machines. Thousands of cluster bomb munitions were flown from arsenals in the USA to Israel and sprayed out across southern Lebanon in bombing raids, or fired into Lebanon using Israeli rockets. Many of these small cluster bombs looked like mobile smartphones, leading Lebanese children to pick them up and lose an arm or eye in the explosion that followed. It was absolute bastardry even by Middle Eastern standards.

Throughout my posting, the polite ambassador from Lebanon, Georges El Khoury, refused to greet or speak with the Israeli Ambassador, and you knew better than to invite them both to a small dinner party.

Israel has a right to defend itself or rescue its own soldiers, but in the past decade it has sometimes decided to act in ways that weaken both its international standing and its core fabric. Equally, just as Fatah Prime Minister Fayyad makes some progress with issues like education and health in the West Bank, his brothers in arms ramp up the random rocket attacks against Israel.

In 2011, on a working visit to Jerusalem, Bethlehem, Nazareth, Amman and Mount Nebo, I was reminded of the many complexities on the ground in this part of the world, especially in the West Bank. During that year there were many stoning incidents – young Palestinians hurling stones at Jewish settlers and Jewish settlers hurling stones at Palestinians.

At Bethlehem University, a student and a professor were savagely stoned by Jewish outpost settlers. (Outpost Jewish settlers are those building settlements adjudged as illegal by both Israel and the international community.) Control Point 300 is the main point of access through the new wall erected over the last few years by the Israeli authorities. Sometimes students can go through this control point in four minutes, but at other times, on the whim of a young Israeli conscript soldier, it can take four hours.

Pope Benedict XVI has often spoken of his deep concern for the Christian populace in the Middle East and especially the Holy Lands. In the aftermath of the summer war of 2006, with Pope Benedict's support, the Vatican and its nunciates in Geneva, New York and Vienna swung into action to help initiate the Convention on Cluster Munitions.

In May 2008 in Dublin there was a gathering of nations to consider the adoption of the Convention, with a large Holy See delegation present, led by Archbishop Silvano Maria Tomasi. Paolo Conversi, a senior Curia lay person, was also part of the delegation. He is a shrewd policy officer working in the Secretary of State office, and supplied strategic backup research.

In the end, 107 nations supported the adoption in principle of the Convention on Cluster Munitions in Dublin, with each nation in turn to consider its own support and ratification. Further plenary meetings took place in Vientiane, Laos, in 2010, and Beirut, in 2011. Ultimately over seventy countries signed up, including Australia (though not the USA or Russia). Arguably the Vatican played a decisive role in tipping the balance. This is more evidence that the diplomatic initiatives and manoeuvres of the Vatican matter more than is realised.

★ ★ ★

The exercise by the Church and its leaders of soft power, but power nevertheless, was further demonstrated by Cardinal Peter Turkson in Ghana after a very narrow election result in 2008. In the first round, John Atta Mills of the opposition National Democratic Congress Party had gained 4,056,634 votes, more than 100,000 behind the government candidate, Nana Akufo-Addo of the New Patriotic Party, who had obtained 4,159,439 votes. A few weeks later, the final result in the second round was John Atta Mills 4,521,032, just 40,586 votes ahead of Nana Akufo-Addo on 4,480,446 votes.

In percentage terms it was ultra-tight – 50.23 per cent to 49.77 per cent – and so often in Africa this kind of situation has led if not to outright civil war then to great violence and turmoil. It was the leadership and soft power of Ghanaian Cardinal Turkson (then Archbishop of Cape Coast) that made the difference. Along with others, he emphasised that this was the result and it had to be peacefully accepted. He used many subtle and less-than-subtle approaches before the two contestants finally accepted the outcome and political power changed for only the second time under multi-party government in Ghana.

It helped that Cardinal Turkson was a member of the National Security Council of Ghana at the time, and through this vehicle he consulted widely during the crisis. His diplomatic skills made a huge and persuasive difference, resulting in the tight election result being accepted largely without violence. President Mills died peacefully in office in July 2012.

It was good training for Cardinal Turkson, who was rightly promoted as a very different (as in non-Italian) type of cardinal to head up the key Pontifical Council of Justice and Peace in Rome.

All of this is a way of saying that through the activities of many senior cardinals, archbishops and bishops, the Vatican has a vital role to play in applying the glue of peace to delicate political processes.

★ ★ ★

Just once during my posting did a government close its embassy in the Holy See, and this came right out of left field.

THE VATICAN AND POLITICS – OIL AND WATER?

The bombshell hit late in the afternoon on a cool and quiet day in Rome. It was Thursday 3 November 2011, and the Irish Prime Minister, Enda Kenny, announced bluntly that Ireland was closing its embassy to the Holy See but it would maintain diplomatic relations, with a nominated part-time ambassador based in Dublin.

The Vatican diplomatic corps went into overdrive – an infrequent happening, but suddenly they were confronted with the most Catholic of countries, which owed much to the support of the Holy See over the decades, severely downgrading its diplomatic links and effectively pulling out of the Vatican. How could this crisis have been reached?

The reaction around Rome was interesting to say the least. At one extreme, a small group of Irish nuns said the action by their prime minister was an absolute disgrace, and predicted it would become a political issue and would eventually be reversed. Conversely, one bishop's reaction was what does it matter? Ireland was a small country and the Church had a host of other links it could utilise.

Somewhere in the middle came a more pertinent reaction from an experienced European diplomat, who said that this would be the first of many downgradings from resident to non-resident ambassadorships. He predicted that for a range of reasons the residential diplomatic corps of the Holy See would be reduced over the next few years from around eighty to barely fifty.

I thought perhaps, but imagine the outcry if it had been, say, Poland rather than Ireland withdrawing a resident ambassador.

And yet Ireland's decision was symbolic in so many ways. To this day I also wonder if Ireland would have done this but for the fact it was between Rome resident ambassadors, the hard-working, thoughtful Noel Fahey had retired a few weeks before from the post and no successor had yet been appointed.

There was another more deadly twist involved, and that was the by-no-means-small matter of the Good Friday Peace Accords and the ongoing fragile peace in Northern Ireland. All peace agreements need a certain amount of glue, and this is particularly so with the peace in Northern Ireland. The Good Friday Peace Accords, backed strongly by referendums in both Ireland and Northern Ireland, were signed on Good Friday, 10 April 1998, and came into effect on 2 December 1999. Despite a few bumps along the way, they have stood the test of time and brought a measure of peace to Northern Ireland.

There are three dimensions to the Accords, known as Strand One (Assembly powers within Northern Ireland), Strand Two (north–south liaison and powers within the island of Ireland) and Strand Three (links across the Irish Sea to Wales, Scotland and the UK as a whole).

Unwritten is Strand Four, whereby the Catholic Church has played a significant role on both sides of the border in Ireland, but also in London and along the east coast of the USA. Many Church heavyweights on both sides of the Atlantic stepped up for the Good Friday Peace Accords and used their influence to build support for it.

It is often overlooked that the brothers of the IRA collected money for their costly campaign from Irish families of New

THE VATICAN AND POLITICS – OIL AND WATER?

York and New England, especially in and around Boston. The knockout blow to the flow of resources from the USA was 9/11.

When the brothers went collecting around the usual places after the Twin Towers came down, suddenly the penny dropped (or the dime, if you like). Irish Americans realised they could not have it both ways. They could not oppose the terrorism that had smashed up the Pentagon and caused the Twin Towers to collapse, while at the same time supporting terrorism in Northern Ireland.

Church leaders had taken the chance to step up for the Good Friday Peace Accords, and with the whole mood of the world changing post-9/11, certain IRA and Sinn Fein leaders also changed both their tune and their foot-dragging. In the decade or so since both the Accords and 9/11, the Church has continued to supply the glue of peace and has been used as an additional conduit for messages and information.

Whilst it will never be officially acknowledged, part of the success of this conduit lay with the Irish Embassy to the Holy See. When the decision was made to close the Irish Embassy to the Vatican, there was complaint and protest from both sides of the Atlantic. Five months later it was still an issue when Cardinal Francis George of Chicago declined to attend a St Patrick's Day dinner at which Irish PM Enda Kenny was due to be present. Australian Cardinal George Pell and many other cardinals expressed their disquiet through various channels.

As recently as 2009, two British soldiers were killed at the front gate of their army base near Belfast when collecting a pizza one Saturday night. At a time when absolute peace in Northern Ireland is still to be achieved, is it a wise step to limit the channel of extra contact that adds to the peace glue? Is it wise to underestimate the influence the Vatican exerts in difficult political situations such as this?

★ ★ ★

Pope Benedict XVI and some of his most senior Curia personnel put a great deal of energy into the 2009 papal encyclical *Caritas in Veritate* ('Charity in Truth'). It was released to coincide with the G8 meeting in L'Aquila (8–10 July), where the 2008 global financial crisis would be a top priority. But there's not a shadow of doubt that it came about a week too late.

A papal encyclical is a letter addressed to the bishops of the world (but usually for a wider audience), indicating the Pope's concern for a significant current issue. It had been widely signalled well ahead that such a letter was in the pipeline. It was coming, it was coming; it got delayed, it got further delayed as problems emerged in the final stages of drafting and with getting the necessary translations right.

It was clear that the Vatican and the Pope had decided: 'We've got all these leaders coming; this is our take on the failings of the modern world that have led to this massive global crisis.' But even for it to have been in the briefing papers of the leaders as they headed to L'Aquila, it would have needed to come out at least one week earlier. Most of the leaders were landing in Rome on the day when it was formally released.

THE VATICAN AND POLITICS – OIL AND WATER?

And the media launch plan for the encyclical was, as usual, essentially nonexistent. There were no controlled strategic leaks, no phalanx of cardinals briefed and ready to step up in each of their locations to endorse and explain the encyclical. There was no special one-off interview by the Pope with, say, CNN or the BBC. It was as if *Caritas in Veritate* should stand alone, drawing attention purely on merit.

If it had come out in time for G8 leaders to properly consider it, it would have been a pointed reminder of the pillars of integrity that a businessman ought to pursue – in his own interest as well as for the sake of the world. It would have prompted the leaders to make the stand necessary to allow regulators to go after the bankers who had broken the law and ruined lives. To quote page 107 in part: 'Finance therefore – through the renewed structures and operating methods that have to be designed after its misuse, which wreaked such havoc on the real economy – now needs to get back to being an instrument directed towards improved wealth creation and development. Financiers must rediscover the genuinely ethical foundation of their activity, so as not to abuse the sophisticated instruments which can serve to betray the interests of savers.'

It was interesting to see the Governor of the Bank of England, Mervyn King, lash out along the same lines in a major *Financial Times* weekend interview. It is interesting to reflect that, as Mr King asserted, there was little integrity about the unsustainable, toxic instruments making certain city kingpins – especially bankers and derivatives traders – loads of money. (Staff of the Royal Bank of Scotland and Lehman Brothers come to mind, though perhaps there was a whiff of integrity in the air that late Friday afternoon in 2008 in New York when Tim Geithner and others pulled the plug on Lehman Brothers.)

The Vatican Bank, the mighty Institute for Religious Works (IOR), is used to handling loads of money, I might add, and whilst its board and leadership were shaken up in 2010, it seems not yet to be fully reformed and done with money laundering. As well as lacking transparency, it continues to operate using clunky management and budgeting structures that belong to another century. I say this on the ground that the IOR has had repeated trouble in adopting all relevant provisions of the Basel Accords (global banking standards). In an unprecedented move, in May 2012 the Board voted out Bank President Ettore Gotti Tedeschi due to lack of progress on this score. For a short period in early 2013, visitors to the Vatican Museum were unable to use ATMs or credit cards because the Bank of Italy had blocked electronic payments over the Vatican's continued failure to comply with requirements. It is to be hoped that the Vatican learns to practise what it preaches.

Be this as it may, Pope Benedict's encyclical raised eyebrows and discourse on the issues of ethics in capitalist systems, the ultimate responsibilities of company directors and the constraints on them, and the need to be sensibly profit-driven but not to the exclusion of morality interfacing with capitalism. And so it gained a degree of currency, and ended up withstanding a great deal of scrutiny to remain a wise and thoughtful document.

★ ★ ★

THE VATICAN AND POLITICS – OIL AND WATER?

More recently, the Vatican has been supportive of the formation of the world's newest – and predominantly Christian – nation, South Sudan. The creation of this new State on 9 July 2011 was achieved without any full-scale war, but sadly very nasty conflicts continue among minority groups, particularly along the declared border between Sudan and South Sudan. This is one of the very difficult circumstances that arise when new boundaries are suddenly laid down – often to clean up the actions of diplomats of 100 years ago, when borders were drawn through the tribal areas of Africa with the use of rulers, and no knowledge of circumstances on the ground.

Physical rulers and maps were used years ago by the British and French colonial officers to draw boundaries that cut across African tribal groups and their homelands. The result has been genocide too often, such as in Rwanda. In the case of South Sudan, Vatican officials had both knowledge and up-to-date feedback from crucial corners of the world. Foreign Minister Archbishop Mamberti, originally from Corsica, had spent years on a posting at Khartoum and in the Horn of Africa. He proactively raised the complex issues associated with creating South Sudan both in his meetings with UN representatives in New York and of course with many colleagues in Rome.

The Vatican has been helping displaced ethnic South Sudanese to relocate from Sudan to the newly formed State. As part of the deal, UN-monitored returnee flights operated, conveying southern tribal refugees from Khartoum to Juba. Foreign Minister Mamberti was very active in facilitating both the independence of South Sudan and support for returnees and refugees to the new southern State.

The Vatican also created a relief organisation known as 'Solidarity with South Sudan', which unusually features priests and nuns (from over 200 Catholic orders) working together. It is led in country by a brilliant Sri Lankan, Father Callistus Joseph, and at headquarters in Rome by a no-nonsense Irish nun, Sister Patricia Murray (whose team of five includes one Australian).

In June 2012, six months after the end of my posting, I was fortunate enough to be able to attend a briefing given by the Solidarity representatives in Juba, where I met down-to-earth Brother Bill Firman, rightly proud of the progress the organisation had made with farm training. It was a good follow-up to the briefings by Sister Murray and others in the board room of the Australian Embassy to the Holy See. It was great to hear at the coalface some of the good news and some of the bad news.

The good news is the sustainable agricultural training projects, helped by Solidarity and others doing a lot of work to equip people to grow their own food. Solidarity is also involved in teacher training and a range of initiatives on the health front, including post-war counselling.

The bad news is the ongoing bombing, which even led Hollywood actor George Clooney to travel into the Nuba Mountains along the border area of South Sudan and Sudan, where tribal minorities are being bombed quite regularly by old Russian bombers flying down from the Sudanese capital

THE VATICAN AND POLITICS – OIL AND WATER?

Khartoum. (Clooney was actually arrested in March 2012 for protesting outside the Sudanese Embassy in Washington.) Other issues include food shortages, a lack of skilled workers and infrastructure, and high levels of corruption.

Mid-year 2012, I paid a two-day visit to South Sudan as part of Australia's UN Security Council campaign. The capital, Juba, very much reminded me of Dili in the early days of East Timor's independence. (Hardworking NGOs, exhausted diplomats, plus Australia has a number of Defence Force personnel stationed in South Sudan, acting in coordinating roles.)

I met with senior members of Solidarity with South Sudan, and I can say with some assurance that the organisation is making a huge difference. Bit by bit, real progress is being made on the ground in Juba and many parts of South Sudan, with many governments such as Australia also helping with aid projects. Full marks to the Vatican for its work, which has such a practical dimension and makes a difference to the lives of so many people.

★ ★ ★

But for all these occasions where the Vatican has used its soft power to make a real difference, there have undoubtedly been times when it has not done enough.

At my own expense, in the final year of my posting I travelled to Sarajevo for the canonisation of several nuns raped and murdered by Nazi troops in World War II. It was Sarajevo at its best, with large friendly crowds, and a huge canonisation ceremony in an auditorium built for the Sarajevo Winter Olympics back in another era, before the breakup of Yugoslavia. Somehow this huge building survived the dreadful shelling by Serb forces located in the hills above Sarajevo during the bitter conflicts of the 1990s.

The Yugoslav Wars led to many horrors, including the shocking Srebenica massacre of 1995, when over 8000 men and boys were marched out of the Dutch-manned UN compound into the hills, to be murdered one by one by the troops of the Bosnian Serb Army under the direction of General Mladić.

It was said to me often enough during my time in Rome that during the Yugoslav Wars the Holy See knew a great deal about what was going on, especially in heavily Catholic Croatia. It must be admitted that whatever the Holy See knew about the agony of Yugoslavia's breakup and its blood-filled aftermath, it, like so many others, was not able to bring about an early cessation of hostilities. Thousands of innocent people died in clashes that too often were fuelled entirely by an appalling brand of religious and ethnic cleansing. The lack of an army, navy or air force obviously limited the extent of the Vatican's involvement, but undeniably it ended up being very supportive of Croatia, and very agnostic about support in other directions where Islam or the Orthodox Church predominated.

To be fair, I think the Vatican was really on the side of peace and stability and human rights – but Europe as a whole and many other leaders also failed innocent civilians during this period, as they watched the massacre lead to direct bombings of Serbia, until finally there was the realisation that the fighting had to be stopped. US President Bill Clinton and one or two others stepped up and the former Yugoslavia accepted an uneasy peace, with a convoluted set of boundaries and tensions to this day, such as those between Kosovo and Serbia.

It is sobering to realise that these events took place in the heart of 'civilised' Europe, just two decades ago. Now that the world has moved its focus to the Arab Spring and the oil-rich Middle East, the Yugoslav conflicts have been forgotten to some extent – and yet it is to be hoped that some lessons were learnt.

★ ★ ★

In more recent times, the huge consternation whipped up against Pope Benedict XVI over some misjudged remarks concerning the Muslim faith proved that words can indeed be bullets. The remarks were part of a speech delivered in September 2006 at Regensburg in Germany (where Pope Benedict once served as Professor of Dogmatic Theology). They quoted a fourteenth-century Byzantine emperor who referred to forced conversions within Islam, calling them 'evil and inhuman'. Taken out of context, the comments sparked riots throughout the Muslim world, and caused enormous difficulty for some Catholics, including a group of missionary nuns in India – as a direct consequence, their lives were put in jeopardy.

Soon afterwards the Pope made an official visit to Turkey. Father Felix Körner of the Gregorian University in Rome was in Ankara at the time; he later told me that he came out of his quarters on the morning of the Pope's arrival, and was informed by his Muslim neighbour: 'We are going to kill your Pope today!' Fortunately, Father Felix was quickly able to defuse the situation by saying with a smile, 'Well, you tried to kill Pope John Paul II a few years back in St Peter's Square, and you failed. I am very confident you will fail again this time.' The Muslim smiled then burst into laughter in return, the situation was defused, and very fortunately Father Felix was proved correct.

As the Vatican continues to wrestle with the aftermath of the Arab Spring and the ongoing exodus of Christians from the Middle East, let us hope that this kind of incident, where words uttered by popes are twisted to become incendiary bombs, is not repeated any time soon.

★ ★ ★

So does the Vatican have influence in this secular world of military superpowers? Probably a great deal less than centuries ago, but occasionally, when deft enough, it can, and has, shifted international boundaries (metaphorically and literally). A small marker of this is the fact the EU maintains an ambassador to the Holy See, in a sense from Brussels to the Vatican, no matter that there are strong Belgian, Dutch, French, German, Hungarian, Polish and Spanish and almost every other European country represented by Rome resident ambassadors.

Indeed, the Vatican does matter today on a range of fronts, in terms of the spiritual, geopolitical and physical wellbeing of the world. This applies to the recent few decades but also to the present and the immediate future. It will matter even more if the new Pope can reassert moral authority by cleaning up the Vatican Bank mess and the clergy sex abuse saga.

CHAPTER ELEVEN

The Canonisation of a Great Aussie Battler

Early on the morning of 22 September 1871, Mary MacKillop and her fellow Sisters of St Joseph entered a forbidding and austere room for a formal meeting with the Bishop of Adelaide, Bishop Sheil; four priests were also on hand. Less than thirty minutes later, Mary had been ex-communicated from the Catholic Church for insubordination: an event that would usher in her biggest test of faith.

Mary MacKillop was born in Melbourne on 15 January 1842, the oldest of eight children. Her father, Alexander MacKillop, had been a seminarian at the Scots College in Rome before returning to Scotland and dropping out of priesthood studies, migrating and marrying but never able to hold down a lucrative job.

Top: *This is Ponte Vittoria, the bridge I walked across – over the modestly swollen Tiber River – on day one of my posting when going from the chancery to the Vatican to meet the Protocol Director of the Holy See.*

Right: *Pope Benedict XVI was in a relaxed and expansive frame of mind on credential day. He is pictured here at the end of the ceremony with my family, Judy on the far left, Dominic beside her, and Harrison on the far right.*

Bottom: *At the end of a papal concert in the huge auditorium Paolo Sixto, just inside the Walls of the Vatican. The music of Handel had memorably dominated this concert, under a roof now adorned with massive solar panels, supplying about twenty per cent of the power needs of Vatican City.*

I represented Australia at many key conferences in the three years of posting; this one was at the powerful Gregorian University in the very heart of Rome, a useful distance from the Vatican.
Below: *Professor Anne Cummins (far right) of Australian Catholic University led a group of Indigenous visitors to Rome to present a painting by Yvonne O'Neill (third from left) and a ceremonial Torres Strait Islander headdress by Anson John Marante, ahead of the canonisation of St Mary MacKillop in 2010.*

Mid-morning sometimes meant a dash up to St Peter's Square to meet a group of Australians and explain the workings of the embassy and the Holy See. Here students of Tumut High School, 2010, are making their annual visit courtesy of funding from the Tumut area Blakeney Millar foundation. (Photo Karen Hayes)

Top: *Leaving the special consistory meeting in the Papal Palace with Sister Maria Casey, flanked by the ever-alert Swiss Guards.*
Right: *The always-friendly Cardinal Peter Turkson from Ghana, head of Justice and Peace in the Curia, with Sister Maria Casey, just after the happy announcement by the Pope that Australia was to have its first saint.*

The huge and poignant Monte Cassino War Cemetery, with the large, much-fought-over Monte Cassino monastery just visible on top of the hill, commanding sweeping views of the southern approaches to Rome.

South of Rome, less than an hour by car or train, lies the superb Castel Gandolfo, the Summer Palace of the Pope, with huge gardens, sometimes used for receptions. It also has a small papal farm plus a helipad.

New Bishop Charles Drennan steps out in good clobber, purchased partly in NZ as well as Rome. He is now the Bishop of Palmerston North, but before that was nicknamed by me 'Agent One-007', as he had deep knowledge stretching in breadth from Christchurch to Canberra to Section One of the Curia.

My family about to head to St Peter's in January 2010. On the far right is my mother-in-law, Mary Brewer.

The portrait of Mary MacKillop, hung over St Peter's Square during the canonisation of Australia's first saint.

Getting ready for the canonisation celebrations were Australian Carmelite Sisters (from left to right) Benedicta, Rosemary, Elizabeth, Marie Francis (Prioress), Teresa Jerome and Marie Rose, with Fathers Keith Pecklers SJ (left) and Stuart Moran (right), and yours truly in the middle.

On a quick private visit to Malta I met up with the Rev. Dr Joseph Bezzina, (centre), and the late inspiring, always-cheerful Sandhurst Bishop, Joe Grech (right), to whom this book is dedicated.

Right: *Principessa Elettra Marconi, daughter of radio inventor Guglielmo Marconi, was always active and helpful on the circuit around Rome. Years ago she switched on a radio beam in Genoa that went right around the world to turn on Christmas lights at the Sydney Town Hall.*

Below: *The other key 'Caritas Express' planner from Caritas Internationalis, Monsignor Robert Vitillo, holding the Vatican flag, with various Vatican and Trenitalia personnel involved in the very successful project.*

Left: *Culture supremo in the Holy See Cardinal Ravasi always enjoyed a good joke and pushed some good agendas. Here I am presenting him with a book I co-wrote with Tshering Tashi on the Himalayan Kingdom of Bhutan. This was in part to encourage the Cardinal to visit Bhutan and Asia generally.*

Inside the armoury of the 500-year-old Swiss Guards Regiment, almost directly below the Pope's quarters and next to the Vatican Bank.

Three ambassadors on the rooftop of the Vatican, Christmas Day 2009; from left to right, US Ambassador Professor Miguel Diaz, me and larger-than-life British Ambassador Francis Campbell.

Above: *A working lunch in Colombo hosted by High Commissioner Kathy Klugman. On my right, Papal Nuncio Joseph Spiteri; on my left Cardinal Malcolm Ranjith and hostess Kathy. For two years during Kathy's posting to Sri Lanka there were zero people-smuggling boats from Sri Lanka to Australia.*
Left: *This view of the magnificent Michelangelo Dome of St Peter's is from near the Pope's railway station, with ARA Heritage rail officer Chris Le Marshall on my right, and David T. Morgan, outstanding President of Fedecrail, on my left.*

One of the beautiful gilt-edged coaches used by previous popes, tucked away in the Carriage Pavilion of the Vatican Museums.

Right: *Judy and I before an official function.*
Below: *The small, happy team of the Holy See Embassy for my entire posting; from left to right, driver Stefano Bernardini, office manager Antonia Da-Rin, me, PA Madonna Noonan and Deputy Head of Mission Michael Sullivan.*

THE CANONISATION OF A GREAT AUSSIE BATTLER

To provide for the family, at age fourteen Mary became a clerk in a stationery store, before taking up a position as governess with her aunt and uncle in Penola, South Australia, and meeting there the formidable local parish priest, Father Julian Tenison Woods, who was to have a profound influence on her life. After four years with her family in Portland, Victoria, and a failed attempt to set up a boarding school, Mary returned to Penola at the invitation of Father Woods. With the help of her siblings, in January 1866 she opened a school there in a disused stable.

As rural South Australia developed, both Mary and Father Woods could see the great need to provide a decent education for the poor bush children. Mary was absolutely wedded to the concept that it was through education that the nation would be built and souls would be saved.

In August that year Mary took religious vows and became Sister Mary of the Cross. Others soon joined her, and with the assistance of Father Woods, she formed a congregation (holy community), the Order of the Sisters of St Joseph of the Sacred Heart (SOSJ). The Rule (constitution) of the congregation was approved by Bishop Sheil in 1867.

Some subsets emerged, one group of the SOSJ adopted a brown religious habit that later earned them the nickname 'the Brown Joeys'. The Rule of the order emphasised poverty and a willingness to go where needed, and the sisters ventured into the remote outback, joining in the hardships of isolated farmers and labourers as they taught their children. Directing their efforts at the primary-school level, Mary and her Sisters developed an education model uniquely suited to the harsh conditions of rural Australia, one that was later adopted in part by the South Australian Government, with elements used right around the country.

By the end of 1969, the Sisters had opened more than twenty schools throughout South Australia and were beginning to expand into Queensland. They had also founded orphanages, refuges for ex-prisoners and ex-prostitutes, and homes for the destitute, unmarried mothers and the elderly. 'Never see a need without trying to remedy it' became their motto.

Yet friction soon developed between some clergy members, on the one hand, and Mary and her Sisters of St Joseph on the other. Mary's energy and dynamism meant that she was always going to earn the jealousy of those who preferred to sit on their hands, and so there were some priests who clearly were very uncomfortable with the progress she was making. And there was certainly an element of male chauvinism involved; the fact that she was a woman made her even more of a threat. (Sadly, this issue is still present in the Catholic Church today.)

A further annoyance for Bishop Sheil was the question of who was in control of the Sisters within each parish and diocese. There was an ongoing battle over the central clause in the SOSJ Rule, which stipulated that it was the Mother-General who ran the order – in consultation with parish priests as to where they set up schools and the like – in contrast to the usual model, in which the bishop would decide where the nuns went, and when and how.

This kind of clash has been around in the Catholic Church since time immemorial – for instance, among the

THE CANONISATION OF A GREAT AUSSIE BATTLER

Jesuit missionaries of South America in the seventeenth and eighteenth centuries. The Jesuits wanted to assist and educate the indigenous people, while the parish priests wanted to take the easier path and look after the Spanish and Portuguese planters, who had the money. So eventually the missionary Jesuits were ordered out of the country by Rome. The planters and the complicit establishment elements of the Church in Argentina and Brazil won the day.

Then there are the rumours (widely circulated at the time of her canonisation) that Mary and her Sisters had uncovered cases of possible sex abuse in Kapunda, north of Adelaide. The alleged culprit, Father Keating, was subsequently sent back to his native Ireland (on the excuse of alcohol abuse), but it is thought that this incited the wrath of Keating's colleague Father Horan, who from that point was gunning for Mary and the Josephites. When he became Acting Vicar-General of the diocese in June 1870, he got the opportunity he needed.

Bishop Sheil was often absent from his diocese, leaving it without effective leadership. He was drifting towards the end of his life on earth, and his indifferent health made him vulnerable to the influence of those around him. On the advice of Horan and others, he eventually decided to take the very cruel action of ex-communicating one of the only people really achieving things, especially on the education front, in and around Adelaide.

Much of our knowledge of Mary's life comes from the huge volume of letters she wrote, often in a crossover way to save paper (writing one way then turning the paper ninety degrees). In a famous letter to Father Woods shortly after her ex-communication, Mary wrote that she had been overwhelmed by 'the sensation of the calm beautiful presence of God', barely aware of the axe falling as she knelt before Bishop Sheil. At the time she had been confined to bed for a couple of days due to illness, and she even had to be helped into the room where the meeting took place. She could hardly have had anything worse happen to her, yet she maintained her faith and courage in a way that to most of us seems incredible.

The period after the ex-communication was tough and terrible for Mary and her followers, banned from church property and thrown out on the streets of Adelaide to live. In an ecumenical gesture, many people of different faiths stepped in to help, including the Jewish Solomon family, and a Presbyterian matriarch of the Adelaide establishment, Joanna Barr Smith who became a lifelong friend of Mary.

On 23 February 1872, after reflection by the Bishop, the ex-communication order against Mary was lifted. He died one week later.

Less than a month after the order was lifted, on 19 March, the Sisters of St Joseph were reinvested with their habits and the saga came to an end, with Mary having shown no bitterness throughout. Still, she was anxious to gain official approval for her order at the highest levels. On 28 March 1873 she set off alone for Rome, landing eventually at Brindisi in southern Italy and travelling up to Rome by train, arriving there on the evening of 11 May 1873.

On her own she ventured out of Termini Station to seek accommodation, and start getting to know Rome and key contacts in the Vatican so the work of her visit could commence. Garibaldi and his Unification forces had stormed Rome just a couple of years before, so wearing clerical garb was no guarantee of safety in those tumultuous times.

On 1 June 1873, she personally met with Pope Pius IX, and so commenced a review that led to an ultimate ruling in favour of the Sisters of St Joseph and their constitution, and against the actions of Bishop Sheil. This brave teacher from tiny Penola, South Australia, had gained access to the very top echelons of the Church in Rome and won a notable victory.

Often having to borrow money to complete her travels around Europe, and on occasions having to dress in non-clerical garb for protection, Mary made it to England, France, Ireland and Scotland. Eventually, in late 1874, she left Rome with fifteen young Irish sisters and returned to Australia. The new sisters were highly educated, and would be an asset to the SOSJ as they continued to expand throughout eastern Australia and New Zealand.

Sadly, though, the ruling Mary gained in Rome would be a thorn in her side over the coming decades. The Vatican had overturned the commitment to poverty in the SOSJ Rule, which caused a rift between Mary and her mentor Father Woods, who blamed Mary for the overturn; they were only reconciled right before his death in 1889. And the SOSJs' self-government would see them come into conflict with the ruling Catholic elite in almost every diocese they ventured into – Mary herself was even expelled from South Australia in 1883 by the local South Australian Catholic Church hierarchy.

Eventually this conflict led to the second major blow of Mary's career: when she was stood down in 1885 as Mother-General of the order she herself had founded. Mixed up in this was the slur made against her that she 'drank'. Most of her life she suffered from severe menstrual pain, and it is well known that she took medicinal brandy, but the evidence suggests that she was an absolute minimalist in this regard. Again, she did not look for anyone to blame for this decision against her; she simply accepted it with good grace.

Her health further deteriorated towards the end of her life, but still she was subjected to unnecessary hardship, on one occasion being ordered out of Albury and made to stay in a shanty hotel in Wodonga on the Lincoln Causeway to await the next train to Melbourne the following morning.

In 1899 Mary was finally re-elected unopposed to the position of Mother-General, ensuring a busy final decade of her life. She suffered a stroke in 1902, nevertheless was again re-elected in 1905. She died in North Sydney, aged sixty-seven, on 8 August 1909, after an extraordinary life of serving and inspiring others.

At her death the order had 750 sisters, 117 schools teaching over 12,000 pupils, and 106 other institutions. The Sisters of St Joseph are still going strong today, living and working in Australia, New Zealand, Ireland, Scotland, East Timor, Peru and Brazil, and in refugee camps in Uganda and Thailand.

★ ★ ★

THE CANONISATION OF A GREAT AUSSIE BATTLER

Mary MacKillop's cause for sainthood has been pursued on and off since as far back as 1926, and has involved almost as many setbacks as the life of Mary herself. In 1931 the investigation was suspended until key documents discrediting her banishment from Adelaide were finally unearthed in the Vatican twenty years later. The cause was also placed in limbo for a period over the false claims that Mary was a brandy soak.

Over more recent decades, official postulators (pleaders for canonisation) Father Paul Gardiner SJ and Sister Maria Casey SOSJ actively took up the case. The record of Mary's life was rigorously examined, and the miracles attributed to her – a woman healed of terminal leukaemia in the 1960s and another of terminal cancer in the 1990s, as a result of prayers to Mary – were assessed by a panel of Italian doctors.

Finally, Pope John Paul II beatified her in Sydney in 1994. It is a little sobering to reflect that while he himself was beatified just four years after his death (in the final year of my posting), for Mary, the process took almost a century.

Then, on 19 February 2010, at a special consistory meeting in the Papal Palace, Pope Benedict XVI proclaimed her sainthood and fixed 17 October as the date of her canonisation. There was a good deal of media coverage over this proclamation. It was a bitterly cold day in Rome, but Sister Maria Casey and I worked closely together to get through the aftermath of the announcement and to ensure widespread and accurate coverage back home in Australia.

Sister Maria Casey was sharp and strong enough to stand up to the various hurdles that seemed to appear from nowhere to frustrate the progress towards canonisation. Born in Ireland, at Kildysart in County Clare, Sister Maria migrated to Australia in 1958 and served in many parts of the country, for a period heading up the SOSJ chapter in Western Australia.

In the middle of 2008, Sister Maria was appointed postulator, and shortly afterwards moved to Rome to pursue the work in earnest, taking on the difficult Congregation of the Causes of Saints (which oversees canonisations). Just like Mary MacKillop years before, living in Rome was not easy for Sister Maria; on one occasion she had her handbag and purse snatched on the famous or infamous Bus 64 from Termini to the Vatican.

She lived in a humble annexe to the Convent of the Ursulines on Via Nomentana, not very far from my own apartment. This worked out well, as I was able to give her a lift downtown on many occasions, and keep her abreast of developments as Rome prepared to welcome the estimated eight thousand Australians who would be flooding in from halfway around the world for the canonisation.

At one stage I asked DFAT Secretary Dennis Richardson for clarification about my involvement in the canonisation, and he said yes, this would be a public and diplomatic event and I was definitely to assist in every reasonable way. Why were the scarce resources of DFAT involved? The answer is that any overseas function expected to draw eight thousand Australians or more means a consular effort is justified, to be able to minimise the grief of one kind or another that will inevitably occur.

This would be by far the biggest logistical event for the Australian Embassy during my three years in the Holy See.

THE CANONISATION OF A GREAT AUSSIE BATTLER

On all occasions of this kind, if things are going to flow smoothly you have to do the spadework months before. Sister Maria and I, along with the embassy team, worked very closely for some time to draw up a five-day program, anchored on the canonisation on Sunday 17 October. A donation of wine from the region around Penola where Mary did a lot of her work proved helpful for all the entertaining involved. Some of the planning was done in conjunction with the Canadian Embassy to the Holy See, which was preparing for the canonisation on the same day of Brother André Bessette, a simple carpenter and builder who dedicated his life and work to St Joseph, building a huge oratory of renown in Montreal in the early 1900s.

We learnt in late August that there would be a bipartisan Federal parliamentary delegation coming for the event, consisting of Foreign Minister Kevin Rudd, Shadow Foreign Minister Julie Bishop, Labor Senator Ursula Stephens and the Nationals' Senator Barnaby Joyce. There were rumours that Prime Minister Gillard might attend; after all, she had been at the canonisation dinner at the Sydney Town Hall on 5 August. This was not to be, though several State MPs did turn up and we fitted them in where possible. The Australian Embassy to Italy stepped in to help also.

The formal program began on Thursday 14 October with a welcome dinner at the Australian Ambassador to Italy's residence. We *did* have a kind of gatecrasher, in the form of the Bishop of Port Pirie, the friendly Greg O'Kelly SJ, who had heard the function was on and claimed that Mary MacKillop spent more time in his diocese than any other. I had invited archbishops, but no bishops, as there was not space for them all. I relented on the grounds that Bishop Greg is Australia's only Jesuit bishop, that he had half a point about the activities of Mary MacKillop, and that he had the hide to ask. Co-hosting this dinner was Ambassador David Ritchie, and it was a good eve-of-event occasion, helping to establish contact and also confidence in all that lay ahead.

Friday 15 August was a very big day for the visiting Sisters of Saint Joseph: an impromptu media conference, a prayer gathering, a lamington morning tea hosted by my embassy, then a tour of the Vatican Gardens while I headed off to a lunch for some Australian business leaders.

The highlight of the Friday was the opening of the Rituals of Life exhibition at the Ethnological section of the Vatican Museums, showcasing a rare collection of Aboriginal artefacts that Pope Pius XI had requested in 1925 from Catholic missions in Western Australia and the Northern Territory. The entrance to the Rituals of Life Exhibition was just near the big Vatican Museum cafeteria, so Australia was front and centre in a part of the museum visited by millions each month.

Phase one of the Rituals of Life event was a conference hosted by the museum's director, Father Nicola Mapelli, followed by the opening of the exhibition by Minister Kevin Rudd. Then it was out onto the edge of the Vatican Gardens for a reception with a buffet dinner for 300. The fourth and final phase was a special concert featuring Indigenous dancers and a didgeridoo player, and except for an impossible seating equation, all went

THE CANONISATION OF A GREAT AUSSIE BATTLER

well. Late into the evening the exhausted team, augmented by staff from the Australian Embassy to Italy, finally saw off the last of the guests.

(Two weeks after the canonisation, the Australian and Canadian embassies did a debrief session together with all staff involved. The Australian staff agreed never to undertake another four-part reception involving huge people movement in venues on four different floors, and without full access or control. In short, we got by, but learnt our lesson: keep it simple always.)

On the Saturday, the eve of the canonisation, another busy day unfolded. First up was a function hosted by Minister Kevin Rudd; the parliamentary delegation was now into the swing of things, putting aside any party-political point scoring and soaking up the buzz of the occasion. After this there was a matinée vigil concert of prayer and singing put together by the Australian Catholic University.

Before the evening session of this concert, the official opening of the new chancery of the Australian Embassy to the Holy See took place, with Archbishop Mamberti, the Holy See Foreign Minister, delivering a brief address that was perfect for the occasion. The commemorative plaque was unveiled and everything completed within the allotted sixty minutes, and Kevin Rudd expressed delight at the compact size and great location of the new chancery. Phew to this, as it had cost enough of taxpayers' money, and I had never been interested in anything grander. In terms of work and cost effectiveness, I believe it is a whole lot better than ninety per cent of the other chanceries in Rome.

After the main vigil concert I had to escort the Minister to a nearby seminary rooftop, to do a live cross to *Meet the Press* on Channel Ten with Paul Bongiorno. The Minister arrived fifteen minutes before the cross, due to my having walked the exact route two days before and so able to lead the way and avoid a traffic snarl. He went live to air on the Sunday morning right across Australia.

This incident highlights one golden rule for ambassadors around the world: make sure you have personally gone to each and every venue being used or on the schedule of any ministerial or other VIP visit. Security people said I was going the wrong way and later that I was heading to the wrong building; I had absolute confidence I had the best route and the right building, having done a full recce two days before. Had this not been the case, the Minister would have missed his live TV cross slot and, yes, I would have copped a deserved blast.

Finally the big day arrived. Judy and I (in formal dress) went across to the Ritchie residence to meet up with the delegation and then we all travelled by convoy, with security escort, to St Peter's. As the crowds flocked to the Square, overhead there were clear blue skies.

The visiting MPs and senators were gobsmacked by the setting, complete with huge portraits of the six saints being canonised, Mary MacKillop looking especially clear-sighted and serene. It soon became clear that the Australians supporting Mary MacKillop and the Canadians supporting Brother André were the most energetic groups, but the Spanish supporting Candide Maria de Jesus were not far behind.

THE CANONISATION OF A GREAT AUSSIE BATTLER

Then the proceedings commenced, with trumpets and organ and choir in full flight. The highlights of the long Mass were many: the moment Mary MacKillop was pronounced a saint, greeted by a huge roar from the crowd; ... the presentation of the relics of the six saints (in the case of Mary MacKillop, a lock of hair); ... and Sister Maria Casey, going forward with the other postulators, to be presented to the Pope.

Immediately after the Pope gave the final blessing to the crowd, he repaired to the corner of the basilica to receive key VIPs, including three of the Australian parliamentary delegation (the maximum allowed number). Senator Barnaby Joyce accepted the situation and yielded to Senator Ursula Stephens, Chair of the Parliamentary Christian Fellowship. Within minutes, the papal audience was over and our group moved back through St Peter's Square, with many Australian visitors greeting Kevin Rudd warmly.

There was then a wrap-up media conference, followed by a canonisation lunch hosted by the Sisters of St Joseph, and everyone relaxed with some good-natured banter.

Through all of this, it was helpful that Ambassador David Ritchie took care of the Minister for key parts of the program, including time-consuming meet-and-greets and transfers to and from the airport. Indeed, the other embassy helped greatly, especially the consular staff. Senior Administrative Officer Paul Given had secured a van to act as a mobile Australian consular centre, providing information to all and sundry at St Peter's Square, particularly Australian visitors. It was nicknamed 'Kanga Two' and was appreciated by all who used it.

Many months after the canonisation of Mother Mary MacKillop, there was a gathering to launch a superb DVD on the happenings in Rome. Here, from left to right, are Cardinal George Pell, Archbishop Philip Wilson, Tim Fischer, head of the Sisters of Saint Joseph Sister Anne Derwin and the ever-helpful Sister Maria Casey, pouring the water. These four represented the 'gang of four' in charge of canonisation arrangements.

On the Monday morning, Kanga Two travelled down to St Paul Outside the Walls ready to handle the thousands visiting for the Australian Thanksgiving Mass. Cardinal Pell was chief celebrant and gave a powerful opening greeting and later a brilliant homily. Many attendees said afterwards that this was one of the most moving Masses they had ever attended.

The last formal function of the canonisation was the final farewell dinner at the St Regis Hotel, with a celebratory atmosphere, and for key embassy staff some relief that the parliamentary delegation had departed Rome that afternoon happy with all arrangements.

THE CANONISATION OF A GREAT AUSSIE BATTLER

★ ★ ★

Months beforehand, DFAT Secretary Dennis Richardson had warned me I should not underestimate the media focus that Mary's canonisation would attract. He pointed out that the month of October sits neatly between the end of the football season and the period when cricket gets serious, and before the Melbourne Cup. If you're doing anything big in Australia, October is a great month for publicity and momentum.

It might seem surprising to compare Mary's canonisation with these major sporting events, but it turned out Dennis was right. I've still got a laminated copy of the front page of the Melbourne *Herald Sun* on the Monday, which was totally thrown over to coverage of Australia's first saint – it was amazing. And the joy of it was that clearly many non-churchgoing Australians thought that this lady had achieved a great deal, and that the recognition being conferred was worthwhile in the circumstances of all that she had had to overcome.

It is hard to argue with the assertion that Mary MacKillop was one extraordinary Australian who achieved much for the disadvantaged, especially in country areas, and reached out way beyond the traditional confines of the Roman Catholic Church. Formal commendation of her life and work is a salute to a genuine hero of our nation.

But perhaps more than that, Mary was a woman who got put down over and over again, but bounced back up every time. She overcame incredible family odds, and endured the great hardships of life in country Australia at that time, to introduce an education template that worked brilliantly, especially in country areas. And she picked herself up after not one but two great putdowns: her ex-communication from the Church she loved, and her demotion from leading the very order that she had created. She endured a hazardous journey to Rome at a time when it was overrun by Unification forces, and experienced constant knockbacks throughout the remainder of her life.

She was a determined and graceful hero, standing up against the male-dominated Church and society of her time, helping pave the way for women to play a wider role in Australian life. In short, you could say she was a great Aussie battler.

Cardinal Pell, at the thanksgiving Mass the day after her canonisation, made it very clear that the Church of that era owed Mary MacKillop many apologies. I have nothing but admiration for this incredible lady, to which so much injustice was done, but who rose above it all to achieve so much. It was a great privilege to be present at the final stage of this humble teacher's journey from ex-communicated nun, cast out onto the streets of Adelaide, to fully fledged saint.

CHAPTER TWELVE

Anti-Semitism in the Vatican?

Decades ago, with a friend from the Victorian State Parliament, Bill Baxter, I made my first visit to Europe and to the Eternal City of Rome. We had taken a long train trip right around the south of France and along the Mediterranean coast. Eventually we arrived at Termini Station in Rome and, like millions before us, caught the bus to St Peter's Basilica and *that* square. Whether you are an atheist or a person of faith, it has to be said that nothing prepares you for the beauty and grandeur of the Bernini Colonnade and the huge façade of St Peter's itself. Yes, I stood in awe back in early 1975, and watched the movements and activities of the oldest Church in the world under the then leadership of Pope Paul VI.

I returned early in the mornings whilst we stayed at Rome to further soak up this breathtaking atmosphere, but also to dwell on the contradictions within the Vatican in rapidly changing times. This was partly prompted by the news at that time that Herbert Kappler, the SS Commander in Rome during the Nazi occupation, had been diagnosed with cancer. Applications were being made for his release from the Italian prison at Gaita where he had then been an inmate for nearly thirty years. As the mastermind of a massacre of over 335 civilians at the Ardeatine Caves outside Rome in March 1944, his early release was not favoured. Kappler had unsuccessfully sought refuge in the Vatican when the Allied forces arrived, and this started me thinking about the Vatican and its role during the huge event that shaped the years just before I was born.

Thirty-five years later, during my posting, I followed this up with more detailed research. The impact of World War II continues to this day, and the Pope of that time, Pius XII, is on the radar screen of the baby-boomer generation – probably the earliest pope they remember.

On 25 July 1943 Fascist leader Benito Mussolini was ousted from office and negotiations commenced with the Allies, who had already landed and occupied parts of southern Italy. Upon learning of this, Hitler feared a total switch of Italy from the Axis side to the Allied side and so ordered the Nazi occupation of Italy. Despite sporadic resistance, Rome was soon under the thumb of the Nazis, led by Supreme Southern Commander Albert Kesselring, and SS Commander Kappler. (Ironically, much is known of the activities of the Nazis in Rome due to Nazi lieutenant Nikolaus Kunkel, who finally gave a comprehensive interview to *L'Osservatore Romano* decades later. This was published in early 2001.)

ANTI-SEMITISM IN THE VATICAN?

At stake were the lives of around 8000 Roman Jews and also a handful of escaping prisoners of war. At stake also was the sovereignty of Vatican City and the Holy See, along with the Papal Palace and estate of Castel Gandolfo, about one hour south of Rome. In fact Castel Gandolfo commanded a strategic location with sweeping views across all the southern coastal approaches to Rome, including the approach ultimately used by the US army.

For many cruel months during the Nazi occupation, Rome and its population suffered horribly as the SS dished out rough justice. Food supplies ran down and a form of civil war existed amongst the Italians. The underground movement supporting the Allies and the Vatican became more and more isolated, with restrictions by the Nazis on movement around Rome.

By September 1943 plans had been adopted for the rounding up of the 8000 Jews living in Rome and their dispatch to Auschwitz-Birkenau, that terrible Nazi-created farm of death. In a last-minute twist, an alternative plan emerged to use Jewish forced labour to help build up the defence structures required around Rome, especially to the south. We now know that telegrams were sent from Rome to Berlin marked 'VERY, VERY URGENT' canvassing this alternative. However, the final definitive order was sent to Kappler on 11 October, containing the key words 'proceed with the evacuation of the Jews without further delay'.

It was on Saturday 16 October that the axe fell. The roundup of Jews was carried out with ruthless SS zeal. Just one week later a special train (X70469) departed Termini with 1002 Roman Jews on board. On arrival at Auschwitz, suddenly the

Jews would be ordered out of their cramped wagons, subjected to the Nazis' cursory examination and flick of the hand, and dispatched, either to labour gangs or to the gas chambers. For most, it was death: only fifteen survived the war.

The question remains today: could this particular roundup have been completely prevented by those in Rome?

In answer to this, all eyes turn to Pope Pius XII, who had served as a papal diplomat in Munich and Berlin before his election as pope in 1939. So he not only spoke German fluently but also knew the power structures of Germany intimately, and had observed first-hand the emergence of Adolf Hitler and the Third Reich.

To arrive at a balanced judgment, it is essential to step back through the decades of colossal spin – I might add brilliant spin – that has more to do with enhancing the cause of the American Jewish lobby than with historical accuracy.

Looking at the saga over six decades later, it is best to cut through to some key facts that all reasonable-minded people accept did happen in the darkest days of World War II. Fact one is the existence of a big split within the Jewish community of Italy before and during World War II. Many Jews were very pro-Fascist and anti-Communist, while others were anti-Fascist and pro-Communist. This meant there was no real unity, and without unity, communications and strategies were less than perfect in preparing for the Nazi occupation and all that it could be expected to bring.

Overlying this was an instruction from Mussolini that Jews who had fought for Italy in World War I, when Italy was on

ANTI-SEMITISM IN THE VATICAN?

the side of the Allies (but in the main with disastrous generals), would be exempted from any labour restrictions or other anti-Jewish measures. This helped create a false sense of security. Many Jews said at the time that they knew the Nazis were coming but in Rome things would be different, and the remnant Italian authorities would help ensure that the Jews were not subject to any kind of roundup. The Nazis were also aided by the basic lie that was maintained until the bitter end: that all the Jews they rounded up were going off to work in labour camps and had nothing to fear.

Fact two was the order of Pius XII to open up the convents and monasteries, as well as Vatican City itself, to those fleeing the Nazis, particularly Jews. It could be said that ultimately the Nazis' Jewish extermination policy was a failure in Rome, since about 7000 of the 8000 Jews escaped the roundup. Hundreds went into Vatican buildings and into monasteries and convents outside the Vatican walls, and many hid with brave gentile Italian families, or in the countryside. Others took the route of disguising themselves as non-Jewish, indeed as practising Christians.

Fact three is the contribution of nuns and priests, generally acknowledged, even at Yad Vashem, the giant Holocaust museum in Jerusalem – their work in providing shelter in convents and monasteries is rightly praised. Counterbalancing the panel saluting nuns and priests is an ugly panel slamming Pope Pius XII. After representations by the Vatican, the wording accompanying the panel was modified in 2012.

It was a deadly game of cat-and-mouse for each family, and for each convent or monastery giving shelter. Those caught by the Nazis harbouring Jews were arrested and given the death penalty, both in Rome and all over occupied Europe. Jews were to be exterminated by order of Hitler and the Nazi hierarchy.

For the large Ursuline convent on Via Nomentana, there was an added risk, since the Nazis had occupied their front house, between the main convent building and the front entrance. The Nazis were staying in the compound and observing a great deal, yet just over 100 Jews were bravely sheltered in this convent.

Meticulous diaries kept by senior nuns at the time and held in the archives of the convent are spellbinding to read – detailing how the volume of food brought into the compound had to be played down, how there were frequent blackouts, and how water on occasions was cut off; how Allied bombing of the railway lines nearby came very close to damaging the convent.

Related to this is fact four, namely that Pope Pius XII gave orders to help raise a gold ransom demanded by SS Commander Kappler in exchange for protecting the Jews of Rome. This ransom was collected and paid, but sadly it proved futile, as no protection was forthcoming. Indeed, after the war the gold was found in a set of boxes, unpacked and unused.

More importantly, as mentioned, Pius XII ordered that where possible shelter be provided in Holy See territory to Jews on the run. The October 1943 Vatican directive was (and I quote from the recent words of Cardinal Bertone): 'to house Jews persecuted by the Nazis in all religious institutes, to open the institutes and also the catacombs'. This one man, Pope Pius XII, made a difference. If absolute proof is sought then this incredible quote provides it.

ANTI-SEMITISM IN THE VATICAN?

The Pope had serious concerns about the safety of the Curia and the independence of Vatican City during the Nazi occupation. He authorised that a conclave proceed in Spain should he be killed. (Fortunately he lived for many years after World War II, dying in 1958.)

★ ★ ★

Finally the Allies came to the rescue, fighting their way northwards and eventually winning the Battle of Monte Cassino. Fortunately the Nazis decided not to make a stand in Rome. After losing Monte Cassino, two hours to the south of Rome, they quit the Eternal City and raced north before they could be cut off.

As the Allied soldiers flooded into Rome, singing broke out in the streets and the Pope appeared in St Peter's Square. The relief was palpable, especially for the hidden Jewish population. They stepped out gingerly from convents and monasteries, and started the process of picking up the pieces of their lives.

Yet within months an ugly blame game broke out in Jewish circles. The Jewish community wanted to hold others accountable in addition to the Nazis, and the patrician Pope of the time was an easy target. So a distorted view of history was in the making from the very days following the liberation of Rome.

After the examination of a great deal of historical material, my conclusion is that the Holy See and its head of government, Pope Pius XII, took action that led to the rescue of thousands of Jewish people from the Nazis. Could it have done more?

That will always be debated. The Pope failed to prevent one trainload of 1002 Jews from departing Rome for Auschwitz; he failed to prevent or stop the Holocaust conducted by the Nazis across Europe; but he did provide sanctuary for many.

There is some evidence that after the war the Vatican helped facilitate a Nazi escape pipeline involving Croatia, allowing Nazi war criminals to make it to Latin America. There is also evidence that news of the Holocaust was relayed to the then Papal Nuncio in Turkey – none other than Pius XII's successor, Pope John XXIII. Again, let the facts and truth come out as soon as possible.

Now, I accept that the ultimate high court of world Jewry ensconced in New York and the East Coast of the USA has a different view. They remind us that Pope Pius XII never actually uttered the word 'Holocaust'. They have taken a neat tactical course that says until all the World War II archives of the Vatican are released, they will cut Pius XII no slack. Further, the moment any suggestion is made to consider Pius XII for beatification and sainthood, they hit out at close to full power and use all media avenues to stamp it out.

In my 1000 days in Rome, I kept encountering this at various levels. At one stage the capable Israeli Ambassador stated that there must be a recognition of the life-saving work of Pope Pius XII during the Nazi occupation; within twenty-four hours he had to put out a statement of clarification, which one monsignor called 'an excruciating backdown'.

The media skills of the American Israel Public Affairs Committee and others pushing the cause of Israel far outweigh

ANTI-SEMITISM IN THE VATICAN?

the best the Vatican has to offer. Take brilliant Israeli spokesman Mark Regev, partly educated in Melbourne. He can spin with great effectiveness on any issue. In 2010 he made a plausible case for the Israeli military's killing of Turkish civilians on the high seas: no mean achievement.

I suspect, but have no proof, that these tactics are about representing a cause and maintaining influence and power rather than promoting a balanced and accurate portrayal of this dark chapter of World War II. The American Jewish lobby is run by hardliners who get their daily feed from Jerusalem and Tel Aviv, and will cut no slack in terms of Israel's policies in the West Bank, not allowing a debate as to whether that is actually in Israel's worst interests long-term. (In my own view, Israel, with its aggressive settlement expansion through the West Bank to the River Jordan, has become a ticking time bomb of its own making. Amid all this, Christian minorities will continue to flee the birthplace of their religion.)

I am happy to state that I am alive today due to the actions in Vietnam years ago of a Jewish national service soldier, Richard Edelman. At another level, the democracy of Australia is alive and well due to the brilliant leadership of Jewish World War I General Sir John Monash. I state this to head off the inevitable attacks on any review and praise of the work of Pope Pius XII.

Yet again, in the second decade of the twenty-first century let me say it is time to learn and relearn the facts about Pope Pius XII and the role of the Catholic Church during World War II, to strip away the tactical slurs and brilliant media spin, emanating particularly from New York. The raft of accusations that have been made against Pope Pius XII has waxed and waned over the years, but in the immediate aftermath of Nazi occupation, outside the Jewish community there was general praise for the work of the Vatican in helping to rescue Jews. 'Pope Pius XII has fully espoused the Jewish cause to the point of offending the sensibilities of his flock ... We never imagined that our Pastor, the Vicar of Christ, the head of our Church, could be one day regarded as the most influential defender of the interests of the Jewish people.' These were the words of Fascist leader Roberto Farinacci on 17 January 1945.

Even more dramatic was the salute of Dr Cecil Roth, a Jewish leader from London, speaking to a key Zionist forum in the USA years later: 'Only in Rome has the colony of Jews continued its existence since before the beginning of the Christian era, because of all the dynasties of Europe the papacy not only refused to persecute the Jews of Rome, but through the ages Popes were protectors of the Jews.

'Some Jews have the feeling that the papacy has a policy of persecuting Jews. But you must remember that English history is definitely anti-Catholic and many views of Catholicism may have been coloured by English history. We Jews, who have suffered so much from prejudice, should rid our minds of prejudice and learn the facts. The truth is that the Popes and the Catholic Church from the earliest days of the Church were never responsible for the physical persecution of the Jews.'

However, the last say might best rest with the tour guide who showed me over the magnificent Great Synagogue of Rome. At the end of the tour I asked how the synagogue building

ANTI-SEMITISM IN THE VATICAN?

survived the Nazi occupation. Her reply was clear. She said it was due to one person, Pope Pius XII. She explained that during the occupation he had this and several buildings added to a special list of protected historic buildings. It was in part a use of the Lateran Treaty provisions put in place in 1929 under Mussolini – and it worked.

As stated, 16 October was the day the Nazi SS started the Rome roundup in earnest. If on the anniversary of that day the Jewish media (speaking on behalf of the Israeli Government) expressed acknowledgment and thanks for the role of Pope Pius XII, the Vatican and many parts of the Roman Catholic Church in helping to save thousands of Jews, then this would be a first step towards a more balanced and accurate portrayal. In memory of one decisive Pope, perhaps, just perhaps, one day this will happen.

★ ★ ★

Although there is still a reluctance to proceed with beatifying Pope Pius XII, I encountered no overt anti-Semitism within the Vatican over my three years there. Of course, there is the odd 'bad apple', such as Bishop Richard Williamson, a Holocaust denier who caused the Pope great grief soon after my arrival in Rome.

What happened was that the Pope lifted an ex-communication order against Bishop Williamson on 21 January 2009, the same day as Williamson renewed his denial of the Holocaust in a media interview. By 4 February the media attacks on the

Pope and the Vatican resulted in a formal statement from the Vatican saying that Williamson must recant and apologise. The Pope emphasised that he had not been aware of Williamson's renewed Holocaust denial when he had lifted the order, and of course he assured all and sundry that Holocaust denial is unacceptable.

But the damage had been done. At one stage during a busy week, the Chancellor of Germany, Angela Merkel, rang the Pope to share her deep concerns about the saga. In Germany Holocaust denial is a serious crime, and later Williamson was found guilty of this crime, as the interview had been given on German soil.

Another incident that caused a stir among the Jewish community was a sermon by Father Raniero Cantalamessa, the Preacher to the Papal Household (and the only person who preaches to the Pope). Once a year in public, during the early evening Good Friday solemn Mass, in the presence of the Pope and thousands of pilgrims, Cantalamessa bursts forth.

In 2010, his Good Friday sermon quoted a letter he had received from a Jewish friend, likening the media's treatment of child-abuse cover-ups in the Church to 'the more shameful aspects of anti-Semitism'. The Vatican rushed to dissociate itself from Father Cantalamessa's remarks, but the timing was certainly unfortunate. Easter is traditionally a sensitive time between Christians and Jews, for obvious reasons (though my personal feeling is that both groups in and around Jerusalem two thousand years ago let the Romans off too gently for their Pontius Pilate role).

ANTI-SEMITISM IN THE VATICAN?

★ ★ ★

Seven decades on from the Holocaust, sadly anti-Semitism is alive and well in many parts of Europe, and even Australia. Walk through certain parts of Sydney and Melbourne today and you may well encounter anti-Jewish graffiti. The 2008 global financial crisis only seemed to give legs to these messages of hate: 'It's the fault of the Jews *again*.'

With the advent of social media has come a new method of delivering such bile. And it was actually an Australian expert who came to Rome to brief an Italian parliamentary committee on this subject in 2010. Dr Andre Oboler's work is all about tracking anti-Semitism in the social media. I had a long working session with him, and until then I had not realised the extent to which anti-Jewish feeling is out there on the Internet.

I passed on his key messages and warnings to a few in the Curia who understand fully the power of the Internet. Pope Benedict himself has opened a Twitter account, which is all about getting the right messages out to counter the massive negativity on social media, including anti-Semitism. At the start of the second year of my posting, the Pope made an official visit to the Great Synagogue of Rome, to demonstrate that the Catholic Church was serious about improving relations with the oldest Abrahamic religion.

So now this important work to eliminate both subtle and direct anti-Semitism falls to Pope Francis, who needs no great encouragement, having witnessed the deadly attack on the Israeli Embassy in Buenos Aires, a few years back.

As the Vatican struggles to completely erase the memories of its supposed failures of half a century ago, let us hope that its embracing of new technology is just the start of a modernisation process that will see the scars of anti-Semitism dealt with comprehensively.

In turn, this will further cement the work of former chief rabbi of Rome, Israel Zolli, who did much to save Jews, but because he converted to Christianity after World War II was airbrushed from the history books. Clearly the World War II Bishop of Rome, Pope Pius XII, and the then Chief Rabbi of Rome, Israel Zolli, made a difference and saved many lives during the Nazi occupation of Rome. Those who refuse to recognise this do so – in the main – for spurious tactical reasons.

CHAPTER THIRTEEN

Towards Religious Freedom

The world is a very troubled place in the second decade of the twenty-first century. With the collapse of the Soviet Union in the early 1990s, it had been hoped that lasting peace might be the dividend. But the ensuing years of great turmoil in the Balkans were not good for progress and prosperity in Europe, or for the world. Then the world witnessed 9/11, two Gulf wars and, more recently, the Arab Spring, and it became clear that the focus of the world's tensions had merely shifted to the cauldron around the Mediterranean. And in all of these wars, religious conflict has been a common factor.

These things may have occurred a long way away from Australia, but they are certainly not irrelevant to our interests. As a signatory to the Human Rights Charter of the United Nations, Australia (like the Vatican) is committed to a respectful acknowledgment of the sovereignty of every country, but also to upholding the rights and freedoms of all peoples on earth. There are many countries that should know better but still don't allow full-scale religious freedom, and still employ their secret police to monitor Church activity. And in the 'enlightened' twenty-first century, the world has simply got to do better on this score.

Moreover, some of the greatest religious persecution in the world is occurring in Asia, right on our doorstep. Because of our proximity, because we speak of 'the Asian century', Australia is committed to building stronger links with our dynamic neighbourhood, and to supporting the upswing of their economies. Yet there are serious thorns in the side of regional stability and progress.

The Catholic Church in Burma has had a very hard time under the current repressive military regime, but it is Vietnam and China that remain on everybody's radar screen. They are both countries with constitutions that are very clear-cut on religious freedom, but at the grassroots level the situation is quite different. This issue was an especial priority for Kevin Rudd, during his time as both PM and Foreign Minister.

Vietnam is very much a work in progress, with key Catholic priests being threatened and put under pressure. Meanwhile, there is a very difficult relationship between Rome and China at the moment, particularly on the issue of bishops. The objective has been for the Vatican and Beijing to reach a situation where both were happy with the number of bishops and the people appointed as bishops of the Roman Catholic Church in China.

TOWARDS RELIGIOUS FREEDOM

And this, for a period of time during my posting, was exactly the case. A few clergy had been acknowledged by Beijing and Rome as being acceptable to be ordained as new bishops.

Late in my posting, however, the two authorities drifted apart again. I suspect this was due to a more aggressive attitude at the provincial level rather than any decision in Beijing. As a consequence, certain bishops were arrested and put in confinement. The Vatican has strongly objected to this hard-line attitude in the twenty-first century, but at this stage things seem to be going backwards.

The situation has not been helped by the fact that formally the Vatican still recognises Taiwan, and does not have diplomatic relations with China – and is unlikely to have them any time soon, if the current disputes continue. The Vatican has publicly declared that when both sides reach agreement on everything else, and are prepared to enter into diplomatic relations, it will close its embassy in Taiwan and switch it to mainland China. So that card has already been put on the table – some would say a bit too early in the negotiations.

Then, of course, there is our powerful neighbour Indonesia. Something that has always been a focus of my work, as an MP, minister, deputy prime minister and then ambassador, is the fact that Indonesia has the largest Muslim population in the world. Australia has real skin in the game of ensuring that it remains the progressive, secular nation-state that it is: a tremendous ally and dynamic trading partner. The tenth anniversary in 2012 of the Bali bombings was a reminder that, in a roundabout sort of way, this horrific attack by Muslim extremists actually strengthened relations between Australia and Indonesia, not the opposite.

The Vatican is deeply concerned by such appalling acts of terrorism, yet it knows that it will never be able to control radical Islam. It will try to withstand the impact of *radical* Islam by dealing with *moderate* Islam – by having much more dialogue with those elements of Islam that oppose the fundamentalists.

Cardinal Jean-Louis Tauran, the President of the Pontifical Council for Interreligious Dialogue (PCID), is at the forefront of that action. Despite the onset of Parkinson's disease, he maintains a heavy schedule. His various roles within the Vatican and conclave included announcing the election of Pope Francis to the people in St Peter's Square and to the world. Early in my posting he made it a priority to visit Indonesia, and so I went to see him before and after that visit. Afterwards the Cardinal reported that he had expressed the Vatican's continuing respect for the secular Indonesian Government, for the freedom of Christians to practise as a minority religion, and for the main leaders of the Muslim faith in Indonesia.

Pope Paul VI created what is now the PCID in 1964, but it was Pope John Paul II who really pushed interfaith dialogue along. He was the first pontiff to step inside a mosque, during a visit to Syria in 2001. Pope Benedict seemed to take a more cautious approach, but the two big issues for him were preserving Europe's Christian roots and preserving the rapidly dwindling Christian communities in the Middle East. Unfortunately his remarks about Islam in his 2006 Regensburg speech were a big step backwards in this regard, provoking outrage instead of strengthening ties with Islam.

Pope Francis has moved quickly to reach out beyond the Roman Catholic Church, in his first week issuing a special message to the Chief Rabbi of Rome supporting enhanced links between the great Abrahamic religions: Christianity, Judaism and Islam.

I think it is a very good thing that in recent years the Vatican has issued messages of goodwill on the holy days of other faiths, including a special message at the end of Ramadan. And the Church is not unmindful of the need to speed up key promotions in parts of the world where a show of strength is needed. During my posting Archbishop Malcolm Ranjith was promoted fairly promptly to become head of the minority Catholic Church in Sri Lanka, a nation still recovering from a 26-year civil war between the predominantly Buddhist Sinhalese and the predominantly Hindu Tamils. If more proof is needed of the Church's political relevance, then it should be noted that Archbishop Ranjith helped Australian High Commissioner Kathy Klugman send out anti people-smuggling messages to the villages of Sri Lanka, resulting in a two-year period in 2010–11 when there were no Sri Lankan boat people arriving in Australia.

On a flight home to Australia in 2010, I was able to stop off in Sri Lanka to meet Cardinal Ranjith and High Commissioner Kathy Klugman and add weight to that campaign. Alas the good work of the Sri Lankan navy and all others in bringing about the zero boat people requires continuing rigour; more recently the flow has resumed but greater liaison will help stem this tide.

Beautiful Sri Lanka is bouncing back from the civil war with many tourists returning and enjoying the large formal botanical gardens and grand colonial-style hotels, not to mention the huge rail network and luxury trains like the Viceroy Express. Australia maintains a two-pronged approach, restricting the supply side and reducing demand, encouraging clear-cut messages on the danger of people smuggling but also helping to boost the Sri Lanka economy and human rights, so demand to depart Sri Lanka reduces.

In fact, religious freedom and interfaith dialogue were core issues for me during my posting and involved many different activities. The objective behind all of them was clear-cut: to make representations in support of genuine religious freedom and a realistic, respectful dialogue between all the great faiths of the world.

A large part of my work in this area was focused on Christian and Muslim interreligious dialogue, which led to a series of meetings in places like Semarang in Indonesia, in Manila and Madrid, and on the margins of the World Parliament of Religions in Melbourne. Participants at these meetings adopted very well-worded communiqués to encourage further exchange and understanding, and gained a lot more respect for faiths of which they previously had only peripheral knowledge.

But there were a couple of instances during my posting where I was able to go further and make a real contribution to the safety of those suffering religious persecution in different corners of the world.

Ambassadors have to be ready to respond to crisis situations, which often arise both suddenly and unexpectedly. And it was the daily time I spent diving into the DFAT clipping service and the sensitive and classified cables that led to the first of these instances: my work with regard to religious freedom in Fiji.

At the time (2009) the regime in Fiji had just arrested nine Methodist Church leaders and one Catholic Church leader. Their alleged crime was daring to organise the annual gathering of the Methodist Church of Fiji. Relations between Prime Minister Frank Bainimarama's administration and the Methodist Church had got to the level where the Church was banned from exercising the basic right of any religion to meet. (The Catholic leader was arrested because she had agreed to host the meeting.)

I could not think of a less radical body or a more absurd response, and quickly informed DFAT. Some of the DFAT silos had not quite realised we had a Rome-resident Ambassador who could plug into this issue, but once I raised the matter with them, they instructed me to go in to bat for this group, which I termed in the media 'The Nine Plus One'.

Australia became very active with regard to the situation, because we had people on the ground in Fiji. DFAT wanted representations made at various levels and wanted the Vatican to be fully aware of what was happening. The Papal Nuncio for Fiji is based in Wellington, New Zealand; I went out of my way to meet him when he was visiting Rome, and keep myself in the loop. It was also a matter I was instructed to raise publicly at the World Parliament of Religions in Melbourne, and that got a helpful run in the media. It really was necessary for international public pressure to build through knowledge of this crazy circumstance being widely shared. So it was a minor achievement to have gained publicity for this particular case, though it was always going to be in the hands of others as to where it ended up.

It ultimately took months before some sense prevailed. More Church leaders were charged, at one stage as many as twenty-five, then later many of the charges were dropped and the ban on the annual gathering of the Methodist Church was lifted (though it was later reimposed). It has been an issue that has run hot and cold ever since. The whole saga was a sharp reminder not to take religious freedom as a given, even in a so-called Commonwealth country with years of democracy behind it, give or take the odd coup.

★ ★ ★

The second incident I was involved in came about in an equally unexpected way and arose from Christians being killed and injured in a cathedral. I received a surprise request from the Pope seeking in effect religious freedom for some of the wounded, a request that I later came to refer to privately as 'Project Baghdad', or the Visa Via Vatican (VVV) pipeline.

In January 2010 I was at a function in the Vatican when I bumped into the Sustituto, Archbishop Fernando Filoni. The

Sustituto was in many ways the equivalent of the Deputy Prime Minister, so I had a certain sympathy for him, as I recalled my own busy days in that capacity during the Howard Government. He asked me to come into the Vatican and see him around sunset the following evening.

I thought to myself, 'What on earth could the Sustituto want to raise with me?' Had I offended him in some way over the busy Christmas period?

I turned up the following evening with a degree of trepidation. After brief pleasantries, the Sustituto handed me a formal papal letter of request, asking that Australia approve for migration a handful of Christian Iraqi bomb victims who had been evacuated to the Pope's hospital in Rome in the aftermath of a dreadful attack that killed over sixty innocent civilians in a Christian church in Baghdad. Let me just say the number seeking entry to Australia was less than the number of apostles, and the Sustituto added that just three other countries were being asked to assist these poor victims, in line with the requests of the victims themselves and based on where they had family relatives.

I replied that of course I would immediately pass on the request to the Australian Government. I also advised that we had certain migration and humanitarian refugee programs, but this would be a matter for the Government to decide on. I would give him its response as soon as possible.

As I reflected on this over the following weekend, I smiled at the Vatican's ways and how it had let it be known there were other countries processing requests from the same group of victims. (Indeed, I later discovered through some shrewd networking and from a non-Canadian source that Canada had worked very quickly and within a fortnight the handful of victims seeking to join their extended families there had been approved and quickly evacuated. Ambassador Anne Leahy had moved swiftly and so had the Canadian Government.)

So there was a competitive edge pertaining, which would no doubt help the Vatican but not me manage an outright no from Canberra if this eventuated. At the same time, I knew the applications had to fit within existing Australian categories, including those relating to proper ministerial discretion, if there were to be a chance of a yes from Canberra. Further, there was the problem of the huge volume of applications already requiring processing in Canberra at any given time.

Australia is often painted as hard-line and lacking in human decency when it comes to the question of refugees. For some applicants the process of determining refugee status and security clearance is extremely slow, and it can take years before they learn of their fate. Thousands are accepted, while thousands more arrive by commercial flights (with passports and valid visas) but then overstay their visa terms and rarely draw any criticism.

I am not in a position to make any comment on the vexed set of complexities relating to boat people currently, but I do highlight the fact that Australia over the Howard years, and since then under Rudd and Gillard, has officially accepted thousands of migrants but also thousands of refugees. All of this is on the public record.

Now, with Project Baghdad, a handful more were under consideration. I quickly lodged the necessary paperwork and waited about a month before phoning Kevin Rudd's Chief of Staff, Philip Green. I pointed out that for anything to happen on this, Kevin Rudd would need to raise it with Immigration Minister Chris Bowen direct. Rudd's office would also need to liaise with the Immigration Minister's office for any chance of fast consideration and a favourable outcome.

My phone call to Phil Green was deliberately an hour ahead of Parliamentary Question Time when I and the world knew the two ministers would be together on the front bench. And indeed, Foreign Minister Rudd raised the issue directly with Immigration Minister Chris Bowen. They were sitting together at the time, and, as Kevin Rudd told me in a conversation weeks later, he simply asked whether, given the particularity of this unusual request from the Holy See involving bomb victims, they could get this file considered as soon as possible.

So I give credit where it is due: to two ministers and their key staff and to Departmental Secretaries Dennis Richardson and Andrew Metcalfe. As a result of their efforts, I had advice from Canberra in reasonable time. On this occasion it was in the affirmative, authorising the entry to Australia of a handful of Iraqis who had had their lives shattered whilst attending a church service.

My memory bank as an ex cabinet minister and Nationals Party leader of how best to prosecute requests when Federal Parliament is sitting had not failed me.

I should add that Canberra was not always favourably disposed to special requests, and neither should it be. There must be due process, and on this occasion it had been efficient process, also in compliance with the provisions of the relevant Australian law. I quickly informed the Sustituto and every other person who was in the know, gaining some traction for Australia, but behind Canada, which had got there first.

It is food for thought that the Vatican remains deeply concerned over the depopulation of Christians in the Middle East. In the case of Project Baghdad, the Vatican only proceeded with looking after some very traumatised Christian bomb victims after weighing up all factors involved in the case, and wishing to see that life was made as comfortable as possible for each victim after the injuries they sustained. The Vatican had the wellbeing of the individuals in mind, but this does not take anything away from its general strong desire to encourage Christians to keep living in the homeland of their faith in the Middle East.

Around the tenth anniversary of the Iraq War, it is also food for thought that there were forty-one Christians, including two priests killed and over sixty injured in the hail of machine-gun fire and bombings, it was later asserted, by Al-Qaida elements in a cathedral in downtown Baghdad on a Sunday night. There was no known Al-Qaida presence in Iraq before 2003. It is one of the negative outcomes of a war that Dick Cheney, George Bush junior and Tony Blair in particular were so keen to prosecute, on what they now accept as being a false premise, relating to weapons of mass destruction.

TOWARDS RELIGIOUS FREEDOM

So why make parts of Project Baghdad public, several years after it happened? Firstly, I think it is out and about anyhow if you know in which annual report to look, and I think the public has a right to know, believing that in all matters large and small, as much as is wise and practical, there should be transparency within the big beast of government. Secondly, it was an example of ministers being ministers in the best tradition of the Westminster system, rather than risk-averse and departmentally dominated. Sadly, on both sides of politics, there are too many 'grey' ministers who have never had a job outside of politics. I support West Australian Labor MP and Minister Gary Gray's assertion that our parliaments need the widest possible diversity among the ranks of new MPs; chances are those who have done things beyond politics will bring skills that allow them to manage, rather than be managed by, their departments.

Life and death remain cheap in places like Egypt, Iraq and Syria as battles continue, including within Islam itself, such as with Sunni versus Shia; more bombings of markets and public places in Baghdad have occurred in 2013. The call of George W. Bush in mounting the Iraq War leaves a bitter legacy; the call of the Vatican against that war was consistent and strong throughout, led by Pope John Paul II. The work of the Vatican to ease the burden was small but very direct and helpful to some unlucky but lucky Christians who now live where religious freedom exists both in theory and in practice.

CHAPTER FOURTEEN

The Pope's Railway

Just occasionally a serendipitous moment comes along when an ambassador's role of promoting Team Australia coincides with his own personal interests. And there were a couple of times during my 1000 days in Rome when the parameters of my job happily overlapped with my much-publicised love of trains.

Around mid-2010, I approached Caritas Internationalis – a federation of Catholic organisations doing relief and development work in poverty-stricken countries worldwide – and asked whether it had a special anniversary coming up. Then the second question: Would it be interested in naming rights and participation in a special train charter from the Pope's platform in Vatican City to Orvieto in Umbria and back?

Planning ahead, I could see a win-win opportunity to raise money for the important work of Caritas Internationalis,

THE POPE'S RAILWAY

boost the profile of the Pope's rather disused but operational railway and, if it went well, indirectly enhance the standing of the small Australian Embassy to the Holy See. (On the other hand, if it was a disaster then I would accept responsibility and take a lower profile for a period or even accept being recalled.)

Previously I had made soundings with Cardinal Giovanni Lajolo (President of the Pontifical Commission for Vatican City State), who is in a sense the stationmaster-in-chief of the Vatican. I had also spoken to other Vatican staff, including the Customs Director, whose office controls the mechanism that opens the huge steel gate allowing trains in and out of the Vatican. There was general support for activating the railway for this first time in years.

The Vatican's railway was constructed after the signing of the Lateran Treaty in 1929 between Pope Pius XI and 'Il Duce', Benito Mussolini. The treaty sorted out the respective sovereignties of Italy and the Roman Catholic Church, creating the Vatican City State, and also allowing for a private railway into the Vatican. The railway has been used mainly for goods transport, and only by the Pope on special occasions.

Caritas advised that its Sixtieth Anniversary Conference was coming up in May 2011 and the opportunity to ride on a 'Caritas Express' would be welcomed on 21 May, the Saturday before the conference. Key heritage arms of Trenitalia, the main Italian train operator, were also sounded out and expressed a willingness to take the project further, in a way that took account of its significance.

Given the broad level of encouragement from these key stakeholders, plus critical members of the diplomatic corps, I decided to commit real time and energy to the project and wrote a discussion paper that set out its objectives, draft budget and broad parameters.

At the same time I alerted FEDECRAIL (the European Federation of European and Tourist Railways) and key UK heritage train personnel of the prospect of the Caritas Express and the desirability of reserving the date for a trip to Rome, pending formal confirmation, ticketing details and the like.

I then invited Caritas and Trenitalia to each nominate a key person so that we could start to meet regularly and work through details. Enter Monsignor Robert Vitillo from

Man-about-town but also Italian Railway Heritage Operations supremo Luigi Cantamessa, meeting with me at the entry gate to the Vatican Station, to discuss arrangements for the Caritas Express.

Caritas and Luigi Cantamessa from Trenitalia, who had the advantage of actually being a qualified steam-train driver as well as having responsibility for Italian railway heritage. The three of us were the troika that drove the project forward, at all times in close liaison with the Vatican and especially with Cardinal Lajolo.

We began to meet regularly, especially when Luigi was in Rome from up north where he was based, and when Monsignor Robert came to Rome from his base in Geneva. Together we inspected the Vatican station and also looked up the list of available Italian Railways rolling stock of a heritage character. (In the end Luigi chose an impressive series of heritage carriages, including one originally built for Italy's royal family.) In addition we travelled up to Orvieto to meet local officials, inspect the funicular from Orvieto railway station up to the main part of the hilltop town, and select enough large restaurants to handle lunch for the crowd off the train on the appointed Saturday.

Later the troika visited Trenitalia HQ near Termini Station in Rome to sort out more of the details in relation to the train. It was resolved to position the passenger carriages at the Pope's platform four days beforehand but provide for the steam locomotive to be positioned on the Saturday morning, due to operational limitations. After all, it takes a few hours to build a fire and create the steam to propel the locomotive, and we needed to ensure there would be enough coal and water in the tender to complete the outbound task, and this could only be done a few hours before departure time.

As the deadline drew closer the final arrangements fell into place, including an online booking system that actually worked. I told as many people as possible why they should consider fronting on Saturday 21 May for some steam train fun and for a good cause. I made my own donation and bought my 100-euro ticket for the Ambassador Class. The other option was a 60-euro ticket for the International Class, although the actual difference between the two types of carriage was very little.

★ ★ ★

The big day dawned nice and sunny across central Italy and up and down the Rome–Orvieto rail corridor. I knew this would greatly help, as there was not much protection against the elements on the walk from St Peter's Square, through the security barrier and the Vatican Gardens to the Pope's station and platform. I assisted many of the visitors who had come over from Great Britain through the security barrier, and by 8am there was quite a crowd gathered on the platform to welcome the punctual arrival of steam locomotive 685 089, in all its glory.

Two cardinals in full regalia soon materialised through the steam: Cardinal Óscar Andrés Rodríguez Maradiaga from Honduras, the President of Caritas Internationalis, and Cardinal Lajolo – the former to travel on the train and the latter to stay behind in the Vatican, as he had to preside over a tribunal that Saturday morning.

There were official Vatican, media and steam buff photographers everywhere, plus a growing crowd of onlookers, both within the

THE POPE'S RAILWAY

wall of Vatican City, and on the Italian side of the wall, beyond the giant arch through which we were about to travel.

By this stage I was desperate for a cup of coffee, and just as I was thinking about this, the laid-back but colourful Australian senior administration officer Paul Given emerged through the crowd with two cups of coffee, one for him and one for me. I felt immediate beatification, or at the very least a promotion of Paul was called for, but typically Paul just vanished back into the crowd. Two years later Paul landed the ultimate DFAT gig, Acting Deputy Head of Mission to the Holy See for five months which included the period of the exciting unexpected conclave.

There was an official welcome and blessing of the Caritas Express by the two cardinals, who then ventured onto the footplate of the locomotive, at which point, on cue, the locomotive emitted both white steam and black smoke. One ambassador mused whether this was a deliberate sign from the Holy Spirit about the next conclave, and if so, to which cardinal the white steam attached!

All tickets checked, it was now a case of a blessing of the train by Cardinal Maradiaga then all aboard, whistles blowing, and away we steamed through the arch into Italy. From the arch it was straight on to the eighty-year-old connecting viaduct, across the viaduct, and so within one minute, we had traversed the full length of the Vatican private railway, the shortest private railway in the world.

Anticipating the needs of many, the troika had arranged for a false-start (so-called photo run), a steam out through the arch so the moment could be captured by all photographers, including those travelling on the train. This happened with some precision driving by the crew and led to some superb images, especially for those with the right angle to capture the dome of St Peter's in the near background.

The Caritas Express made history as the first-ever train from the Pope's platform available to anybody who wanted to buy a ticket. It was also the first steam train to travel out of the Vatican in the twenty-first century, and it looked a great sight. Indeed, as it gathered speed through the suburbs of Rome, many people standing on platforms awaiting regional trains were waving and looking on with a degree of incredulity.

At Orte, over halfway to Orvieto, in accordance with the well-laid-out plans, the Caritas Express came to a smooth halt and engines were changed. Two electric heritage locomotives were added for the remaining stages, and soon enough we were underway again. On arrival at Orvieto, the mayor and a bevy of local officials turned out to welcome us and escort everybody to the funicular base station for the short ride to the top.

The superb Umbrian town of Orvieto was looking 'in the pink', and the train patrons soon spread around the various nominated restaurants for lunch and then a stroll around the various gift shops, many of which sold local pottery products, including large colourful dinner plates.

At the given time, everybody assembled in front of the cathedral, with its delicately designed façade, to listen to a welcome from the local bishop and to split up into groups to tour the cathedral and all its delights, spanning many centuries.

THE POPE'S RAILWAY

Then it was back to the train, with many weakening and buying gelatos on the way down the hill.

On the way back to Rome everything ran smoothly, with one monsignor electing to ride in the locomotive cabin for the last leg. The more interesting deputy heads of missions crammed into one compartment for an impromptu party all the way back to Rome. Again, planning ahead, the troika had elected not to return to the Pope's platform, since we did not want the responsibility of 200 well-lubricated steam buffs and others scattering through the Vatican Gardens on sunset.

So it was that the Caritas Express glided to a gentle halt at platform one at Termini Station. As it came through the last kilometre of approach tracks, many other trains sounded their horns in welcome and salute. Everyone disembarked with big smiles and cheerful farewells. And with that, the project had been safely completed, raising about 15,000 euros for Caritas emergency funding for the 2010 Haiti earthquake victims and other needs.

The troika was mightily relieved that it had all gone off so well. A good cause had been helped and important rail heritage saluted, but there had also been a lot of fun along the way. The only remaining task for me was to write some letters of thanks and look through the various collections of great photos that had been taken of the train.

Five months later, Pope Benedict XVI elected to travel by train from the Vatican to Assisi for a day of prayers for peace. He did the trip in a modern 'Silver Arrow' and again everything went smoothly, and the train did the trip up and back in record time. As there is no overhead wiring on the Pope's platform, a diesel locomotive was used for the first kilometre outbound through the arch and the last kilometre back in after the long day.

In fact the year of 2012 turned out to be a record year for movements on the world's shortest private railway, and I was happy that the troika had made a contribution in helping to bring this about. I do hope that from time to time, permission will be granted by the Vatican for more outings of trains of a similar nature to the Caritas Express.

★ ★ ★

My second encounter with the Pope's trains took the form of a deep mystery – and the discovery of a scandalous situation, which took me almost the entirety of my posting to get to the bottom of. In fact, the saga continues to this day, with no likely end in sight.

Just near Piazza Navona, in an eighteenth-century palazzo, lies the superb Museum of Rome. In that museum there is an account of the political rumbles against the papacy after the French Revolution, culminating in Garibaldi's seizure of the Papal States in 1870 and formation of a united Italy. It was a very fervid time on the streets of Rome.

The first railway of the Papal States had been constructed in the 1850s, and for the next two decades, the Pope did a lot of train travel around the States, which stretched from Bologna to Rome, and down to Naples. A special train – consisting of a papal throne carriage and two other carriages – was constructed in Paris to enable this. But when the Pope lost the Papal States in 1870, these carriages fell out of use, since the Pope went into seclusion inside the Vatican until 1929, when finally the Lateran Treaty was signed with Mussolini and a railway built into the Vatican.

By that stage, the original carriages were too old to be used. And no other papal train was ever built; when the Pope uses a train today, he uses modern carriages supplied by the Italian Railways.

I was determined to see these three historic papal railway carriages at least once during my posting as Australian Ambassador to the Holy See. This was partly out of personal interest, but also out of general interest, to develop another subject for dialogue in and around the Vatican Curia.

Hidden away in a long, deep gallery under the main plaza of the Vatican Museums is the Carriage Pavilion of previous popes, part of the Vatican Museums. All diplomats to the Holy See were ushered through this extraordinary pavilion on one occasion early in my posting. Astonishingly beautiful gilt-edged coaches with magnificent carvings were all on display, right through to the early papal motor vehicles, and even one of the famous 'Popemobiles'. I went there with high hopes of seeing the original three papal railway carriages, but sadly there was no sign of them.

At a dinner in the Vatican I asked Monsignor Nicolas Thevenin, a senior member of the Pope's household, about this mystery. Monsignor Nicolas knew a great deal about trains and we shared a deep interest in the historical impact of railways around the world. His great-grandfather had been the president of the French railway company that built a narrow-gauge railway from Beirut to Damascus, sadly no longer in existence. Monsignor Thevenin, just to remind you, is a delightful human being, and over my time in Rome we would become great friends. In fact he has now been promoted to Papal Nuncio to Guatemala.

He told me that the carriages still existed, but were owned in a technical sense by the Municipality of Rome. In fact, he recalled that they had been on the ground floor of the splendid Museum of Rome, but had been moved out a couple of years ago.

This aroused my interest, and once I'd enlisted the help of my office manager and researcher, Antonia Da-Rin, the hunt was on. Alas, it turned out to be nearly three years before a breakthrough came.

Through her perfect Italian and great contacts, Antonia finally tracked down a clue: the Centrale Montemartini, a museum located in a former power station in Ostiense, in the south of Rome. Many ancient statues and other treasures were moved here in 1997 during renovations at the famous Capitoline Museums – which are also owned by the Municipality of Rome. When she rang the Centrale Montemartini, she received a very curious response to her questions: 'Well, we can't say the papal carriages are down here, but you may come and have a look at the museum.'

This sounded like a good lead and was enough for her to alert me. And on my very last weekend in Rome, I finally got down to the south of the city to visit this museum as an individual tourist accompanied by British rail expert and fellow tourist Bill Parker of the Bream Flour Mill rail repair and revamp workshops. Ploughing around out the back of the massive power station, to my absolute joy we came across three carriages wrapped in white plastic, sitting out in the open air.

For a train buff like me, the carriages, with their magnificent parquetry, and the throne carriage in particular – which had a middle section with an elevated roof – were wonders to behold. Bill and I agreed they were railway jewels from yesteryear. Yet here they were, sitting outdoors right near the Tiber, exposed to high levels of humidity, deteriorating before my very eyes.

I subsequently went into bat for these three unique pieces of rail heritage. I alerted parties in the Vatican to the matter but they said they had no room for them, as they already had the beautiful Carriage Pavilion full of papal carriages and motor cars. I also wrote to an official at the Capitoline Museums, who never formally replied.

But the final twist in the tale emerged some time after the end of my posting. In October 2012, Judy and I returned to Rome as private citizens for a number of activities over a couple of days. I dashed down to Ostiense to see what had happened to the three carriages.

Victory! They had been moved fifty metres into an undercroft area of the old powerhouse station, still wrapped, but at least out of the direct impact of sun and wind and rain. And I think there had been acute embarrassment, at various levels, that they had been kept outside for so long.

But there in the undercroft they remain, because there seems to be nowhere else for them to go.

The solution here is blindingly obvious. I have no doubt that a well-run railway museum somewhere in the world would be happy to take the three carriages, restore them to their original beauty, have them on display for five years as a way of meeting the costs of restoring them, and then return them to Rome. The obvious location for them in the Vatican would be in a long, empty, dead-end railway tunnel already existing, at the far end of the Pope's railway station. Then they could be added to the official tours of the Vatican Gardens.

The solution awaits; I would urge that they not be forgotten, because they are absolute gems of examples of the early use of trains, and the design and parquetry are unique among all the railway carriages I've seen in the world. They would be up there in the top ten trains of the nineteenth century, anywhere in the world – especially the throne carriage, which bears comparison with icons like the Queen Victoria carriage in the British National Railway Museum in York. If that museum can spend millions on restoring the Flying Scotsman – which is only twentieth century – then surely the original throne carriage of the Pope deserves a better fate than to be hidden under plastic at the back of a museum on the outskirts of Rome.

As both ambassador and private citizen, I believe I have achieved a minor triumph regarding these three neglected train carriages. Now that my appearances in Rome will consist of nothing but occasional tourist trips, I can only hope that others will step up to help carry on the fight. In breaking news the dynamic head of the Baltimore and Ohio Railway Museum, just north of Washington DC, General Courtney Wilson, has commenced investigations and negotiations to help rescue and revamp the original papal train.

CHAPTER FIFTEEN

Filth in the Church ... Light in the Tunnel?

In early 2005 an elderly cardinal prepared to deliver Easter meditations on the Way of the Cross at the Colosseum in Rome. His name was Cardinal Ratzinger, a man with deep knowledge of the workings of the Church both in his native Bavaria and around the Vatican. A great theologian and a sharp observer of many things, he decided to issue a bold declaration.

'How much filth there is in the Church, and even amongst those who, in the priesthood, ought to belong entirely to Him.'

Within weeks Cardinal Ratzinger was elected as Pope Benedict XVI and in a position to deal with the issue very directly. During his pontificate, he has expressed an understanding of the bitter anguish of victims of sexual abuse, and has met with

FILTH IN THE CHURCH ... LIGHT IN THE TUNNEL?

many of them, especially during visits to places as far afield as Australia. In particular, he has empathised with the hurt and disappointment of thousands who have been abused by clergy, or are parents of children and teenagers who have been abused.

Sexual abuse by Catholic clergy has been well documented, in the USA especially and in our own country, and also in European countries including Belgium, Germany and Ireland. But what about Italy? The fiction is maintained by some in Italy that sex abuse by the clergy is not a big issue there, as it is essentially an 'Anglo' problem – which of course is a totally wrong assessment, but rather convenient for elements of the Italian media and even for some in the Curia.

Cardinal Ratzinger's clear recognition and public reference to 'filth in the Church' so soon before his elevation to the papacy should have been a clear signal to all in authority to be transparent about sex abuse by the clergy and proactive in dealing with it.

There has certainly been some slippage in Church standards in the decades following the free and easy 1960s, now regarded as being a time when attitudes changed greatly in the West with regard to sex, particularly promiscuity and homosexuality. Worse, however, was the prevalent practice of shuffling known sex abusers between parishes, without alerting parents to the dangers. This soft-shoe shuffle was and is unforgivable, yet it was not faced up to for years.

The issue of what young bishops knew in, say, Ireland and the USA a couple of decades ago and what they recall today, as senior archbishops and cardinals, is a contentious one. What is often missing is an up-front apology and clear remorse – not at the papal level but further down the chain.

Too often those in Church leadership positions stumble around on radio interviews as if advised they must not say sorry to the victims for fear of creating legal exposure. Indeed, perhaps they have been so advised, but there are sets of words that could be cleared and used that have no legal ramifications but would make it clear how the Church now regards clerical sex abuse and how deeply saddened it is by the knock-on effects for the victims.

Marcial Maciel Degollado was born in 1920 just south of Mexico City. After studying for the priesthood, in 1941, at just twenty-one years of age, he founded a dynamic new Church organisation, the Legion of Christ. The Legion of Christ expanded quickly after World War II and Degollado continued to lead it successfully – whilst also leading a kind of double life. He is credited with fathering at least three children and also sexually assaulting a number of young seminarians. Eventually the victims stepped forward.

As a priest he was obviously way out of line, yet as a megafundraiser for the Church, he was very successful and found favour in the Vatican under various popes. His magnetic personality clearly meant that he had no great difficulty in getting away with sex abuse for many years. But eventually the complaints mounted up and led the Vatican to open an investigation and force him out of the leadership of the Legion of Christ. The Vatican nailed him, but not until after his death in 2008, and tragically after he had wrecked the lives of many.

FILTH IN THE CHURCH ... LIGHT IN THE TUNNEL?

The various cases involving large numbers of priests in places such as Boston and Philadelphia who were shuffled around parishes after carrying out sex-abuse crimes leave a deep-seated anger, including amongst the fair-dinkum honourable priests of the USA who are unfairly besmirched. It should be said Cardinal Bernard Law, former archbishop of Boston, has expressed his remorse that he did not do more to deal with and expose the sex abuse in his diocese around the turn of the century, but it was not a good look or outcome that Pope John Paul II promoted him to a key position in Rome, albeit one in which Cardinal Law worked hard until his retirement.

Now, around Rome the argument is aired that the Catholic Church is often singled out by the media for an unfair level of criticism. Further, many of the cases still gaining headlines relate to sex-abuse crimes carried out thirty or forty years ago.

So what was my response when I heard this? Whilst I acknowledged that many other organisations had their share of sex abuse cases, especially various youth movements that failed to drive out adult leaders who were known paedophiles, the Catholic Church and all Christian churches had a clear responsibility to act forthrightly against sex abuse by clergy or never be trusted in any fundamental way, especially on the education front.

Beavering away in Rome is a young Jesuit from Germany, Father Hans Zollner, whom I met at a reception at the German Embassy to the Holy See in my first year of posting. His readiness to help me with translations from German into English, and to explain so much of his work at the Gregorian University, was very helpful. He was part of the outward-looking Gregorian Jesuit brigade – which includes people like the Rector François-Xavier Dumortier, previous rectors such as Father Imoda, and also Father Norman Tanner, Father Keith Pecklers and Father Felix Körner. I picked their brains as much as I answered their questions on Australia.

As head of the Gregorian Institute of Psychology, Father Hans Zollner battled away on key issues relating to young seminarians, developing templates that ensured adequate standards so that those with sexually deviant or criminal tendencies, especially active paedophiles, would be detected and dealt with in a proper way. To bring further focus and momentum to the issue of sexual abuse, the Gregorian team convened an international symposium in early 2012 entitled Towards Healing and Renewal.

At last a high-level, Vatican-supported conference was taking place in Rome on an issue that many thought could be ignored or simply swept under the carpet. Jesuitical dedication and tenacity had paid off. The Pope sent a message of support and several key Curia heavies attended and spoke, including Cardinal William Levada, Prefect of the Congregation for the Doctrine of Faith (CDF).

In his comprehensive address, Cardinal Levada restated the recent history of the tightening up of Canon Law relating to the sex abuse of minors. Pope John Paul II made a promulgation on 30 April 2001, which was added to in a promulgation made by Pope Benedict XVI on 21 May 2010. The Cardinal then reaffirmed the thrust of the 'Circular Letter to Assist Episcopal

Conferences in Developing Guidelines for Dealing with Cases of Sexual Abuses of Minors Perpetrated by Clerics', released by the CDF on 3 May 2011, and highlighted the fact that the consideration of victims was its first priority.

Up-and-coming Archbishop Luis Antonio Tagle of Manila also fronted in Rome to speak at the symposium, notwithstanding a heavy dump of snow across the city at the time. He said that perpetrators in the Church must accept responsibility for their actions, and that 'geographical transfers' of offending clergy were not acceptable.

Gradually the establishment figures of key parts of the Church are starting to get it, and episcopal conferences are starting to get it – some more quickly than others. The Australian Catholic Bishops' Conference made a strong declaration back in 2001 and moved speedily to adopt a set of guidelines called 'Towards Healing'. In addition, various civil inquiries and State parliamentary inquiries have been commissioned in Australia over the past decade.

But in the absence of a fully transparent front-foot approach by the Catholic Church and other churches over the years, it was inevitable that the pressure would build in Australia for a comprehensive Royal Commission. In November 2012, following allegations and comments by senior police personnel, including Detective Chief Inspector Peter Fox from the Hunter Valley, Prime Minister Gillard returned from an overseas trip and within forty-eight hours changed the policy of the government and announced that there would be a Royal Commission into institutional sex abuse of minors, with comprehensive terms of reference issued later. The Commission is headed by Justice Peter McClellan, Chief Judge at Common Law of the NSW Supreme Court, and involves not only the Catholic Church but many other institutions as well – as it should. It will hopefully bring some closure for Australians very badly dealt with by abusive clergy.

So progress is slowly being made in combating this evil that has wreaked havoc throughout recent generations within the Catholic Church, the Anglican Church and other churches and organisations. But of course it should never have occurred at all. Surely the exposure of the various scandals, especially of the soft-shoe shuffle of paedophile priests – allowing them to find new victims and offend again, as detailed in a stinging Grand Jury Report in Pennsylvania not so long ago – will cause many would-be sex abusers to desist.

In the developing world, especially in Africa, a more uneven pattern applies. Once again Father Hans Zollner is among those working through programs to ensure that the relevant guidelines are available throughout Africa. Cardinal Peter Turkson speaks of the issue in an upfront way, upsetting some but also reminding everyone interested that 'sex tourism' drives a lot of paedophelia in parts of coastal Africa and Asia.

Judging the current state of affairs versus the era of the Borgia papacies (1378–1655), it has to be said that progress has been made over the centuries in cleaning up the Church, and for that matter cleaning up Rome, but there is still a long way to go to reach absolute compliance with Canon Law. A huge organisation operating in over 150 countries will always have the odd rotten egg, but it is how surveillance is maintained and how the rotten eggs are dealt with that matters. Total transparency is surely one of the keys to all of this.

Alas, in May 2012 another twist emerged in the saga of the tainted Legion of Christ. The current head of the Legion, Father Alvaro Corcuera Martínez del Río, admitted in a letter to members that he knew around six years ago that a certain Father Thomas Williams had fathered a child and yet was not prevented from preaching on TV and writing books about right and wrong. The cardinal appointed to investigate the Legion, Cardinal Velasio de Paolis, said he learnt of this particular twist about a year earlier.

Significantly, Father Alvaro as the current head begs forgiveness in his letter for being an ineffective leader and 'not being more diligent in setting proper restrictions and enforcing them'. Hypocrisy exists the world over, but this case is a reminder of the distance the Church has yet to travel in delivering full, dynamic transparency concerning all aspects of sex abuse and sexual activity by those preaching from a declared belief in chastity.

On the good news front of sorts, in the same month of May Pope Benedict XVI sacked a bishop in Sicily for alleged fraud and financial corruption, now the subject of a police investigation. Popes need these headaches like a hole in the head, yet when these types of matters reached Pope Benedict's desk (not always the case), then action was forthcoming. An organisation like the Vatican must be led from the very top. The German Cardinal said there is filth in the Church; it must indeed be dealt with, and that means, from the top down, no allowance of sitting on hands, no cover-ups.

There is filth in the Church of various kinds. It is being dealt with and sometimes this process is too slow and too cautious, but if the pope of the day has his way and if his cardinals and other key leaders follow his directions, then I am confident that by degrees there will be light in the tunnel.

CHAPTER SIXTEEN

Papal Resignation?

> *I resign the papacy out of the desire for humility, for a purer life, for a stainless conscience, the deficiencies of my own physical strength, my ignorance, the perverseness of the people, and my longing for the tranquillity of my former life.*

With these extraordinary words, Pope (later Saint) Celestine V resigned the papacy in Naples on 13 December 1294. He had been elected pope on 5 July, just five months earlier.

Meeting and watching the undeniably brave and dedicated Pope Benedict XVI over the course of a three-year posting caused me to contemplate the big question: Will Pope Benedict XVI return to the Celestine template for departure from the Chair of St Peter, in accordance with Canon Law and his own utterances? Will he resign abruptly? In fact he did, very abruptly and about a year ahead of when I was predicting; he resigned with effect at 2000 hours Rome time, Thursday, 28 February 2013.

In the first few weeks of my posting, the mountain city of L'Aquila was battered by a huge earthquake that even rocked Rome, about eighty kilometres away. More than 200 people were killed in their sleep on that dark night in March. At the same time, the Vatican and the Pope were being buffeted by a raft of sex scandals involving a minority of clergy, most notably in Belgium, Germany, Ireland and the USA but some other places as well.

In addition to this was the Bishop Williamson Affair, opening up old wounds of anti-Semitism and revealing a disconnection at the very top of the Vatican that left the Pope exposed to attack from way beyond Israel and the New York Jewish lobby. Here was a pope of German descent – an aspect leaving him especially exposed on anything relating to Holocaust denial – lifting an ex-communication order against a bishop known for denying the Holocaust, at the very time when that bishop was renewing his attack.

As I have said, he later revealed that he had not known of Williamson's latest Holocaust denial when he had signed the decree lifting the ex-communications of Williamson and three others. He had a right to feel greatly let down by many near the top, but, manfully, at no stage has he ever indicated this.

On top of this, there was a papal tour to the complex cauldron of the Middle East in the pipeline, where great tact and diplomacy would be required as the Pope sought to reach out

PAPAL RESIGNATION?

to the Christian minority without further escalating tensions in this volatile region.

What happened next was instructive. Whilst meeting many victims of the dreadful L'Aquila earthquake it was clear that he was genuinely moved. Some victims raised the issue as to why the Pope had not officiated at the huge funeral Mass a fortnight earlier, and why Secretary of State Cardinal Bertone, the number two in the Vatican hierarchy, had been sent instead.

The earthquake had badly damaged the church of Santa Maria di Collemaggio, but the still-intact main door was unlocked and the Pope was shown in to pray at the tomb of Pope Celestine V. Television footage showed him in deep prayer and thought, possibly reflecting on the fact that Celestine was a pope who had chosen to resign – not the only one to do so in history, but certainly one who did so in direct and honourable terms, in accordance with Canon Law.

In a gesture that was purposeful and clearly reflected a great deal of respect for the Pope who had resigned, the new Pope placed his own pallium (Y-shaped vestment) on the glass of the tomb and prayed. He then looked at all the damage inside the church and was clearly moved by what he saw. All of this was noted carefully by some senior Vatican watchers and tucked away in their memory banks.

Within weeks Pope Benedict XVI had two more stumbles, one physical and one metaphorical. Whilst on holidays in northern Italy, he fell and his arm had to be put in plaster. Then on a papal flight to Cameroon, he answered a pre-submitted written question, making comments on the hot-button issue of

HIV-AIDS policies and condoms. This led to a huge distraction on his tour of Africa, which was otherwise very successful, with massive colour and happy crowds in both Cameroon and Angola. It was the Pope's first visit to Africa, but sadly much of it was drowned out by the condom controversy.

Towards the end of 2009 the Pope appeared to 'lift' as he got ready for a new year, one that would see him create twenty-four new cardinals, canonise several new saints, and attempt further reform of the Vatican finances and the secretive Vatican Bank, alas with spectacular failure, through no fault of the Pope.

In February 2010, he conducted a consistory meeting to which Australians were invited, led by Sister Maria Casey SOSJ, the postulator for the cause of Blessed Mary MacKillop. It was a privilege to be present upstairs in the beautiful Clementine Hall for the occasion and observe the Pope announce the canonisation of Australia's first saint. Pope Benedict looked well and was clearly back on the front foot, and appeared to remain so throughout that busy year.

But what happened on 4 July 2010? The Pope returned to the tomb of Pope Celestine, about two hours' drive east of Rome, and once again he meditated and prayed. This second visit was to mark the 800th anniversary of the birth of Celestine V, and to do so with a well-thought-out-homily delivered by the Pope. Benedict highlighted the simple life of this monk who became pope, a monk who through long periods of silence found peace and God. Later in the day he praised the simplicity of the life of Celestine V and contrasted it with aspects of the consumerism of today.

PAPAL RESIGNATION?

On the law of averages, in a five-year pontificate there are at least a dozen ex-popes whose centenaries or multiple centenaries of birth occur, so perhaps there are a dozen out of 250 papal tombs that the Pope could have visited, and most are in or around Rome. Yet he chose the tomb of Celestine V and went twice in a fifteen-month period.

It was then that I became convinced that Pope Benedict was thinking of resigning but I thought not for a couple of years. As the matter related to the head of state of the country I was accredited to, I cabled Canberra with an intimation around that time.

Shortly thereafter, the Pope moved directly to his summer palace at Castel Gandolfo and granted a set of extensive interviews to a German journalist, Peter Seewald. Over several days, with two recorders running, questions and answers flowed, after which a transcript was submitted to the papal household for review. The transcript was signed off on by the Pope, so we know it was deliberate when he had this to say, responding to the question, 'Have you thought of resigning [as Pope]?':

> When the danger is great one must not run away. For that reason now is certainly not the time to resign. Precisely at a time like this one must stand fast and endure the difficult situation. This is my view. One can resign at a peaceful moment or when one simply cannot go on. But one must not run away from danger and say that someone else should do it.

Peter Seewald had a follow-up question on the matter of a papal resignation: 'Is it possible, then, to imagine a situation in which you would consider a resignation by the Pope appropriate?'

'Yes,' replied the Pope, adding (and I quote exactly):

> If a Pope clearly realises that he is no longer physically, psychologically and spiritually capable of handling the duties of his office, then he has a right and, under some circumstances, also an obligation to resign.

Was this the Pope laying down a marker? I was now absolutely convinced. He was seriously contemplating what has been nicknamed the monastry option, whereby he would resign at a date in the future and quickly repair to a monastery, either in Rome or in his beloved Bavaria, in or around Munich, where he once served as archbishop.

So after the 2009 *annus horribilis*, here in the high summer of July 2010 was a confident Pope raising the option of resignation, stating emphatically the pope can resign and in certain circumstances has the duty to do so. In all of this Pope Benedict was referring to the issue in mainly abstract terms, but clearly ruling that those terms could apply to him. In any event, these remarks were drowned out by comments in the same set of interviews relating to HIV-AIDS and condoms, all detailed in the excellent book *Light of the World*, published in the US, the UK and the Vatican.

What, then, does the current version of Canon Law (the laws of the Catholic Church) say about the issue of papal resignation?

PAPAL RESIGNATION?

Section 332, clause 2 of Canon Law states: 'If it happens that the Roman Pontiff resigns his office, it is required for validity that the resignation is made freely and properly manifested but not that it is accepted by anyone.'

In other words, the Pope can act alone but not under any kind of duress. He must in practice affirm his resignation to at least two cardinals to ensure clarity of intention, but no individual or unit of the Church has the power to reject the resignation so tendered. The language in clause 2 is curious, but it means that the papal resignation in fact must be accepted and stands immediately.

I would contend that it is no big deal if and when a papal resignation happens. As modern science and health care extend longevity, more and more popes will live to an age beyond what they adjudge is needed to meet the physical and mental and all other requirements of the papacy. To put it bluntly, they may no longer have the capacity to be able to properly lead the worldwide Roman Catholic Church.

The one thing I think had become certain in my mind is that Pope Benedict XVI would and did take this exceptional step the moment he reached a stage when he felt no longer able to properly continue. Why? Because he laid out the template to do so and because his love of God and the Roman Catholic Church ensured his desire to see adequate leadership at all times and beyond his pontificate. In short, he wanted to do the right thing.

★ ★ ★

Another development influencing the Pope's hand may have been an ugly 300-page internal report by senior cardinals on corruption within the Curia – corruption of all kinds apparently. This may have been the straw that broke the camel's back, causing Pope Benedict to say to himself: No I am not going to linger even another year, my successor will have to read the report and act. For whatever reason, the Pope was pulling the pin and doing so with no turning back.

So it was that the cardinals gathered for a consistory meeting in the Sala del Consistoro within the Papal Palace, up on the second level and next to where ambassadors are ushered through to see the Pope. It was a cool Monday morning, Monday 11 February 2013, and the Pope entered and prayed and then read his now famous 'Letter in Latin', announcing his irrevocable resignation, set down on the morning of 11 February 2013 to take effect on the 28th.

Only a handful within the meeting hall knew what was coming. The looks of utter amazement and disbelief clearly showed this to be true. Many senior Italian Curia officials and clergy had always been dismissive when I had raised the possibility in polite conversation around the dinner tables and conference rooms of Rome, saying this will never happen.

This I did often in 2011, the last full year of my posting when I had more confidence and standing, and had worked out to my satisfaction that the Pope was seriously thinking of resigning. But I had the likely date for this action absolutely wrong, thinking it would be in 2014 or 2015. One memorable response was that it was not only unlikely but it would be the wrong thing for a pontiff to do. The brigade saying it will never happen were big in number, as they possibly had most to lose, in the inner Vatican circle. Some added they would not let it happen.

Pope Benedict XVI outwitted them all, staying with the template he laid out in mid-2010. I am advised he told only a handful of people of his decision and not until the Sunday before the Monday, when he took the world by surprise and methodically laid out his resignation.

This papal resignation created modern history and a new dynamic for conclaves, as well as being a marker of his papacy, which will be remembered for ever more. It was a brilliant decision, a tipping point and a turning point with the Roman Catholic Church, and will, I feel, come to be recognised as such in the future, more than in the immediate aftermath.

As the world now recalls Pope Celestine V's papal resignation of 1294, so the world will also recall Pope Benedict XVI's resignation of 2013, for ever more. I feel strongly it is the first of frequent resignations by popes in the twenty-first century.

★ ★ ★

In relation to papal resignation generally, one wise person plugged in on both sides of the Tiber told me that we do need people to speak up with regard to papal resignation possibilities, if only to ensure that Pope Benedict, now that he has resigned, is not treated as an outcast and so that any future pope can consider the option and not see it trampled on by elements of the old guard in the Church and Curia.

Against this is the overarching need for the pope of the day to maintain stability and unity, a need arising from the lingering centuries-old fears engendered by the great East–West schism and the Reformation. In more recent times there have been various threats, most notably in Europe, with fears of wholesale defections of priests pressing for reform.

In Ireland Father Tony Flannery has helped found the independent Association of Catholic Priests of Ireland with about 850 members. Father Flannery has refused to confirm his acceptance of the policies and teachings flowing from Rome, declaring it would be 'a lie' for him to do so. In Austria there is also a loud independent priests' organisation with a reform manifesto espousing controversial views on issues such as celibacy which have been utterly rejected by Rome. At the same time Pope Benedict tried to reach accommodation with ultra-conservative organisations such as the Pius X Society in France. The thought of adding to the instability of these turbulent times with an ill-considered resignation would not be acceptable; but the option of an enlightened resignation, at exactly the right time, for all future popes should be maintained.

CHAPTER SEVENTEEN

Jesuit Pope Francis Arrives

As things often go in Italy, within minutes of white smoke emerging and the new Pope being announced from St Peter's balcony out went the clanger of the decade, the Italian Bishops' Conference issued a statement formally congratulating Cardinal Scola of Milan on his election as the 266th Pope. They were totally wrong; an Argentinean non-Italian but of Italian descent had won.

As papal conclaves go, the March 2013 conclave was to be like no other on several scores and reflects the fact that in many ways the Roman Catholic Church in 2013 was under a degree of challenge and, once again, at the crossroads.

Yes it was the first conclave in centuries with a living ex-pope nearby. As Pope Benedict XVI said he would do, he repaired to Castel Gandolfo about fifty minutes south of Rome, where the Papal Summer Palace is, on his last day of his pontificate, remaining there throughout the month of March 2013, whilst an apartment was being prepared within Vatican City in Rome.

Actually, if I were him I would elect to live in retirement at Castel Gandolfo permanently: good security, a spare large Vatican villa overlooking the papal farm and a climate all the year round that is better than Rome or even his beloved Regensberg and Bavaria.

The glistening headquarters of the Vatican Observatory is nearby, and a terrific library containing, as mentioned elsewhere in this book, some of the very early writings of Copernicus. He can also walk across to the Observatory HQ for many good and lively discussions, or even take in a sharp lecture or two.

However, with his retirement the action and focus was now back on Vatican City conclave and the good news was that the Italians inside the Vatican Walls quickly found the stove and temporary chimney, to be erected on the southeast corner of the roof of the Sistine Chapel.

The number of voting cardinals had contracted, firstly with the resignation of Cardinal Keith O'Brien of Scotland and secondly with the sad news that the only Indonesian cardinal and retired Archbishop of Jakarta, Cardinal Julius Darmaatmadja, announced ill health would prevent him attending and voting in the conclave.

So as things stood, there were 115 voting cardinals sitting down in the Sistine Chapel to select the 266th Pope, with the Anglo bloc down in numbers and the Italian bloc as large as ever, comprising twenty-eight of the 115 voting cardinals. This

Anglo situation has come about in part by the failure of the Vatican Curia to take account of the eightieth birthday last year of the tall media-savvy UK Cardinal Cormac Murphy O'Connor. So he is out of the conclave based on age and the RC Archbishop of Westminster, Vincent Nichols, is not yet in as he was not made a cardinal in the rushed group of six late in 2012. The result is there was no voting cardinal from the UK, thus any geo-political objection from the UK to an Argentinean pope evaporated. Curiously around the time of the conclave, the Falkland Islands voted ninety-nine per cent to remain British.

It is an example of the segmented planning and thinking in the Vatican that somehow nobody alerted the Holy Father Pope Benedict to the 'voting vacancy in the UK', when he drew up the last list of new cardinals, the list that will go down as perhaps the 'Extraordinary Six'. However, another reason advanced, in my view a little unfairly, is that Archbishop Nichols is considered too liberal for preferment and the granting of a red hat.

Then again there are at least fifty countries with active branches of the Roman Catholic Church that did not have voting cardinals at the conclave, including New Zealand and Thailand.

As the cardinals gathered in Rome, methodical preparations took place within the Vatican for the conclave to elect the new pope. Pope Benedict XVI allowed the lifting of the customary fourteen days between the throne of St Peter falling vacant and the conduct of a conclave. This was in part to ensure the new pope was elected before Easter. Further, there were early indications the new pope should not be from Rome or from the Roman Curia. Various public utterances by cardinals en route to Rome and statements by some ranking Vatican officials clearly pointed to a new dynamic applying to the March 2013 conclave.

Some key cardinals were attracting media as leading contenders, demonstrated by the thousands of media representatives present. Around the city of Rome, impressive Cardinal Marc Ouellet of Canada, aged sixty-eight, also capable Cardinal Leonardo Sandri, an Argentinean Italian aged sixty-nine, came to the fore, along with several others, such as Cardinal Peter Turkson of Ghana. This list included the Italian dark horse who enjoyed his Sydney visit greatly in 2008, Cardinal Frederico Fernando Filoni, a man who as papal nuncio in Iraq was nearly killed by a car bomb and was the only ambassador to stay in Baghdad during the US-led invasion of 2003.

All of the above have extensive language skills; for example, it is nothing for them to switch between English, French and Italian, as well as handle German and Spanish and other languages. Cardinal George Pell in a farewell interview before departing for Rome, emphasised in particular the need to have a new pope who can readily communicate in this century of massive 24/7 classic media and social media demands.

Cardinal Pell, aged seventy-one, joined several others in their early seventies in contention but ultimately none of the aforementioned were elected. All of them were on the scene and fully engaged in the conclave process, attending the ten congregation meetings or assemblies of cardinals to discuss key issues and size up contenders, immediately ahead of the conclave like no other.

White smoke signalling the election of a pope emerged on the evening of Wednesday 13 March. Less than an hour later Cardinal Tauran whispered the announcement and left several key TV anchors absolutely silent because they did not hear a name they were familiar with and had to await verification. It would have helped if Cardinal Tauran had repeated the announcement in clear tones.

The Al-Jazeera news anchor was silent for what seemed an eternity. I was watching on a small television set five thousand feet up at the Grand Hotel, in the city of Nuwara Eliya in the centre of Sri Lanka, and I soon worked out it was the Jesuit cardinal and the only Jesuit in contention.

It was the election of a bolter, indeed for those of us who believe in the Holy Spirit, guidance was clearly provided. It was a total rank outsider from Argentina who reached the magical seventy-seven votes first up; not only a Jesuit cardinal but at the ripe old age of seventy-six, one Archbishop Jorge Mario Bergoglio of Buenos Aires.

What happened in the conclave can only be surmised from some utterances on the record by cardinals reflecting on the joy of the outcome and suggesting that the quietly spoken Cardinal Archbishop of Argentina led the way early on and throughout the five ballots. It is suggested that the supremo Dean of the Cardinals, Italian Cardinal Sodono, linked up with Cardinal Bertone to push for a contender other than the leading, much-favoured Cardinal Archbishop Scola of Milan.

Cardinal Sodono himself was too old to vote in the conclave but had enormous influence, formally and informally, giving the final address to the cardinals at the special Mass in St Peters just before they entered the conclave. So the bloc of twenty-eight Italian cardinals appears to have splintered again; for the third consecutive papal election the choice was in favour of a non-Italian. In 1978 second time around it was a Polish Pope, in 2005 a German Pope and now in 2013 an Argentinean Pope of rare colour, action and movement.

So will he be a 'label conservative' — branded a conservative but not so in fact? Then again who thought the very conservative German Pope would take the radical step of resigning, so beware any labelling. In a bold decisive move, the first Jesuit Pope, the first Southern Hemisphere Pope, the first Pope known to have but one lung, adopted the name Pope Francis in honour of St Francis of Assisi.

As I have said, it is a lack of transparency that is wrecking the authority of the Church, the inability of many senior Italian Curia and others to be on top of the problems with clergy sex abuse, with harmonised, efficient administration and with the struggling Vatican Bank, among others. Relations between the Holy See and Ireland are so bad that the Government of Ireland has still not reappointed a Rome-resident ambassador.

Pope Francis comes from a humble background, the son of Italian parents who migrated to Argentina; his father was a railway worker and even once upon a time, a train driver from the beautiful northern parts of Italy, in fact from Torino. I have been to the north of Italy many times, as my wife's great-grandfather Battista de Piazza, as noted already, grew up at Grosotto next to Tirano and made his way across northern Italy to Genoa, to embark for Australia in the gold rush era of the nineteenth century.

The young Argentinean elected to pursue a vocation with the Society of Jesus, later heading up the Jesuits in Argentina during the so called 'Dirty War' period when the generals were in charge. He took action, largely behind the scenes, to secure the release of two Jesuit priests arrested by the generals. They came out alive after five months' incarceration; sadly thousands were never sighted again.

A study stint in Germany has ensured the new Pope speaks German, as well as Italian and Spanish, and, it is said, a smattering of several other languages, including English. His clear preference is to speak Italian and Spanish. He will need to communicate well in whatever language, but as Bishop of Rome, his fluency in Italian gives him a flying start, and more so his warm, friendly and spontaneous approach, which is about 180 degrees from his immediate predecessor.

The overall worldwide head of the Jesuits is often called the 'Black Pope' with the actual Holy Father being called the 'White Pope'. Now we have a 'White Pope', a Spanish-speaking Jesuit from Argentina, and a 'Black Pope', a Spanish-speaking Jesuit from Spain. This is a story of what happened in the first week of the new papacy; the receptionist, at the tiny desk just inside the front door of the modest Jesuit HQ picked up the telephone and said, 'Pronto.' A voice came through saying, 'This is the new Pope and I want to speak to the Father-General of the

Presenting books to the 'Black Pope', the supreme head of the Jesuits, at Jesuit HQ in Rome; that is, to Spanish Jesuit Father-General Adolfo Nicolás.

Jesuits, Father Adolfo Nicolás.' The receptionist said, 'Do not play jokes. The White Pope never rings out of the blue to speak to the Black Pope.'

Pope Francis had to patiently explain that it was in fact the new Pope and please put him through so he could invite the head of the Jesuits to an early meeting and dinner. One embarrassed receptionist quickly found Father Adolfo and connected the Black Pope to the White Pope. Things are going to be a little different in many ways around the Vatican under Pope Francis. Already there were alterations to the huge Easter program of 2013. The new Pope greatly reduced the length of the Holy Saturday Vigil service. He also washed the feet of prisoners on Holy Thursday. I wish Pope Francis every success with the shake-up he plans to deliver.

The enthronement Mass that followed in superb cool, sunny conditions on Tuesday 19 March in St Peter's Square demonstrated how much was already changing, Pope Francis wore an old iron cross, not gold, and normal black shoes, not red ones, and he accepted a gold-plated silver papal ring, not a pure gold one. Over 130 delegates attended, including Chancellor Angela Merkel of Germany and President Cristina Kirchner of Argentina, with many other Latin American leaders.

Robert Mugabe, long-serving President of Zimbabwe who is banned from travelling to Europe but not to the Holy See, seized the chance to come to Rome with his wife, Grace. Often enough these people, once clear of the Vatican, are sighted on huge shopping expeditions around the Via Veneto. Many royal families were also represented, including those from Belgium and Spain.

The Mass of enthronement was held not only in dry, sunny conditions, perfect for the large outdoor ceremony with thousands in attendance but there were no ugly incidents or people getting crushed in the crowd. Further, the Mass and ceremony appeared somewhat simpler than previous enthronements, with a short homily from the new Pope talking about 'reality' amongst other subjects. Earlier in the day he had met with Bartholomew I, the Ecumenical Patriarch of Constantinople and head of the Greek Orthodox Church. They prayed together in what was also a first on a papal enthronement day.

Clearly this Argentinean Jesuitical one-lung Pontiff is going to be very different, as demonstrated by his leaving his open vehicle to hug members of the crowd when travelling to the Mass. This shows an open spirit that I pray might never be overwhelmed by the office and the higher echelons of the Curia.

His first set of major tasks will be appointing the tenure of right personnel to the twenty key positions at the top of the Curia. Logically he has extended the term of all of the incumbents for the transitional period, but some tough decisions are called for, clearing out the dead wood and those now past their prime.

In particular I commend the selection by Pope Francis of a G8, or group of eight cardinals, nicknamed COCOA, as in Council of Cardinals of Advice. It is not a cabinet but it will provide vital advice to the new Pope, and should be a counterbalance, as seven of the eight are non-Italians who are based a long way from Rome.

I not only wish Pope Francis all the best for a successful bold beginning, but for a successful pontificate overall, ending in a properly timed papal resignation after a few frenetic years at the top. In this regard I pray for him.

CHAPTER EIGHTEEN

Grand Finale Year

Many had warned me that my posting as ambassador would start slowly and build steadily, with the last year always being very busy, a kind of 'grand finale' year. Indeed it was, with less time on the ground in Rome as DFAT sent me to more and more conferences, from Buenos Aires to Belgrade and beyond.

At the same time I was completing a 70,000-word manuscript for a book on trains, signing off on the editing and helping organise a book launch to coincide with my mid-year annual leave. My weekends were therefore kept very busy on this personal work, but at least there were few big Vatican commitments on weekends, except for Easter, and Sunday 1 May 2011.

This was the very special Sunday that drew a million people to St Peter's Square and the surrounding streets, to celebrate the beatification of Pope John Paul II, the Slav Pope who did so much to help the world. The President of Poland, accompanied by a huge official delegation, was front and centre, along with most of the diplomatic corps and various other VIPs.

However, dominating all were the thousands of proud Poles, many of them having endured long train or coach trips, travelling through the night, determined to be present at this salute to their famous countryman.

Polish Ambassador Hanna Suchocka was cool, calm and collected throughout the build-up to Beatification Sunday, handling various negotiations to ensure a smooth presidential visit, and organising a raft of other arrangements to help the thousands upon thousands of visiting Poles soak up the day.

After the long Mass in St Peter's Square the simple wood coffin of Pope John Paul II, quietly brought up from the Crypt below, stood in front of the main altar for several days. It was a reminder that this man, who for the last twenty-six and a half years of his life had been surrounded by pomp and circumstance, had grown up in very humble conditions in occupied Poland.

Later, the papal coffin was placed behind a marble casing in a side chapel of St Peter's. This has since become a very popular place for prayer, affording more dignity than downstairs in the Crypt, where there is always much bustle and congestion.

This deep-thinking anti-Communist came along at the right time to make a real difference to the world. He visited a record number of countries during his pontificate, and became the second longest serving Pope in history. No wonder a million people of many faiths turned up to witness his beatification. It was one of those very special days that was a great privilege to attend as Australian Ambassador to the Holy See.

★ ★ ★

My final year also gave me the opportunity to kick along a campaign that many in Australia had been working on for some time: a bid (in partnership with New Zealand) to be one of the host nations of the Square Kilometre Array (SKA) radio telescope.

The world's largest and most powerful interferometer (linked array of radio telescopes), the SKA will be 10,000 times faster and fifty times more sensitive than all other radio telescopes. Scientists hope it will help them answer fundamental questions about the origin and development of the universe – proving Einstein's General Theory of Relativity, among many other things. Scheduled to commence in 2016 and be fully operational by 2024, the project has ten member countries, including both Australia and Italy.

Italy is campaigning to have a further HQ role, and so to some extent Rome was a hub in the decisions associated with the project. The Holy See did not get to vote on the decision, but my involvement was all about building support and understanding of the strength of Australia's case. It was important to ensure that the Vatican Observatory, as a key world authority, was fully briefed. (This was the observatory that corrected the Julian Calendar by ten days and created the more accurate Gregorian Calendar, nearly 500 years ago.)

So during my posting I found myself in frequent contact with the Director of the Observatory, Father José Funes SJ, a sharp-minded Argentinean. And in my final year, while I was still chair of the Greater Asian Group of Ambassadors, I arranged to take the entire group to the Vatican Observatory headquarters for a briefing.

Since 1935, the Observatory has been located in the grounds of the Pope's summer palace, Castel Gandolfo, just south of Rome. A revamped monastery houses a collection of manuscripts and meteorites to die for, including the first drawings by Copernicus showing the earth going around the sun (and not vice versa, as had been believed previously). Operational telescopes are maintained on the palace rooftop, including a solar telescope to enable the observation of sunspot activity.

Following a lecture on the work of the observatory, as mentioned earlier I took the Asian ambassadors up onto the rooftop to watch these spots erupting on the surface of the sun, before we moved off to a local restaurant for a working lunch. One ambassador kindly observed that it had been the most colourful and interesting day of her posting to date.

On another occasion, as the countdown to the decision grew closer, I took a party that included Kim Carr (then Minister for Innovation, Industry, Science and Research) out to the Observatory. The Minister was very impressed by all he encountered, ending the evening at the rooftop observatory, sampling the mountain breezes but alas, not seeing any stars due to a technical hitch as well as light cloud cover.

GRAND FINALE YEAR

Eventually, in mid-2012, the decision was made on the location of the SKA: a major site was to be in Western Australia, with a second site to be developed in southern Africa. Australia's prospects had waxed and waned at different stages of the campaign, and this decision was a gritty win. DFAT was not the lead department on the SKA bid, but stepped up and helped as much as possible, with many ambassadors in key SKA countries pulling out all stops. The Embassy to the Holy See played a tiny, modest part in that.

★ ★ ★

The big final occasion of my posting was in one sense internal to the Church, but in another sense part of the fabric of my job, if broadly defined. This was the opening of Domus Australia ('Australia House'), a joint project of several Australian dioceses. Domus Australia provides boutique guesthouse accommodation in the heart of Rome, complete with an excellent conference centre (the Cardinal Knox Centre) in the basement. The conversion of a previously rundown, backwater monastery into the sparkling Domus Australia has been nothing short of remarkable.

There is no doubt that the commitment and leadership of the Archbishop of Sydney, Cardinal George Pell, made the difference in bringing the project to fruition. Under his supervision of the project through the indefatigable Danny Casey, he micro-managed deftly, right through to ensuring 'Australian size' shower cubicles, convenient and larger than the average offered by European hotels.

Cardinal Pell was also the key influence in securing none other than the Pope for the official opening and consecration of the building. Due to the good organisation behind the scenes, the event went very smoothly. Pope Benedict arrived right at the appointed moment, greeted and escorted into the chapel by a beaming Cardinal Pell. The Pope initially looked very tired but he soon rose to the occasion and moved quite quickly around the various parts of Domus Australia that he was scheduled to see. Then, as promptly as they had arrived, the pontiff and his small entourage were gone, heading back across the Tiber to Vatican City.

Domus Australia continues as a glistening practical salute to Australian Vatican linkages and is drawing its fair share of the tourist trade. By the way, you do not have to be a practising Roman Catholic to stay at this jewel in the heart of Rome! For the first year of operations and beyond, capable kick boxing expert Father Anthony Denton was the Rector, and Gabriel Griffa, an Argentinean Italian led the strong Domus Australia staff team. Clearly Cardinal Pell and Danny Casey had anticipated the elevation of the Buenos Aires Cardinal to Pope by appointing an Argentinean Italian to head Domus, some eighteen months before the famous March 2013 conclave!

★ ★ ★

It was in fact at Domus Australia that I decided to have my farewell reception in January 2012. The occasion began with a brief concert featuring Thomas Aquinas's *Panis Angelicus*, Bach's Toccata and *Fugue in D Minor* and the great Australian work from Sydney World Youth Day, *Receive the Power*. Then it was downstairs to the bright Cardinal Knox Centre for the reception. It was a happy place to formally say goodbye to many.

The very last day of my posting was good, bad, sad and hilarious in that order.

It was Friday 20 January 2012 and a clear, cool, sunny day. Having completed my packing at the apartment, I headed downtown to do something I honestly had been unable to fit in before: to finally enter the Colosseum and behold the jewel of the former Roman Empire. I vividly remembered catching sight of it as I first sped into Rome three years earlier. Now, as I quietly walked around a near-empty arena, I found comfort in the solemnity and tranquillity surrounding me, despite the blood that had soaked these stones so many years ago. It was a good way to say goodbye to the city of Rome.

I am not a deeply devout person, but I do try to maintain my commitment and faith as a Christian, and so I took these few minutes to review the three years of posting in Rome and to express my thanks by way of a prayer to my Maker. I did think in some ways that I had not been exactly the best of Christians, having sampled too much of Italy's delectable food and wine, and engaged in *la dolce vita* by degree. It was certainly not the case that my time in the Holy See had created a holy me. The reality was possibly the reverse – Holy See, unholy me!

After a last lunch with the embassy staff at the incredible tiny bookshop ristoranti around the corner, a last gaze out the windows of my office to take in the Dome of St Peter's, and a final sweep of the desk and drawers – leaving some transitional notes for my successor, along with a welcoming bottle of Italian grappa – I sadly quit the chancery for the last time.

On arrival at the airport check-in counter, a gremlin arose, a very bad gremlin, in fact. Check-in officials decreed I must have a transit visa to pass through New Delhi (even for less than twenty-four hours) en route to Bhutan for the Government. I was to accompany Australian High Commissioner to India and Ambassador to Bhutan Peter Varghese on this two-day mission. It was a purposeful detour for bilateral talks and for the UNSC campaign. For an hour it looked like I would miss all flights and be spending an extra weekend in Rome but DFAT at the coalface in Rome and New Delhi came to the rescue with a visa arrangement to be obtained on arrival at New Delhi airport but only carry-on baggage permitted.

This was in the end a hilarious perfect solution, as my two heavy suitcases would go slowly but directly to Australia and I would travel light into Bhutan, I had one final glorious Italian beer in the small VIP lounge and boarded on time, after all. For the record the last suitcase turned up via Boston USA two months later, no matter as I had many boxes to unpack ahead of this.

Then, after the brief detour for meetings in India and Bhutan – the meetings in Bhutan with the King and PM of Bhutan and others were particularly successful – at last it was home, sweet home. It was just great to see Judy, Harrison and Dominic waiting for me at Tullamarine Airport.

GRAND FINALE YEAR

Over the next few days on the Fischer farm, I noticed two big differences: the brightness of the daylight during the long summer days, and the fact that the trees of southeast Australia were back with a vengeance after years of drought. The leaves were glistening again with lots of new growth. For these and a raft of other reasons, it was terrific to be home.

To Rome I will return many times, I am sure, but in a different phase of life. As I reflect on the events of this chapter, I am convinced that nothing could match the joy, the highs and occasional lows of my grand finale year of diplomatic posting. It was a special buzz, the last year – but then again, so were the whole 1000 days.

It had been a totally unexpected experience that left me feeling absolutely exhilarated, even if a little travel-weary. It is for others to judge my contribution, as a junior head of mission resident in Europe leading a small embassy for Australia. For my part I believe I did as much as I could in respect of the issues in my remit. Did I boost Australia's profile and use whatever leverage I could from the establishment of the first Rome-resident Australian Ambassador to the Holy See? Yes I did – in roundabout ways, but also in very direct ways. In conjunction with the Australian Embassy to Italy, I would say that Australia's profile in this great hub of the world had been lifted a great deal.

In appreciation of this, I reiterate my thanks to my wife Judy, to Ambassadors Amanda Vanstone and David Ritchie and their teams, and to DFAT, led by Secretary Dennis Richardson throughout my posting. I particularly thank my own embassy staff: Deputies Anne Giles and Michael Sullivan, PA Madonna Noonan, Office Manager Antonia Da-Rin and driver Stefano Bernardini. In addition I thank Kevin Rudd in his two capacities, initially as prime minister and also as foreign minister, as well as Foreign Minister Stephen Smith. Many ministers and shadow ministers fronted up in Rome over my 1000 days, all on their best behaviour; it must have been the proximity to Pope Benedict XVI!

I likewise sincerely thank the Holy Father, Benedict XVI, Pope Emeritus, who rarely gets a fair go in the world media and deserves a great deal better. I thank his extended team for their helpfulness and courtesy, in particular the hard-working Director of Protocol, Monsignor Fortunatus Nwachukwu. I thank all the faithful clergy in Rome, especially the Australian brigade, and many others, too many to mention.

Let me conclude this chapter with the observation that some time after returning to Australia, I do not miss the city of Rome as much as I do the many friends and good people I worked with closely. However, you move on, keeping in touch from afar.

I must confess, when breaking the farm slasher as I try too quickly to rebuild my farm skills, just occasionally I do wish I were stepping out across the Tiber after a quick coffee in Café Nero, heading past Castel Sant'Angelo and up to the Vatican for a meeting or two, listening out for all soft and subtle or even loud drumbeats signalling change, large and small.

CHAPTER NINETEEN

In Salute of DFAT but Not Every Diplomat

DFAT is skinny as government departments go but, when given a chance, it is up there with the best in delivering on policy and logistics. Though headquartered in Canberra, it has embassies, high commissions and consulates in about 100 different locations around the world. It could be said that, despite recent budget cutbacks – felt especially at HQ level – DFAT has a certain standing in being one of the more senior departments in the Federal Government pecking order – though certainly below Treasury and, some would argue, below Defence. It is younger than the Federal Government of Australia by many years, and as such has had to fight for its place in the sun more often than not.

There is an ongoing triangular battle between the International Division of the Department of the Prime Minister and Cabinet (PM&C), the international divisions of Treasury and the international efforts of the Department of Foreign Affairs and Trade itself. So it is not even a given that DFAT maintains absolute supremacy with regard to its bailiwick of foreign affairs and overseas trade. It has to earn that place, and continue to earn it, against some heavy hitters sitting in Treasury and, most notably, PM&C, not to mention the various powerful spook outfits such as ASIO, the Defence Signals Directorate and the Office of National Assessment.

Yet when other departments stuff up overseas, again DFAT has to maintain silence if not a stiff upper lip. The post-GFC stimulus package saw $900 cheques from the Australian Government scattered all over Tuscany and the Greek Islands, in fact wherever people who had spent at least ten years and one day or more in Australia had retired to, all because Treasury forgot to put in the clause paying out the $900 only to people living in Australia — actually domiciled in the country. When the Federal Department of Agriculture and Minister Ludwig pulled the pin on the live export trade of cattle to Indonesia abruptly, it was left to DFAT to try and clean up the mess.

The position of ambassador to the OECD, headquartered in Paris, rotates every three or four years, depending on the personalities, between Treasury and DFAT. So *there* is one key overseas posting that is not automatically held by DFAT. Normally DFAT would be the peak department representing Australia at various overseas conferences, but a particular set of issues might arise — for instance, the environment and climate change — and the departments involved also take their place at the international table. This is not going to change any time soon under either government; nevertheless, it *is* curious that over recent years PM&C has muscled in on the area.

Further, as Australia's ambassador in Washington, Kim Beazley, has highlighted, many senior MPs these days have direct contact and friendships with senior Congressional personnel, and bypass the embassy completely.

The broader point is: don't for a moment think that DFAT is the only source that Cabinet can turn to. And this is why the performance of embassies and high commissions has got to be a cut above the average, because any loose policy work, any wrong-fitting ideas, will be slaughtered.

Even more important than policy is keeping an eye on the bottom line. The mantra of productivity dividends that departments of finance apply as a lazy way of bringing about cutbacks, by saying that every department will give a two per cent productivity dividend, rather than looking at each embassy line by line, can lead to some stupidity, such as the case in 1996 of DFAT having to offer up the embassy in Denmark for closure. And guess what? In 2000, under the same government, it was reopened, and will never close again while Tasmanian Mary Donaldson, now Princess Mary, is part of the royal family of Denmark.

DFAT also has to overcome the accumulated prejudices and assumptions of many decades. Throwaway lines are often bandied around in Cabinet and Parliament, and indeed in the media at times, that DFAT is full of pinkies (left-wing types) who know what is best for the world, regardless of the policies and priorities of the government of the day. Further, it is alleged that diplomats on postings enjoy living in exotic places with a bevy of servants, being driven around in chauffeured cars, eating and drinking for their country, and just occasionally reporting back to headquarters – in short, leading a carefree life, too often suffering from ambassadoritis or homitis, *hom* standing for head of mission.

Nowhere are these allegations more keenly felt than in the gruelling rounds of Senate Estimates – the chance for senators both mischievous and magnificent to get stuck into DFAT on expenditure relating to the upgrading of chanceries in Rome and various other diplomatic activities. It's always an opportunity to apply that anti tall-poppy lash we Australians so love.

Senate Estimates preparations are enormous. Every embassy is required to provide a brief to DFAT as to what might be a subject of questioning in the hearings, and woe betide you if you haven't anticipated the latest twist in the clever mind of Senator X, Y or Z. (The smart thing is to *feed* Senator X, Y and Z a set of questions, having previously supplied the answers to DFAT, and complete the loop. I never quite got around to doing that, though I was tempted!)

Nowadays, with modern communications, you can in fact monitor the actual Senate Estimate hearings via the Internet. And often they were grinding on in the middle of the night in Canberra when it was in the middle of the day in Rome. On occasions I could hear an official struggling when I knew a clear-cut answer to the question: for instance, that the new Holy See chancery came in *under* budget. But on that occasion there was a little bit of confusion and so it hung in the air and the DFAT official said, 'We'll come back with further information.' And by the time DFAT comes back with further information on issues like this, they are already in the minds of the public: 'Oh, millions are being spent on the upgrade of chancery X in capital city Y; for what purpose?'

I think DFAT has got better at handling Senate Estimates, but there is still plenty of room for improvement. The next time a senator smirks and shoots at the operational budgets of, for example, embassies in Europe, straight away the senior DFAT official should say: 'Well, Senator, would you have liked the survivors of the *Costa Concordia* to have waited weeks and then gone to Berlin to get new passports, or would you rather that there had been an emergency consular centre established by dawn on that Saturday on the wharf, accounting for all twenty-three Australians by sunset, and processes commenced for the reissue of their passports? Your choice, Senator.'

So I think DFAT has the right to get a lot more aggressive in the face of mischief that senators on both sides often undertake, and to make sure that there is a more balanced picture of what the department does on the ground. As mentioned, Ambassador to Italy Amanda Vanstone once saved an Australian company $18 million: no mean effort.

I do think the role of Senate Estimates is exactly as it should be. It allows for the monitoring of activities like those of a former ambassador to a Latin American country, who managed to smuggle Mercedes-Benz vehicles into Australia at reasonably frequent intervals, until he was finally caught and dealt with.

But Senate Estimates should be balanced: criticisms where they're deserved, and genuine praise where it's deserved. And DFAT officials giving evidence need to be on the front foot. If they're being pinned on subject X, they should be able to counterbalance that by explaining why it led to breakthrough Y.

DFAT is not clever at putting out good-news stories, and ensuring those good-news stories get a run. It has to be said that the department is deserving of a lot more praise than it gets.

DFAT's achievements over recent decades under the Hawke, Keating, Howard, Rudd and Gillard governments have been considerable, but often where a small or large victory is obtained, others will take credit. And the 101 things DFAT does well are always overwhelmed by the shrill media coverage of the odd thing that goes wrong. Hundreds can be rescued from a country where war has broken out (such as Lebanon in 2006 and Libya in early 2011), with DFAT pulling together huge logistical efforts, but the one person who had a delay or difficulty with evacuation arrangements will be the lead item on the news.

Foreign ministers over the years have tried hard: longest serving Alexander Downer, as well as Stephen Smith, Kevin Rudd and Bob Carr, have never been shrinking violets in the media, and have sometimes championed particular activities of DFAT. But a minister can only do so much; good promotion requires skill on DFAT's part, *especially* at the Senate Estimates hearings, because if they go wrong, the headline is (as it has been) 'Massive Amount Spent on Reception for Olympians

IN SALUTE OF DFAT BUT NOT EVERY DIPLOMAT

Arriving in London', or whatever. In hindsight the headline might have read: Male swimmers in the diplomatic swim but can they in fact swim, let alone swim fast.

Still, DFAT can be proud of the APEC (Asia–Pacific Economic Cooperation) and Regional Interfaith Dialogue forums, its role in East Timor and much more, as has been detailed in writings by other authors – not to mention the UNSC campaign, as described in this book. It can also be proud of much on the consular front, and really has proved itself to be a department that punches above its weight.

Yes, it could be said I am biased, and yes, there are aspects of any unit of bureaucracy that need constant monitoring – notably the silo mentality that also infects the Vatican, with information not always readily exchanged between units or departments.

One part of this equation is the interface of diplomatic staff with the media, the extent to which this is permitted and the need to ensure that the foreign minister knows early of major developments and of course announces all good news. I have no argument with this, but within the overall paradigm, it is sometimes desirable for ambassadors to speak up and do media on the spot.

Fortunately DFAT has moved along this pathway in recent years. Not once was I told to remain silent on an issue, and generally ambassadors and high commissioners are encouraged to respond to media queries and requests as soon as possible, but only after notifying the Media Liaison Service back at DFAT HQ. It is now at least five years since one high commissioner was told to cease giving radio interviews after a major bombing involving Australian citizens took place in London. It is even longer since an ambassador has had to be pulled out of a posting for misbehaviour.

★ ★ ★

'Read your DFAT briefing notes ahead of key meetings' was an item of good advice I received on my way to becoming minister for trade in 1996 from former Minister Doug Anthony. The alternative is easily imagined: a minister, at the end of a busy week, finds himself meeting a visiting overseas VIP. He tries to wing it, glancing at the brief literally as the VIP sits down opposite him. Result? Relevant VIP departs Australia frustrated and a win-win opportunity is lost.

DFAT is still helping to deliver very good briefing notes, and while diplomatic networking is mainly on location, I found it wise never to ignore my DFAT contacts back home. Go native, forget about DFAT HQ, and see how long you last … generally only as far as the next round of postings.

From my own experience, I can say without hesitation that DFAT's support of small embassies is outstanding. Small embassies are a necessary part of the foreign affairs footprint of an OECD nation of over twenty-two million people. It is tempting to centralise in, say, Berlin for continental Europe, with FIFO (fly-in-fly-out) teams to deal with ministerial visits to, say, Vienna or Zagreb. The problem is that the necessary local contacts and knowledge evaporate under that approach.

IN SALUTE OF DFAT BUT NOT EVERY DIPLOMAT

When Australians are stranded after a ship sinks off the Italian coast, it is most necessary to have feet on the ground quickly and local connectivity.

In any event, many small embassies have to cover a raft of nearby or even far-away countries. The Australian Ambassador to Austria is credentialled to places that do not adjoin, such as Bosnia-Herzegovina and Kazakhstan, seven hours' flying time from Vienna. The Australian Ambassador to the Holy See could at a future date take up extra roles easily, such as Ambassador to San Marino (four hours' drive northeast of Rome) and Ambassador to the Sovereign Order of Malta (headquartered fifteen minutes' walk northeast of the Australian chancery).

Certainly DFAT and the Australian taxpayer would get more value if ambassadors stayed at post for four rather than three years, given the considerable cost of travel, accommodation, nine months' language training, family transfer and so forth. You spend the first year really getting to know the place, in the second year starting to deliver, the third year hitting your straps, and then you're gone. A way not to jam up promotions back down into more junior levels of DFAT would be to make sure the hardship postings keep rolling over every two years as a counterbalance – for example, Tehran, Iran; Beirut, Lebanon; and Kabul, Afghanistan.

Unexpectedly some colourful Australians who reside permanently overseas step up for embassies and for DFAT. Painter Jeffrey Smart allows one of his great works, at least a print of same, to hang in the Holy See Ambassador's office or at least it was there whilst I was ambassador. I met him through another dedicated Australian, Anna Sturgess; he was still painting in his nineties in Tuscany and very sharp and quick witted when asked for a comment on fellow Australian artists, such as Russell Drysdale.

Another issue that bubbles up from time to time is the appointment of ex-parliamentarians as ambassadors: Kim Beazley to the United States, Amanda Vanstone to Italy, Tim Fischer to the Holy See, and over the years many more but not too many.

Most senior diplomats from DFAT will tell you it is a healthy thing to have a handful of ambassadors who are ex-parliamentarians with governmental connections. They bring a different set of skills, and they can enliven and change people's perspective of the role of an ambassador. The recent ambassador in Brussels Brendan Nelson, former leader of the opposition, did an outstanding job. I have heard career diplomats say he has irrevocably expanded and altered the role of the Australian ambassador based in this very difficult post, which includes the European Union and NATO.

Australians don't often think about these things, but if they do, their reaction is: 'Oh, jobs for the boys.' But, while admitting my own partiality, I think that there *is* a legitimate case for the particular skill sets that former parliamentarians bring in injecting some variation into the diplomatic corps. I certainly found this in the case of the ex-politicians in the Holy See corps. But equally, if half the postings were political, this would be excessive, indeed very wrong, and would create severe morale problems in the younger ranks of DFAT. Career diplomacy should always be the dominant model.

IN SALUTE OF DFAT BUT NOT EVERY DIPLOMAT

By and large, Australia is well served by its diplomats and by DFAT, but final judgment on this will always be forthcoming twice a year at Senate Estimates and daily on the front page of tabloids. Australia is a long way from the hubs of the Northern Hemisphere, where so many decisions are made on commerce and on other matters. We are naturally insular – but we can't afford to be, because we are an exporting nation. This is why we need DFAT to be successful without and within overseas, but also within the pecking order of the government of Australia.

CHAPTER TWENTY

Which Way the Vatican?

Is it the Pope's butler or the Pope's banker who has set the Vatican up for a mighty fall? Will these two, accused of much, be found not only guilty in their inadequate performance but also guilty of helping to break the will of the German Pope to continue in his role. Will their sagas put back or speed up the cause of sweeping reform of the Curia?

These questions arise from the month of May 2012, when the Pope's butler was charged with leaking sensitive emails and letters from the Papal Household to an Italian newspaper, and the Pope's chief banker was voted out by the Vatican Bank board. All of this I observed from the safety of 'Grossotto', Mudgegonga, the family home and cattle farm in a mountainous part of northeast Victoria.

Whilst it is not for an ambassador of just three years' standing to pontificate about the future of the Holy See, I will chance my arm in a respectful way to at least ruminate about some negative aspects and also some pieces of good news, after a lifetime of following papacies from afar and then three years close up.

On the negative side of the ledger, there are some time bombs ticking away – none that threaten the existence of the Vatican, but serious issues nonetheless. These are best raised and dealt with sooner rather than later, in my view, but I am the first to admit this is stuff way beyond my remit as a humble parishioner down under.

What I *can* say with certainty is that they are all, sadly, influenced by the Vatican's cumbersome, top-down, high-handed leadership style. In the case of many of these key problems, which are already causing negative publicity, increasingly the Vatican seems to be discouraging free-flowing debate, preferring instead to demonstrate that it is still in control with a show of force from on high.

Overarching all is the 'fifty per cent' problem: the 'glass ceiling' that exists between the leadership of the Roman Catholic Church and the women of the world. This is especially true of the developed world, where many outstanding women have shown leadership skills equal to and often better than their male counterparts. The key is surely to find a formula where the traditional structures of the Church are not done away with, but where every effort is made to be inclusive of women. There are key positions that women can fill in the existing structure, but rarely do they get the opportunity to do so.

When women occasionally crack the top positions they are sometimes allowed to drift from certain core aspects of their remit and so are kneecapped when their term is up for renewal. Does anyone ask how Christian in attitude is it for senior male clergy to allow this to happen under their very noses, rather than stepping forward and providing counsel and guidance?

A classic example of this occurred halfway through my posting, right in the midst of preparations to blow the starting whistle of the Caritas Express. Just when all our plans seemed settled, the news broke that the Secretary of State, Cardinal Bertone, was formally removing the right of the Secretary-General of Caritas Internationalis, Dr Lesley-Anne Knight, to contest a second consecutive term. The position was due to be discussed at the Sixtieth Anniversary Conference, to be held a few days after the running of the train.

I didn't want to get caught in the crossfire of this controversy, but I sought out and spoke with three cardinals, and they fortunately made it clear that the ruling of Cardinal Bertone should not be seen as a reason to suspend our one-off train ride out of the Vatican. Yet, unwittingly caught up in the Machiavellian machinations of this incident, I learnt a few hard facts about the way the Vatican operates.

Caritas Internationalis is a fantastic organisation, achieving a great deal in relief and development work worldwide – way beyond what any government could do. And Lesley-Anne Knight has been a big part of that. But this move to roll a black marble against her ostensibly arose from the Vatican's desire to ensure that Caritas remained, at its core, committed to a strongly Catholic focus, as opposed to the more pragmatic approach pursued by some Caritas programs. Elements of Caritas argue that this more pragmatic approach is often dictated by local conditions, for instance in isolated parts of Africa or Latin America.

Now, most well-led organisations, seeing a senior figure in the establishment drifting off the correct *modus operandi*, would counsel that person and help guide that person back to what was deemed to be correct. Most organisations would make that effort, as part of a humane approach, but also as part of a good management approach: if you have a manager going about things the wrong way, you would try to fix the problem rather than just sacking them. Lesley-Anne Knight was summarily dismissed with nice words and a long letter, but where was the guiding communication from within the Vatican that could have avoided that happening? And the answer is pretty clear: there was none, because the Vatican is clunky; it doesn't work in that humanised, modern-management way.

But an element of chauvinism doubtless applied as well. In some ways Lesley-Anne Knight was a modern version of Mary MacKillop: she was active, she was dynamic, and in the process of getting things done, she may have raised eyebrows among the conservative elements of the Curia.

Rightly or wrongly, the Vatican is often seen to be happy to wage war against and besmirch its thousands of devoted female workers, for instance in the USA over recent years. An Apostolic Visitation of Institutes of Women Religious of the USA was announced by Rome in December 2008: a method used to uphold discipline and look into the welfare of sections of the Church. Women religious had not been consulted before the announcement, and it caused great angst and upset. The

Visitation continued in a heavy-handed way until January 2012, leading to a set of key meetings in Rome with US female religious leaders. Many female clergy in the USA expressed their deep disappointment at the shoddy handling by Rome as they went about their many good deeds.

All of this devised by the all-male Curia and driven allegedly by some US cardinals, perhaps to create a distraction from the dominantly male clergy sex-abuse saga. A textbook example of all that is wrong with the Curia and its use of power.

This leads me to the second ticking time bomb: sex abuse within the Catholic Church. Enough has been said on this subject in a previous chapter, but it is rightly on the list of ticking time bombs and is not unrelated to the collective standing of the priesthood that sees many quickly clamber into civilian clothes when travelling to avoid being noticed.

It also has an impact on the number of people entering the seminaries to become priests or joining various religious orders. This is the third ticking time bomb: the declining numbers of people being attracted to the dedicated and devout life of the priesthood. A degree of cross-subsidisation is certainly helping – for example, Indian priests heading off to developed countries in the English- and Portuguese-speaking worlds to fill increasing numbers of vacancies, especially in the parish networks.

I have no particular suggestions to turn this around in our increasingly materialistic and often sex-driven Western society. One obvious solution often floated is to revert to the practice of the first thousand years of Christianity and allow married priests more widely than is currently the case. The practice was discontinued (in line with some of the teachings of the Apostle Paul) to ensure that priests concentrated on their primary duties, but marriage of priests is not precluded by any doctrinal determination. A limited number are allowed in certain Eastern rites in communion with Rome and converting former Protestant priests are allowed to continue as Catholic priests even if happily married. It would be curious to stipulate divorce in that situation!

Going even further and admitting women to the priesthood is another matter. Following an apostolic letter put out by his predecessor John Paul II, Pope Benedict said that, while not quite enshrined in Canon Law, this is simply not possible.

So there is quite a sharp division between what is flexible and what is regarded as essentially doctrinal, in which there is no flexibility. And any Catholic clergy not wanting to be stripped of their role should be sensibly conscious of that view.

This was precisely the issue at stake when the popular Bishop of Toowoomba, Bill Morris, was forced to take early retirement (in effect, sacked) by the Vatican in May 2011.

Toowoomba is a vast outback Queensland diocese staffed by aging clergy, with virtually no young men stepping up to fill the ranks. Over his eighteen years as bishop, Morris had already been disciplined by Rome for encouraging 'group absolutions' rather than individual confessions to a priest – a practice declining in popularity and difficult to administer in such a huge diocese. But it was an Advent pastoral letter he wrote in 2006 that sealed his fate in Rome. Acknowledging the staffing crisis in the Toowoomba Diocese, he suggested the Church should be open to all options, such as ordaining women and married men, welcoming back former priests, and recognising Anglican, Lutheran and Uniting Church orders.

Following repeated requests to resign from high in the Vatican, an Apostolic Visitation by a US archbishop, and even a personal audience with the Pope in June 2009, the bishop finally declared his decision to retire in a letter read out to all congregations in the diocese during Mass, just hours ahead of an official statement from the Vatican. It was this unusually public declaration of his position that prompted headlines around the world.

I learnt about the matter backwards from Australia rather than from within Rome, which was quite proper, because it was a matter internal to the Church, and nothing to do with the Australian Ambassador. It led to a very strong campaign of letter-writing to me from Australians, and I had to remain absolutely neutral about it. The vast majority of people who wrote to me were very angry, and felt that the decision was in no way justified. I wrote back to as many of them as I could, pointing out that they might like to bring their comments to the attention of the Papal Nuncio in Canberra, or pass it on to the Australian Catholic Bishops' Conference – the national body of bishops.

In fact, a sequel to the Bishop Morris saga occurred in October 2011, when this body visited Rome. Every few years, in turn, the Catholic bishops from each country visit for about a fortnight, to report in at HQ. These days they tend to meet as a group with the Pope and others, to receive guidance and to sort out areas of difficulty. These visits are called Ad Limina visits.

WHICH WAY THE VATICAN?

My embassy put on a big reception at the Vatican Museums to welcome the Australians to Rome.

During their Ad Limina the Australian bishops raised the controversial sacking at the highest levels within the Vatican. They were seeking a more detailed explanation as to why there'd been such a serious parting of the ways. According to their statement on this matter (which is publicly available), they obtained a better understanding and cleared the air with the Vatican Congregation of Bishops on what was, I understand, quite a complex raft of issues. I for one was pleased that that outcome was reached.

Having stepped down from my role in the Vatican, I still do not feel in a position to judge the correctness of the decision. On the one hand, according to Bill Morris and reports later commissioned by his supporters, he was removed without due process and without the right to be heard. Allegations by marginal elements within his diocese were accepted without proper examination by the Vatican hierarchy, which was anxious to be seen to exert its authority at a time when it seemed to be losing its grip in the wake of worldwide sex-abuse scandals. On the other hand, this outspoken outback priest had been causing headaches within the Holy See for years with his stubborn refusal to tow the doctrinal line and yield to numerous Vatican requests. I shall leave it to others work out which of these positions is closest to the truth.

Certainly, though, massaging and managing difficult decisions is an area where the Church could do a lot better. I think it took too long to explain the processes, and to provide a more detailed explanation in the Diocese of Toowoomba. However, I was pleased to see that the new Bishop of Toowoomba particularly invited Bill Morris to his induction in mid-2012, where Bill received a huge round of applause. I felt that invitation was a meaningful gesture that brought a degree of closure to a very fraught situation.

★ ★ ★

The list of large and small ticking time bombs continues as the twenty-first century unfolds, involving more and more change. Then again, the Roman Catholic Church has survived the breakaway of the Orthodox Churches, the huge split during the Reformation and a raft of other enormous challenges. It has had to deal with Roman emperors pre-Constantine who slaughtered Christians and suppressed the Church, conquering Spanish emperors, the invading Napoleonic army, Italian Unification forces under Garibaldi, plus two world wars, Hitler and Nazism, and the surge in Communism under Lenin and Stalin.

But the Church's progress will be helped greatly if it can somehow modernise its clunky, centralised mode of operation and welcome more ideas from outside the ranks of the Curia. This is the clarion call and priority for new Pope Francis.

It appears that aged Italian men have consistently failed to reform the decades-old Vatican Bank money-laundering saga. Perhaps the Vatican needs a female similar to the current International Monetary Fund head Christine Lagarde; perhaps a new position is required in the Vatican, that of cardinal treasurer or chancellor of the exchequer. Millions of dollars flow every day into the Vatican Museums, yet the Vatican still does not have proper management structures and budget structures. That will have to change some time soon or it will pay a heavy price.

The Vatican particularly needs to lift its game in coping with the incessant media cycle. The Pope has a strong group of communication advisors, and every now and then they get a chance to move the agenda along. But the capable, hard-working Father Frederico Lombardi SJ acts as both Vatican spokesman and head of Radio Vaticano, which included until recently the Vatican's television activities. This is in a sense the equivalent of being both Canberra media spokesman and head of ABC Radio and Television as well. Father Lombardi also travels with the Pope on all his overseas visits and remains readily available to ambassadors when information is sought.

Two logical steps that might be considered to boost Vatican media firepower would be firstly to create a papal spokesman position in addition to the current Vatican spokesman, and secondly to appoint a separate head of Radio Vaticano – but again, I am merely a distant observer at a parish level.

The good news is that there are senior personnel in the Curia thinking aloud and looking for ideas on how to boost the Vatican's media presence. This has led to the appointment in mid-2012 of articulate ex-Fox News reporter, Greg Burke from St Louis, who is fluent in Italian, as a senior Vatican media advisor. So don't write off the Pope of the day or the Vatican any time soon, but they are in a competitive space.

Above all, it's my hope that the modernising monsignori, the more dynamic individuals with great intellect but also practical capabilities, of the Curia will be promoted sooner rather than later, and that their ideas and capabilities will be recognised. Some new blood is just what is needed in the Vatican's upper echelons.

Are there inefficiencies in the Vatican? Is there high-level crime in the Vatican? Are there factions in the Vatican, the most dominant being the Italian faction? All of these questions are for others to consider and deal with. Warts and all, the Vatican will be around for a long time to come and hopefully doing everything it can to lift its game on all fronts. As for the Italian group of cardinals and bishops, they are on the back foot, one suspects with the new Pope, especially after the Italian Bishops' Conference managed to congratulate the wrong cardinal on being elected pope in March 2013, issuing a media release incorrectly congratulating Cardinal Scola of Milan! In one sense this says it all.

★ ★ ★

On the good news side, worldwide the Catholic Church is growing annually by about 1.3 per cent – even if that is hard to believe in countries like Australia, where the overall decline in church attendance has been well documented.

Only too well aware of the increasing secularisation of the West, in September 2010 Pope Benedict took the significant step of establishing the Pontifical Council for Promoting New

Evangelisation, writing that the mission of the Church 'has been particularly challenged by an abandonment of the faith – a phenomenon progressively more manifest in societies and cultures which for centuries seemed to be permeated by the Gospel'.

It is perhaps a sad reflection of our materialistic culture that Christian Churches seem to be shrinking in many wealthy, developed countries, while much of the developing world is experiencing outright Church expansion, most notably parts of Africa – Benin, Cameroon and Ghana come to mind.

However, in several countries in Africa there remains bitter conflict between Christian- and Muslim-dominated areas. Fuelled by Muslim–Christian conflict, outright bombing along the South Sudan border with Sudan continues, long after South Sudan's independence was declared on 9 July 2011. And, as mentioned, the Church remains gravely concerned about the continuing exodus of Christians from the Middle East in the face of widespread persecution and violence.

The Church remains strong in places like Poland, perhaps not quite as strong as when it was under Communist suppression but still with a dynamic momentum, in the shadow of the work and standing of Pope John Paul II. In some places in Latin America there is strong commitment and devotion, boosted by the arrival of Argentinean Pope Francis. Asia has some standouts, especially South Korea, as well as the Philippines, and even East Timor. But in fact there are many countries where Christian Churches, and specifically the Roman Catholic Church, are growing in numbers, and where there is a healthy population of men and women with deep commitment.

The Holy See itself continues to experience renewal of a kind, with more and more senior Vatican members being recruited from beyond Italy. I say 'of a kind', because the Italians remain dominant. Moreover, nepotism is part of the DNA of Italy, and many lay positions are still handed down from father to son – or in the case of one Vatican door porter, grandfather to father to son. How do I know? I witnessed Grandma turning up with a cake for all and sundry to salute the appointment of the grandson. A minor matter, yes; a nice gesture, yes; but the ripple effect of this type of preferment goes too far across the Vatican.

Ensuring the best people are recruited for each job and defeating nepotism by degree is in part the responsibility of a secretive committee hidden in the Secretariat of State. It handles the appointment of papal nuncios and their deputies, and has the challenge of getting the balance right and ensuring the necessary rotation.

The Vatican continues to issue well-argued statements, as well as Angelus and Papal Audience messages that are meaningful and stack up, as do many of the congregations such as Justice and Peace. It is a Herculean effort to draft and fine-tune then issue all the key statements by the Pope, particularly at Easter, Christmas and on the occasion of the annual address to the diplomatic corps.

Then there are the many organisations, agencies and religious orders acting out Christ's command to help the disadvantaged throughout the world, and which are massively helped by funding assistance from the Vatican. Caritas Internationalis is one of many Church organisations that has saved the lives of thousands, on occasions working with other Christian organisations such as the capable and dynamic Lutheran World Relief.

On the health and hospital front, the Vatican is a catalyst for much activity around the world, and often in very poor, developing countries. This is visionary work and parallels that of, say, the Jesuit Refugee Service, to be found a long way from the celebrity charity spotlight but helping thousands.

One of the greatest contributions of the Vatican, and indeed the Church worldwide, is in the provision of education at primary, secondary and tertiary levels. This is a mammoth task, and one in which the Catholic school system is often in fierce competition with other private schools and also up against well-funded State school systems. Many of the very best universities, colleges and secondary schools in OECD countries are owned and operated by the Catholic Church.

And I accept that it may not be the view of all, especially agnostics and atheists, but the Vatican remains a bulwark against the worst excesses of modern secular society in the West, with its winner-take-all attitude and deeply materialistic bent. The Christian Churches and the new Pope and key cardinals do much good work on this front.

Pope Francis in fact revealed that on reaching seventy-seven votes in the conclave, a brother cardinal from Brazil hugged him and said: do not forget the poor. As a result he chose the name Francis in honour of the great Saint Francis of Assisi. In his first fortnight, he also shed some of the trappings of office, a good start it has to be said.

Admittedly, all the good works and strong leadership do not generate a guarantee of survival for the Vatican, the danger lurks that it will degrade into a super network of NGOs administering aid projects from air-conditioned offices, dashing around in huge four-wheel-drives. Pope Francis spoke of this risk directly in week one of his papacy.

However, there will always be the need for some approved changes and a fresh new dynamic along the way, taking into account aspects of twenty-first century life without compromising the teachings of Scripture. Two thousand years old and still full of initiatives and activities, crumbling in the eyes of some, but, I feel, the Church and the Holy See will be around for another two thousand years or more.

So will there always be Christians in the world? Yes, there will be. Will the Roman Catholic branch of Christianity necessarily be carried forward by a strong Holy See based in Rome? We should never take for granted the ongoing existence of a structure, even one that has been around for two thousand years, because things do change – as the Vatican's history so far attests. (There's now proof that Hitler was considering invading the Vatican. And had he done so, who knows? The Church may have re-formed in Avignon or Madrid.)

But the point I am making is: there'll be ups and downs in the standing of the pope of the day, the Vatican of the day; but yes, there will still be Christian faith, yes, there will still be a Catholic Church; and its strength will depend on the perceived and actual performance of its leader and its central government.

POSTSCRIPT

Return to Rome

The term 'second coming' has many biblical connotations, and it was the term hurled at me by a smiling US Ambassador to the Holy See, Miguel Díaz, when he welcomed me to a giant reception he was hosting in the Vatican Gardens. It was the week of the UNSC ballot, and the lead-up to seven canonisations being held on Sunday 21 October 2012.

Judy and I had come to Rome for a two-day break, and a renewal of contact with many friends. And what a break it was – almost surreal. We kept bumping into many people we knew in the narrow streets of Rome, as had been so often the case when I was stationed there. In fact in a narrow street near the Jewish ghetto, Judy and I walked into yet another church for a few minutes' silence and found the only other person in the church was our friend Australian seminarian Simon Grainger, also coincidently visiting the church for the first time! Within ten minutes we were participating in a Latin Mass which Simon hastily arranged to commemorate our twentieth wedding anniversary, which we were celebrating on this trip. In typical Australian style, ten minutes after Mass we all adjourned across the road for a beer. It was just another extraordinary, warm and wonderful evening in bella Roma!

It is an added delight of Rome's CBD that you can walk everywhere, and it has a kind of country-town flavour about it. In glorious, mild, sunny autumn weather Judy and I paced the streets, darting into the Pantheon, dashing across Piazza Navona, meditating in front of the Farnese Palace, and of course calling on my former staff at the chancery, plus the two Australian ambassadors.

As a kind of luck would have it, my successor, John McCarthy QC, had not yet presented credentials to the Pope. Informal protocol dictates that ex-ambassadors should move on, and now that John has presented credentials (5 November 2012), I will stay away from Rome for at least a year or so. I might add that he has hit the ground running.

When the big day of the UNSC ballot arrived – Thursday 18 October – I kept looking at the time and calculating when the voting would have commenced in New York for the rotational UN Security Council seats. The moment of truth was about to unfold for Australia.

As the witching hour drew close – morning in New York and near sunset in Rome – Judy and I were due to have drinks with Australian Ambassador to Italy, David Ritchie, and his wife, Jenelle.

On our arrival, David in his professional way told us that the UNSC results had just come through and Australia had been elected on the first ballot, with 140 votes out of a possible 193. In the second ballot Luxemburg beat Finland 131 to 62 – all of this after years of campaigning by all three countries, especially Australia and Finland.

We toasted Gary Quinlan and Caroline Millar and the whole DFAT UNSC team. Within hours extra staff were flying to New York, including former SAO Paul Given from Rome – but only after he had two quick beers with me at one of my favourite Roman watering holes by way of an impromptu farewell.

We now also know that the Vatican staff returning from New York predicted Australia would top the first ballot, as indeed it did. Australia is due to be the rotating president of the UNSC twice during its two-year term, the first occasion expected to be September 2013.

Later, of course, came the debriefs, and the flood of articles examining why the large margin of victory for Australia. Success has a thousand fathers and mothers, but mention was made of several factors. Clearly the work of Caroline Millar and Gillian Bird and others at HQ, plus the envoy networking (including in a small way my own efforts) had been fruitful, capturing new votes and fortifying committed votes. Envoys fluent in at least one other language had made huge progress on their visits, especially Bill Fisher (French so very helpful in the Francophone African countries), Neil Mules (Portuguese), Peter Tesch (German) and John McCarthy (Spanish – not to be confused with John McCarthy QC, Ambassador to the Holy See). Having these language-fluent envoys was smart, and added a lot to our campaign's credibility. But having a permanent representative to the UN based in New York (Gary Quinlan), who was actually on good terms with the other ambassadors voting in the ballot, was also a great help – compared with 1996, when our UN representative, Richard Butler, was on questionable terms with the key UN diplomatic corps.

PM Julia Gillard made a point of going down to DFAT HQ the morning after the big win and congratulating all those present and the department as a whole. I later received a letter of thanks from her, which I appreciated. The Coalition had supported Australia's UNSC bid in principle, though not the timing; nevertheless, Leader of the Opposition Tony Abbott added his congratulations when the moment came. Of course, senior members of government can also take a good deal of credit for the victory.

Did ambassadorial activity in the super-hub of Rome make a decisive difference? The answer is probably no. But did the same activity add momentum to the UNSC campaign wheel through the various activities for which David Ritchie and I had responsibility? Well, the answer is a modest yes.

Yet I must echo the pertinent question of the big 'White Bear', discerning Cypriot Ambassador George Poulides: why on earth were there two candidates from Europe in the same ballot? Why indeed? This was just another helpful twist for

Australia, but not a decisive one; the hard yards still had to be done at every stage of the campaign.

Further, the hard yards continue to be done by diplomats right around the world on a raft of issues and activities: doing battle in support of greater trade access and the abolition of various barriers to trade; getting ready for snap ministerial visits, then the cancellation of same; and so much more. As an ex-ambassador but still Envoy to Bhutan, as approved by Minister Bob Carr, who took over from Kevin Rudd early in 2012, I salute them all; the dedicated diplomats who make a difference in support of the betterment of the world. They cop plenty of flak, occasionally deserved, but by and large they get the job done.

Judy and I raced joyfully over many parts of Rome during this brief visit but we were soon on a jet winging our way home – that is to true home in Australia but for a home away, Rome has much to commend it.

I was back in Europe for meetings of the Global Crop Diversity Trust in May 2013 but not in Rome. Nevertheless the dynamic spirit of new Pope Francis was clearly detectable, pushing a lively agenda here and there and making his first visit to Brazil and Latin America – a kind of huge home coming. Each pope in the modern era will do things his way and this will be true for Francis as it was for Benedict, and there will always be much to be done.

Equally each ambassador to the Holy See will do the job his or her way and this is as it should be, with DFAT HQ keeping a close eye on things overall!

APPENDIX A

Map of Vatican City

Forty-four-hectare capital city of the Holy See

LEGEND:
1. St Peter's Basilica
2. Bernini Colonnade
3. Pope's Palace
4. Sistine Chapel
5. Porta Santa Anna Gate
6. Vatican Museums
7. Vatican supermarket
8. Vatican morgue
9. Pope's Railway Station
10. Governorato HQs
11. Papal helipad

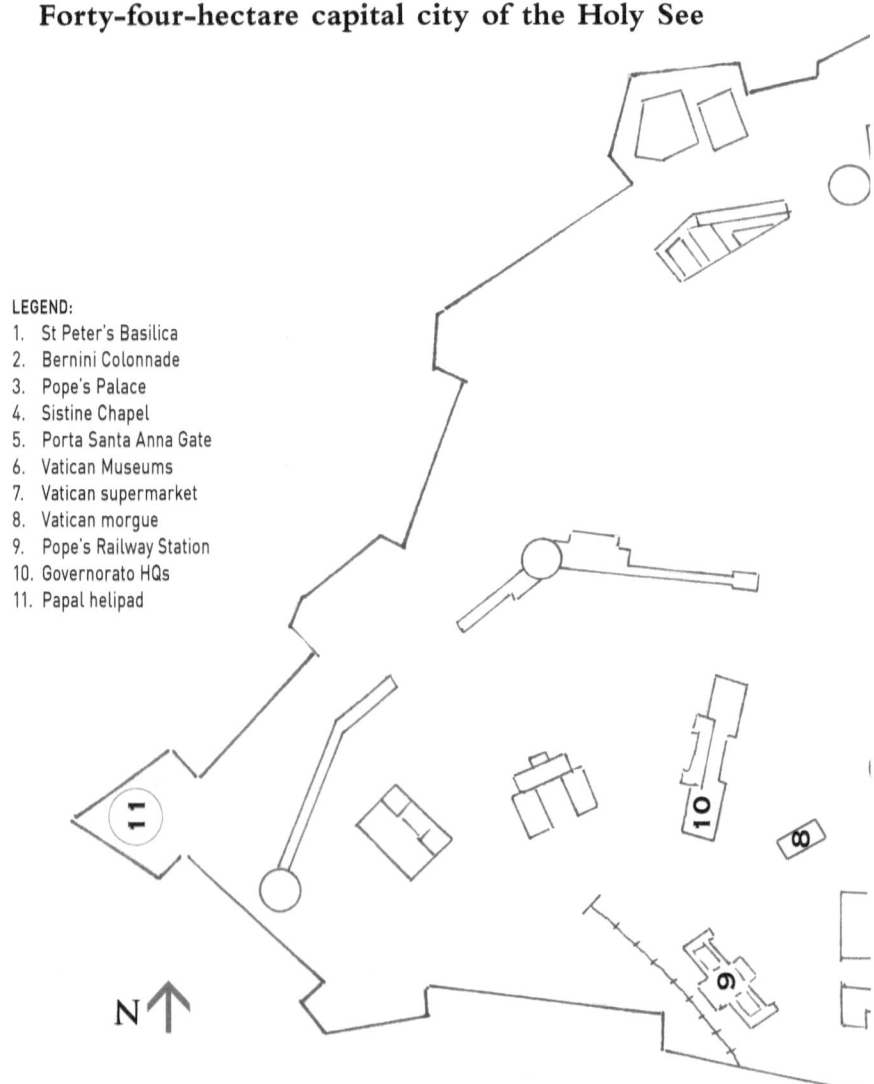

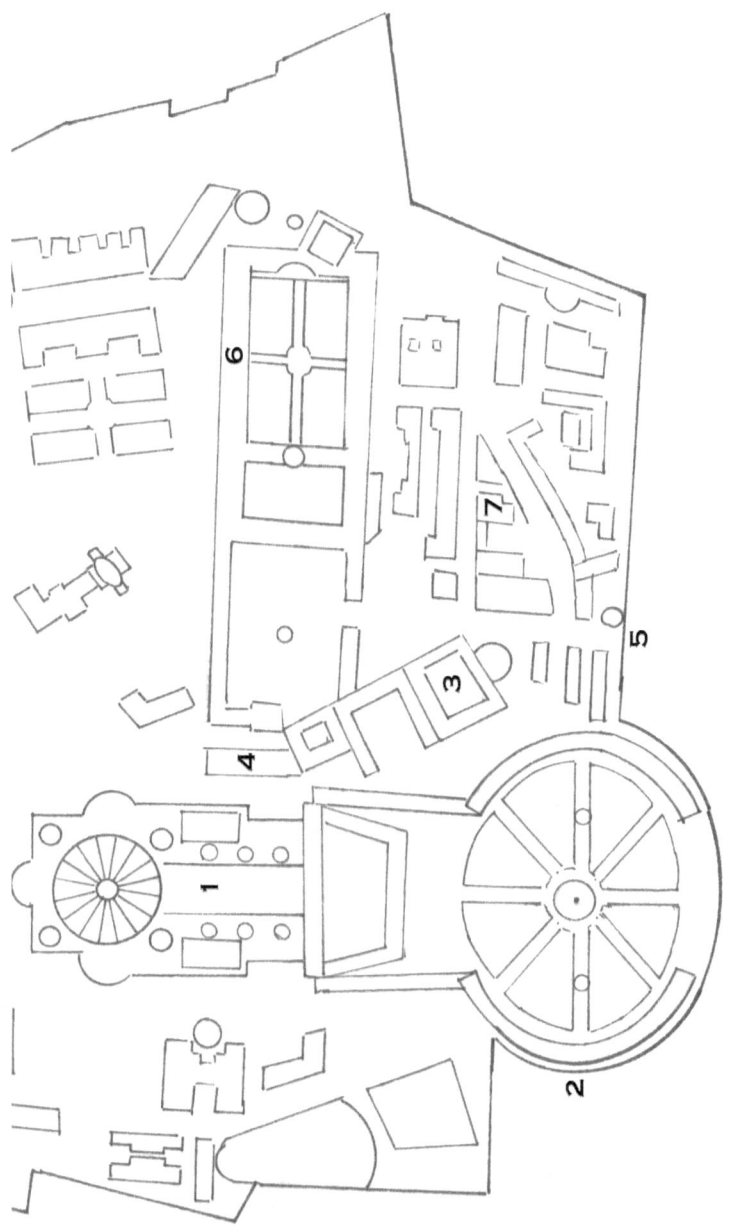

The 44-hectare Vatican City is the sovereign capital of the Holy See and is dominated by St Peter's Basilica (built 1506–1626), and by the Michelangelo dome and the Bernini colonnade. The Pope's railway station is in the southwest corner of the Vatican Gardens, and the Vatican Museums lie on the northern side, from the Sistine Chapel to the outer wall. Note that there is a slight twist and misalignment between the main east–west spine of St Peter's Basilica and the centre line of the sweeping Via della Conciliazione leading up to St Peter's Square. This grand avenue was bulldozed through only in the last 100 years, the project starting with Mussolini wheeling a pick-axe in October 1936, leading to the necessary demolition of many buildings to open up the avenue from the Tiber River and Castel St Angelo to the Vatican City. Map drawn by Dominic Fischer.

APPENDIX B

Map of Castel Gandolfo

The Summer Palace of the Popes and the location of the Vatican Observatory HQ

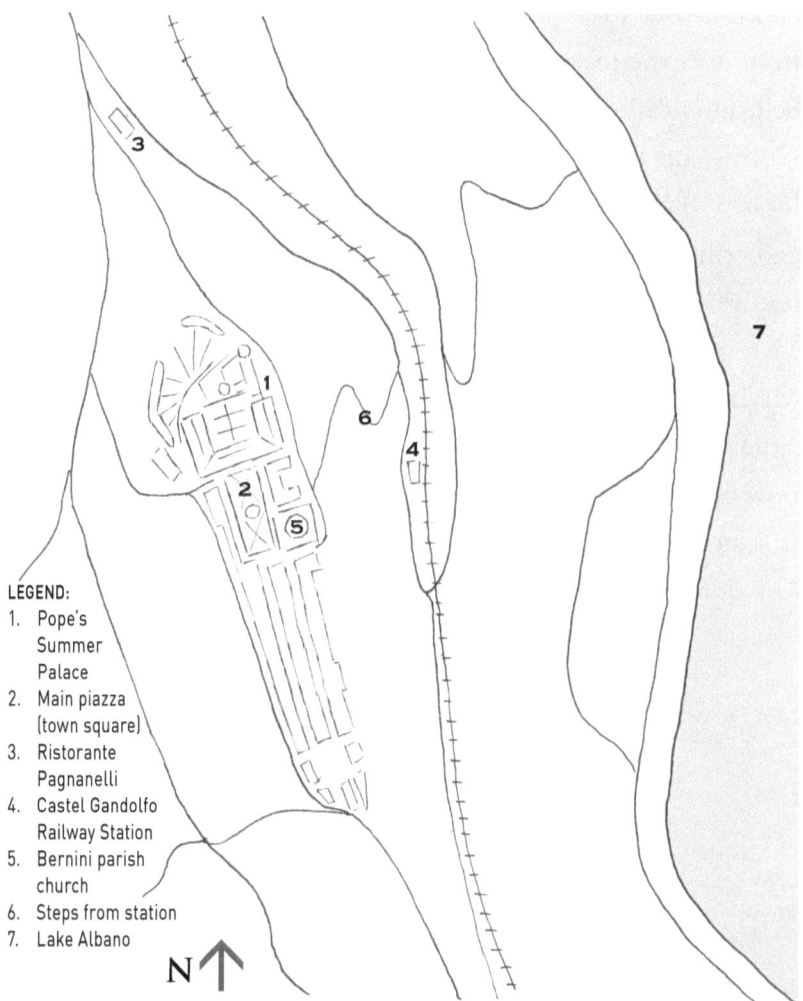

LEGEND:
1. Pope's Summer Palace
2. Main piazza (town square)
3. Ristorante Pagnanelli
4. Castel Gandolfo Railway Station
5. Bernini parish church
6. Steps from station
7. Lake Albano

Castel Gandolfo has been the summer home for Popes – on and off – since 1628. The Papal Summer Palace, with two telescope cupolas on top, adjoins the town square on which the Bernini parish church is located, and all overlooks the large and beautiful crater lake known as Lake Albano. Halfway down the hill to the lake is the Castel Gandolfo single-platform railway station with regular electric trains to Roma Termini, taking about forty minutes. The papal farm and gardens run from near the town square southwards right along to the papal helipad and the new headquarters of the Vatican Observatory. Nearby, on the northern side of the Papal Summer Palace, is located Ristorante Pagnanelli in a pink building. It is a key gathering place with huge multi-level cellars containing 30,000 bottles of wine, owned by Aurelio and Australian-born Jane Mariani. It is now managed by their sons Gabriele and Matteo Mariani. Lake Albano has many summer villas including the large Villa Palazzola, part of the English Venerable College and now operating as a B & B and conference centre of excellence. It is an easy and delightful two-to-three hour walk around the foreshore of Lake Albano. Map drawn by Dominic Fischer.

APPENDIX C

Australian Ambassadors to the Holy See

Ambassadors are listed under the date their credentials were presented.

Non-resident

8 October 1973 – Dr Lloyd D. Thompson MVO (resident in The Hague)

27 August 1974 – John M. McMillan (resident in Ankara; from 1 October 1976 resident in Malta)

5 April 1979 – Brian C. Hill (resident in Stockholm)

26 June 1980 – Dr Lloyd D. Thompson MVO (resident in Geneva; from 2 September 1981 resident in Dublin)

Non-resident (resident in Dublin unless otherwise stated)

25 November 1983 – Sir Peter Lawler OBE

28 March 1987 – Francis W. S. Milne MBE

31 October 1988 – Hon. Brian T. Burke AC

2 December 1991 – Terence B. McCarthy

13 January 1994 – Rev. Fr the Hon. Michael C. Tate (resident in The Hague)

11 January 1997 – Edward J. Stevens

20 May 1999 – Hon. Robert G. Halverson OBE

15 May 2003 – Hon. Dr John J. Herron

18 May 2006 – Anne M. Plunkett

Rome resident

12 February 2009 – Hon. Timothy Andrew Fischer

5 November 2012 – Hon. John McCarthy QC

APPENDIX D

Popes since 1878

Modern popes since the loss of the Papal States in 1870, after the longest-ever 32-year papacy of Pope Pius IX (1846 to 1878).

Pope Leo XIII	1878–1903
Pope Pius X	1903–14
Pope Benedict XV	1914–22
Pope Pius XI	1922–1939
Pope Pius XII	1939–1958
Pope John XXIII	1958–63
Pope Paul VI	1963–1978
Pope John Paul I	1978
Pope John Paul II	1978–2005
Pope Benedict XVI	2005–13
Pope Francis	2013–

APPENDIX E

Departments of the Roman Curia

An explanation of the function of each department has been given in parentheses where necessary.

- A. Secretariat of State (*political and diplomatic functions*)
- B. Congregations
  1. Doctrine of the Faith (*Catholic doctrine*)
  2. Oriental churches (*Churches in Egypt, Sinai peninsula, Eritrea, northern Ethiopia, southern Albania, Bulgaria, Cyprus, Greece, Israel, Iran, Iraq, Lebanon, Palestinian territories, Syria, Jordan, Turkey*)
  3. Divine Worship and the Discipline of the Sacraments (*liturgical practices*)
  4. Causes of Saints (*canonisations*)
  5. Evangelisation of Peoples (*sometimes called 'Propaganda Fide'; missionary work*)
  6. Clergy
  7. Institutes of Consecrated Life and Societies of Apostolic Life (*religious orders etc*)
  8. Catholic Education (*in seminaries and institutes of study*)
  9. Bishops (*selection of new bishops outside of mission territories and oriental churches*)
- C. Tribunals (*judicial bodies*)
  1. Apostolic Penitentiary (*court for matters of conscience*)
  2. Supreme Tribunal of the Apostolic Signatura (*court for normal judicial appeals*)
  3. Tribunal of the Rota Romana (*supreme appellate and administrative court*)

D. Pontifical Councils
   1. Laity
   2. Promoting Christian Unity (*unity with other Christian Churches and with Judaism*)
   3. Family
   4. Justice and Peace
   5. *Cor Unum* for Human and Christian Development (*care for the needy*)
   6. Pastoral Care of Migrants and Itinerant People
   7. Health Care Workers
   8. Legislative Texts (*interpreting the laws of the Church*)
   9. Inter-religious Dialogue
   10. Culture (*relations with different cultures*)
   11. Social Communications (*using media to spread the gospel*)
   12. Promoting New Evangelisation (*missionary work to countries where the Church has declined*)
E. Synod of Bishops (*body of international bishops who advise the Pope*)
F. Offices (*financial bodies*)
   1. Apostolic Camera (*central board of finance*)
   2. Administration of the Patrimony of the Apostolic See (*property administration*)
   3. Prefecture for the Economic Affairs of the Holy See (*oversight of Holy See offices that manage finances*)
G. Pontifical Commissions
   1. *Ecclesia Dei* (*seeking to restore communion with traditionalists who have broken with the Church since Vatican Council II*)
   2. Cultural Heritage of the Church (*contents of museums and archives*)

DEPARTMENTS OF THE ROMAN CURIA

    3. Sacred Archaeology (*cemeteries, monuments etc*)
    4. Biblical Commission (*biblical scholarship*)
    5. Theological Commission (*thirty international theologians who advise the Congregation for the Doctrine of the Faith*)
    6. Latin America
    7. Interdicasterial Commissions (*commissions set up to deal with matters involving several departments of the Roman Curia*)

H. Swiss Guard (*responsible for the Pope's safety*)
I. Institutions Not Connected with the Holy See
J. Labour Office of the Apostolic See (*labour relations of the Holy See with its employees*)
K. Pontifical Academies (*including the Academy of Sciences*)
L. Pontifical Committees

More details can be found at www.vatican.va/roman_curia.

APPENDIX F

Senior Personnel in the Secretariat of State as at 2009

Cardinal Secretary of State (Prime Minister equivalent): Cardinal Tarcisio Bertone

First Section (General Affairs)
Sustituto (Deputy Prime Minister equivalent): Archbishop Fernando Filoni
Assessore (Chef du Cabinet): Monsignor Gabriele Caccia

Second Section (Relations with States)
Secretary (Foreign Minister equivalent): Archbishop Dominique Mamberti
Undersecretary (Deputy Foreign Minister equivalent): Monsignor Pietro Parolin

Australian Desk Officer
Monsignor Joseph Murphy

APPRECIATION

At the outset I must thank my wife, Judy, for her support and guidance not only with writing this book and helping to collate the photos but also with her selfless support of the huge endeavour of the ambassadorship. I thank my sons, Harrison and Dominic, and all members of my family, including Judy's mother, Mary Brewer, who is very good at correcting my convoluted English grammar, and her sister, Rosie Brewer, who helped enormously with caring, travelling with and entertaining her nephews.

I thank all in DFAT who supported my ambassadorship role and my staff in Rome – loyal Deputy HOMs Anne Giles and Michael Sullivan, my PA par excellence, namely Madonna Noonan, first-rate office manager Antonia Da-Rin, and my extremely patient driver, Stefano Bernardini. He put the first mark on the car and on day one of his appointment, I put the second; fortunately both were minor. A truck then put the third one right down one side while the Peugeot was parked in its proper slot on crowded Via Paola. I recommend a Mini Minor for Rome traffic.

I am also indebted to the motivated team from the Australian Embassy to Italy, led by former Federal Minister Amanda Vanstone then later led by former Deputy Secretary of DFAT David Ritchie. Both were strong but very different ambassadors for Australia covering Italy, tiny San Marino and more recently Libya. Within that embassy, many added support to the Holy See Embassy, especially those on the administrative and consular side.

It is fair to say ABC Books and HarperCollins wrestled with this book, which they had commissioned, and I thank them for their perseverance and enlightened processing, especially Amruta Slee, Emma Dowden and Mary Rennie, with Brigitta Doyle and all the team at the modern Sydney HQ. Good advice and thorough manuscript reading always helps remove gremlins, and in this regard I especially thank retired Ambassadors Anne Leahy and Noel Fahey and others I am not allowed to name, for their great help, along with advice from Robert Mickens from the hard-hitting UK magazine, the *Tablet*.

Above all else I thank my friends and interlocutors in Rome on both sides of the Tiber, dedicated people but also kindly in many ways, from the most senior to the most junior. I am eternally grateful to them all and have endeavoured to not breach confidences but equally shine a light on so much that is purposeful but also fun in the eternal city of Rome.

I also owe much to many of all ranks in the clergy, including all the priests associated with Caravita, the wonderful parish church in the centre of Rome, right through to retired senior Curia member Cardinal Edward Cassidy now living in Newcastle.

INDEX

Abbott, Tony 17, 290
Aguzzi, Massimo 25
Alexander III, Pope 140
Al-Gaddafi, Muammar 111–17
Al-Sadr, Habeeb 74
Alston, Richard 17
Anderson, David 27
Archilei, Vittoria 109

Bainimarama, Frank 201
Balestrero, Monsignor Ettore 59
Barr Smith, Joanna 168
Baxter, Bill 181
Beazley, Kim 27, 263, 270
Belo, Bishop C. F. 14
Benedict XVI, Pope (Cardinal Joseph Ratzinger) 1, 3, 18, 22, 24, 26, 28–30, 52, 53, 55, 56, 59, 70, 71, 72, 86, 92–93, 94, 109, 124, 126, 141, 144, 146, 148, 154, 155, 156, 161–62, 171, 177, 191–92, 193, 198, 202–03, 215, 222–23, 226, 229, 241–42, 256, 260, 278, 282–83, 291, 298
  resignation 231–40, 241, 243
Berlusconi, Silvio 114
Bernardini, Stefano 24, 35, 85, 260, 303
Bertone, Cardinal Tarcisio 29, 52, 53, 55, 65, 186, 233, 245, 274, 302
Bessette, Brother André 173
Bishop, Julie 16, 173

Blair, Tony 69, 106, 206
Boncompagni Ludovisi, Prince Nicolò Francesco 109
Boncompagni Ludovisi, Princess Rita 109
Bongiorno, Paul 176
Bonnor, Jenelle (Ritchie) 39, 289
Bowen, Chris 205
Brewer, Judy *see* Fischer, Judy
Brewer, Rosie 48
Brimaud, Ken 62
Bryce, Quentin 86
Burke, Greg 281
Bush, George W. 206, 207

Caccia, Monsignor (later Archbishop) Gabriele 51, 59, 302
Camilleri, Monsignor Antoine 56, 59
Campbell, Francis 69
Cantalamessa, Father Raniero 192
Cantamessa, Luigi 211
Casagrande, Ric 23
Casey, Sister Maria 171, 177, 234
Catherine of Aragon 104
Celestine V, Pope 231, 233, 234, 235, 239
Cheney, Dick 206
Chester, Doug 2
Clark, Alan 7
Clement VII, Pope 105
Clinton, Bill 161

Clinton, Hillary 145
Clooney, George 158, 159
Conversi, Paolo 149
Cribb, Julian 123, 124
Crossman, Richard 7
Crotty, Monsignor Michael 96
Cushley, Leo 58

Da-Rin, Antonia 24, 34, 218, 260
Darmaatmadja, Cardinal Julius 242
de Gaulle, Charles 27, 80
de Laboulaye, Stanislas 67, 80
De Paolis, Cardinal Velasio 229
Degollado, Marcial Maciel 224
Desbois, Father Patrick 100
di Piazza, Battista 7
Diaz, Marion 67
Díaz, Miguel Humberto 67, 287
Doogue, Geraldine 45
Duffy, Professor Eamon 104–05
Dumortier, Rector François-Xavier 226

El Khoury, Georges 75, 147
Electron 241–50
Emerson, Scott 45

Fadden, Artie 19
Fayyad, Salam 148
Filoni, Archbishop (later Cardinal) Fernando 96, 97, 202–03, 244, 302
Firman, Brother Bill 158
Fischer, Carol 5

Fischer, Dominic 3, 4, 6, 26, 27, 48, 60, 258
Fischer, Harrison 3, 4, 6, 26, 27, 29–30, 48, 258
Fischer, Judy (née Brewer) 1–6, 26, 27, 30, 31, 37, 48, 60, 141, 176, 219, 258, 259, 287–88, 291
Fischer, Tony 5
Fischer, Vicki 5
Flannery, Father Tony 240
Fowler, Dr Cary 45
Fox, Detective Chief Inspector Peter 227
Francis, Pope 53, 60, 81, 193, 198, 199, 233, 280, 283, 285–86, 291, 298

Gallagher, Michael 62
Gänswein, Monsignor Georg 57
Gardiner, Father Paul 171
George, Cardinal Francis 153
Giles, Anne 22, 25, 29, 34, 50, 66, 260
Gillard, Julia 44, 131, 136, 173, 204, 290
Given, Paul 36, 42, 177, 213, 289
Gjorgevski, Gjoko 78
Gray, Gary 207
Greco, Francesco 69
Green, Philip 205
Gudmundson, Ulla 72
Gürsoy, Professor Kenan 67

Han, Thomas 77
Harris, Lachlan 16

INDEX

Harvey, Archbishop James 57
Henry VIII, King 104, 105
Hill, Robert 131
Hobbs, Jenny 36, 39
Hogg, John 50
Horan, Father Charles 167
Howard, John 6, 17

John Paul II, Pope 141, 146, 162, 266
Joyce, Barnaby 173, 177

Kaczyński, Lech 69
Kappler, Herbert (SS Commander) 182, 183, 186
Keating, Father Ambrose Patrick 167
Kelly, Father Michael 61
Kenny, Enda 151, 153
King, Merryn 155
King, Dr Ralph 136
Kinnear, Grant 86
Klugman, Kathy 199
Knight, Lesley-Anne 45, 274–75
Körner, Father Felix 161–62, 226
Krivošić-Prpić, Jasna 78–79
Kurmann, Anton 50

Lajolo, Cardinal Giovanni 209, 211, 212
Landi, Antonio Zanardi 68–69
Law, Cardinal Bernard 225
Leahy, Anne 67, 70, 204
Levada, Cardinal William 226
Lewy, Mordechay 67
Luther, Martin 105

MacKillop, Alexander 164
MacKillop, Mary 48, 70, 141, 164–180, 234, 275
Madigan, Professor Dan 45
Mamberti, Archbishop Dominique 56, 96, 133, 157–58, 175, 302
Mapelli, Father Nicola 45, 174
Maradiaga, Cardinal Óscar Andrés Rodríguez 212, 213
Margulis, Professor Lynn 103
Mariani, Gabriele 296
Mariani, Jane 296
Mariani, Matteo 296
Martínez del Río, Father Alvaro Corcuera 229
Martosetomo, Suprapto 75
Maude, Richard 38–39
McCarthy, John 288
McCaughan, Daniel 62
McClellan, Justice Peter 228
McCulloch, Robert 61
McGauren, Peter 17, 228
McMullan, Bob 45
Mekhemar, Lamia Aly Hamada 85
Merkel, Angela 192, 249
Metcalfe, Andrew 205
Michel, Jean-Claude 84
Millar, Caroline 131, 289
Mills, John Atta 149–50
Mladić, General Ratko 160
Monash, Sir John 116, 189
Moran, Stuart 62
Mugabe, Robert 115, 249
Murphy, Monsignor Joseph 58, 302

Murphy-O'Connor, Cardinal Cormac 243
Murray, Sister Patricia 158
Mussolini, Benito 182, 184, 191, 209, 217, 294

Nichols, Archbishop Vincent 243
Noonan, Madonna 24, 34, 260
Nwachukwu, Fortunatus 24, 58, 260

O'Brien, Cardinal Keith 242
O'Kelly, Bishop Greg 173
O'Neill, Tip 133
Orwell, George 24
Ouellet, Cardinal Marc 244

Parker, Bill 219
Parolin, Monsignor (later Archbishop) Pietro 51, 59, 302
Paul II, Pope John 6, 14, 69, 141, 142–43, 144, 145, 146, 162, 171, 198, 207, 225, 226–27, 252, 277, 283, 306
Paul VI, Pope 141
Pecklers, Father Keith 108, 226
Pell, Cardinal George 153, 178, 180, 244, 255, 256
Phillips, Sister Sue 61
Pius XII, Pope 209, 298
  anti-Semitism 182–194
Pyne, Christopher 37

Quinlan, Gary 2, 16, 131, 289, 290

Ranjith, Archbishop Malcolm 199
Ratzinger, Cardinal Joseph
  see Benedict XVI, Pope
Ravasi, Cardinal Gianfranco 102
Rayner, Peter 40
Reagan, Ronald 143–44
Regev, Mark 189
Richardson, David 106, 107
Richardson, Dennis 131, 172, 179, 205, 259
Ritchie, David J. 39, 40, 42, 123, 136, 174, 176, 177, 259, 289, 290
Ritchie, Jenelle *see* Bonnor, Jenelle
Roth, Dr Cecil 190
Rowland, Kay 36
Rudd, Kevin 2–3, 11, 12, 14, 16, 44, 131, 133, 173, 174, 175, 177, 196, 205, 260, 266, 291

Sandri, Cardinal Leonardo 244
Scola, Cardinal Angelo 241, 245, 282
Seixas Corrêa, Luiz Felipe de 67, 133
Shalit, Gilad 147
Sheil, Bishop Laurence 164, 165, 166, 167, 168, 169
Simoes, Armindo Pedro 75
Simpson, Sister Helen 62
Smith, Stephen 17, 131, 260, 266
Solomon 168
Sorondo, Bishop Marcelo Sánchez 15, 40, 45, 101, 119, 121, 123, 124, 125
Starkey, David 105

INDEX

Stephens, Ursula 173, 177
Stone, Peter 137
Suchocka, Hanna 69, 252
Sullivan, Michael 34, 260, 303
Svetek, Maja Lovrenčič 80

Tagle, Archbishop Luis Antonio 227
Tauran, Cardinal Jean-Louis 198, 245
Tedeschi, Ettore Gotti 156
Thatcher, Margaret 69, 144
Thevenin, Monsignor Nicolas 29, 59–60, 217–18
Tighe, Monsignor Paul 58
Tomasi, Archbishop Silvano Maria 51, 149
Tooth, Geoff 136
Tuason, Mercedes 75
Turkson, Cardinal Peter 108, 109, 149, 150, 228, 244

Ueno, Kagefumi 74–75

van Lynden-Leijten, Henriette 45
Vanstone, Amanda 26, 36–38, 40–41, 259, 265, 270

Vegliò, Cardinal Antonio Maria 95
Vitillo, Robert 59, 210

Wałęsa, Lech 144
Wells, Monsignor Peter 59
Williams, Archbishop Rowan 18, 106–08
Williams, Father Thomas 229
Williams, Rowan 18, 106
Williamson, Bishop Richard 191–92, 232
Wilson, Courtney 221
Wojtyla, Cardinal Karol *see* John Paul II, Pope
Woldetatios, Zemede 136
Woods, Father Julian Tenison 165, 167, 169
Wright, Sister Mary 61

Yamaguchi, Hidekazu 75
Yates, Bill 116
Yates, Tom 112, 116
Yelda, Albert 74
Yu-yuan, Larry 76

Zollner, Father Hans 225–26, 228

www.ingramcontent.com/pod-product-compliance
Lightning Source LLC
Chambersburg PA
CBHW022033290426
44109CB00014B/851